BARBARY ENTANGLEMENTS

The Revolutionary Age

FRANCIS D. COGLIANO, CHRISTA BREAULT DIERKSHEIDE,
ELIGA H. GOULD, AND PATRICK GRIFFIN, EDITORS

Barbary Entanglements

REALIZING AMERICAN INDEPENDENCE
ON THE WORLD STAGE

John M. Chamberlin

UNIVERSITY OF VIRGINIA PRESS
Charlottesville and London

The University of Virginia Press is situated on the traditional lands of the Monacan Nation, and the Commonwealth of Virginia was and is home to many other Indigenous people. We pay our respect to all of them, past and present. We also honor the enslaved African and African American people who built the University of Virginia, and we recognize their descendants. We commit to fostering voices from these communities through our publications and to deepening our collective understanding of their histories and contributions.

UNIVERSITY OF VIRGINIA PRESS
© 2025 by the Rector and Visitors of the University of Virginia
All rights reserved
Printed in the United States of America on acid-free paper

First published 2025

1 3 5 7 9 8 6 4 2

LIBRARY OF CONGRESS CATALOGING-IN-PUBLICATION DATA

Names: Chamberlin, John M., author
Title: Barbary entanglements : realizing American independence on the world stage / John M. Chamberlin.
Other titles: Realizing American independence on the world stage
Description: Charlottesville : University of Virginia Press, 2025. | Series: The Revolutionary age | Includes bibliographical references and index.
Identifiers: LCCN 2025008595 (print) | LCCN 2025008596 (ebook) | ISBN 9780813954097 hardback | ISBN 9780813954103 paperback | ISBN 9780813954110 ebook
Subjects: LCSH: United States—History—Tripolitan War, 1801–1805 | United States—Relations—Africa, North | Africa, North—Relations—United States | United States—Foreign relations—1783–1815 | United States—Foreign relations—Treaties | Pirates—Africa, North—History—18th century | Pirates—Africa, North—History—19th century | BISAC: HISTORY / Military / Revolutions & Wars of Independence (see also United States / Revolutionary Period (1775–1800)) | HISTORY / United States / 19th Century
Classification: LCC E335 .C43 2025 (print) | LCC E335 (ebook)
LC record available at https://lccn.loc.gov/2025008595
LC ebook record available at https://lccn.loc.gov/2025008596

Cover art: *Decatur and the Dey of Algiers*, wood engraving by W. Mollier, 1881. (The Miriam and Ira D. Wallach Division of Art, Prints, and Photographs, Picture Collection, New York Public Library)
Cover design: Elke Barter

To Stephanie, ILYM

CONTENTS

Preface ix
Acknowledgments xi
Notes on Language Use xv

Introduction 1

1. The Barbary System: Mediterranean Corsairing at the Dawn of American Independence 19

2. American Sovereignty Checked: Diplomacy and Captivity in North Africa, 1776–1793 47

3. A Minor Power: Diplomacy and American-European Cooperation in North Africa, 1793–1801 79

4. A Coalition of the Willing: The Multinational Tripolitan War, 1801–1805 116

5. Changing Tides: Rising America and the Ebb of Corsairing, 1807–1825 153

Conclusion 185

Appendix 1. The Al Koraschi Ebnallad Letter 193
Appendix 2. Article 11 of the 1796 Treaty Between the United States of America and Tripoli 196
Notes 201
Bibliography 231
Index 241

PREFACE

In 2017 the Barbary Wars were far from my mind. I was aware of them in a general way, given my background as an analyst of US–Middle East interaction for the United States Air Force, especially my previous study of how history has been mobilized to explain and justify modern dynamics. I had written extensively on Arab reinterpretation of the Crusades as a metaphor for, or even explanatory of, colonialism and Arab-Israeli issues, for example. I found analogies to the Barbary Wars to counter-piracy operations off Somali and to the 2011 international intervention in Libya, known in the United States military as Operation Odyssey Dawn, inapt but unsurprising. As far as the "Barbary pirates" themselves, my main thought was that the use of the word "pirate" was inaccurate, owing to the era's privateering rules, but I had not yet examined either issue deeply. Then a seemingly unrelated organizational decision focused my attention on North Africa's relations with the early American republic.

The reorganization of my command came as something of a shock. At the time, I was commanding an Air Force squadron, what I had always imagined would represent the pinnacle of my military career. I was likely to retire at the end of my tour and pursue my love of history as a civilian. But the reorganization cut my command tour short when my squadron inactivated. Major General Rothstein at Air University (the Air Force's graduate school) made me an offer I couldn't refuse. He asked me to stay in service as a full-time PhD student in the history of American involvement in the Middle East and return as a professor upon my graduation. Professor Stacy Holden at Purdue suggested I look into the Barbary Wars and introduced me to T. Cole Jones, Purdue's resident historian of military affairs and the early American republic. The rest, as they say, is history.

I offer you this background because several academics have noted that my military experience seems to inform my reading of the sources, giving me a slightly different perspective when I interpret them. In my mind, the historical method and intelligence analysis are closely related, especially in the importance of not letting one's initial hypotheses color how one interprets the material but instead following where the evidence leads. Having received excellent training in both disciplines, I see few differences between the methodologies, though I accept the wisdom of my colleagues who tell me my approach is noteworthy. I can only hope that it interests, rather than distracts, the readers.

My initial hypothesis when I began researching early American diplomacy in North Africa was that I would see a chauvinistic approach related to what was later described as Western Orientalism. I was pleasantly surprised to see that attitude very rarely among American diplomats and captives alike during the eighteenth century, though it became more common in the nineteenth. I was also surprised to see how focused American diplomats, political leaders, and later military leaders were on the law of nations. Not only did they accept much North African practice as lawful, but they went to great pains to show America's respect for international law to North Africans and Europeans alike. The evidence led me ever further away from a clash of civilizations and toward America's attempts to show it belonged in the international system. I very much hope that you enjoy following that path with me.

ACKNOWLEDGMENTS

This project would not have been possible without the help and support of many. First, and foremost, I cannot express adequately my deep appreciation for the love, patience, and support of my wife, Stephanie Skaff, who has encouraged both my military and academic careers, often at a cost to her own, as we move frequently around the country and the world. My mother, sounding board, and first copy editor, Judith Entwife, spent countless hours helping me bring this project together. She shared my joy of discovery during my research and helped me frame how to present it through the writing. Then she examined multiple drafts and brought my attention to many a typo or unnecessary comma. I appreciate how much clearer she made my prose, and I hope that the copy editors at University of Virginia Press appreciate how much her efforts lightened their own. Most of the edits I got from Ruth Melville related to meeting the house style sheet, though she also found some typos that had evaded both my eyes and Judith's. I'm sure that even with both of them combing through my prose, a couple remain. They always do. Any remaining errors or examples of unclear communication are entirely my own responsibility, and I can only thank them for helping me to expunge so many of them.

This book had its genesis as my dissertation at Purdue University. I owe a profound debt to my adviser, T. Cole Jones, for his guidance and encouragement throughout my studies and on this project. Thank you for taking a risk on a military student with minimum time to complete his degree and for helping me plan to make that possible. Thank you also for all the cogent feedback that has helped make this manuscript better. I would also like to thank my Purdue mentors, David Atkinson and John Larson, who set me on a strong track via their courses in my first semester of study and supported me up through serving on my dissertation committee. I am also grateful to Stacy Holden at Purdue, who first suggested combining my Arabic language skills and military history background to examine the Barbary Wars, and to Andrew Fagal of Princeton University, who pointed me to many obscure records, including obtaining digital access to many that I would otherwise have been unable to review, as much of my research took place during the pandemic travel restrictions. Similarly, thank you to the many archivists and librarians who have digitized vast amounts of material and made it available via subscription databases and even on the open internet. Owing to the vast array of digital material at my fingertips, I was able to continue my research in a time of pandemic with very little disruption and considerable cost savings in travel. Thank you also to the staff of those archives I was able to visit in person.

Frank Lambert's fine study *The Barbary Wars: American Independence in the Atlantic World* served as an inspiration for this study. His placing Barbary contestation in a wider framework and writing in prose that is both scholarly and approachable offered goals worthy of emulation. Benjamin Armstrong and Abigail Mullen at the United States Naval Academy are fine colleagues indeed. Though I was unaware of their work when I started this project, I quickly discovered these two were also writing about American cooperation with European powers, particularly in the "First Barbary War." They were both very gracious to the new scholar entering their field, sharing sources and discussing interpretations. In particular, if you like this book and want a deep dive on the material in chapter 4, read Abigail Mullen's *To Fix a National Character*, which focuses on everyday interactions of the United States Navy, the American consuls, and partners in the Tripolitan conflict. I am also fortunate to have great colleagues at the Air Command and Staff College. I am particularly indebted to my former and current department chairs at the Department of Airpower, Michael "Mongo" Pavelec and Edward "SPED" Redman, for their support in helping me obtain travel funding and time to work on this book and their encouragement of a project so far outside the scope of the department's core field. Thank you also to Paul "PJ" Springer, who mentored me through the academic publication process, from helping me craft the proposal to reviewing the contract. Your guidance and friendship are very much appreciated. Thank you also to the entire department for creating such a strong collegial culture, heavy on both academic inquiry and comradeship. Airpower!

Last, but far from least, thank you to the team at University of Virginia Press. Most especially, I want to thank Nadine Zimmerli for her interest in this project and her steadfast support as she shepherded it through the review and acquisition process. Nadine is a champion. Ruth Melville, mentioned above, helped turn my often MLA-influenced writing into solid Chicago style. I also appreciate Clayton Butler's work on marketing and publicity, and Ellen Satrom and Andy Edwards for supervising my project from "finished" manuscript to actual book. I'm sure many other folks at the press played a role as well, and I am grateful for their efforts, as I am to Bobby Wright, who made the maps to help readers orient themselves. Thank you also to Eliga Gould for his great support and enthusiasm. I was blown away by his review and even more so by the fact that he wanted my manuscript for his book series. I am honored. I am grateful to several anonymous internal and external reviewers who commented on earlier drafts and helped me strengthen the final product. As with the copyediting mentioned above, any flaws remain my own, and I am simply glad they helped me improve this book so much.

NOTES ON LANGUAGE USE

Scholars of the Middle East will note that I have made some choices of terminology that are currently unusual. I do not use the term "Maghrib" to refer to North Africa in general, for two reasons. The first is that the term is the Arabic name for the country (or, in the period of this study, empire) known in English as Morocco, thus potentially leading to confusion. The second is that it implies a similarity and "Arabness" across North Africa that is anachronistic to the era of this study. Morocco was an independent sultanate, while the regencies of Algiers, Tunis, and Tripoli were appended to the Ottoman Empire, with Algiers and Tunis also being directly governed by a Turkish elite. Additionally, I do use the term "Barbary," though I realize it is a somewhat fraught word. I have chosen to use it as it was the dominant term for North Africa, excluding Egypt, in the Western sources of the era, especially in the context of maritime predation. I have tried to reserve its use to contexts of corsairing, or when referencing documents that use the term, but may have unintentionally sprinkled it into other contexts when the phrase "North Africa" seemed overused. The term Barbary was originally a reference to the portions of North Africa in which the Amazigh, or Berber, ethnic group was prevalent. As the words "Berber" and "barbarian" both come from the same Greek root, the Amazigh people are moving away from using the ethnonym Berber, and Barbary is becoming less common for the same reason. No slur or claim of barbarism is meant by my use of Barbary, though the same cannot be said for my primary sources, some of which made much of the linguistic connection between the two words.

In quoting eighteenth- and nineteenth-century English-language sources, I have tried to keep intact the period usages of grammar, spelling, and punctuation to the maximum extent possible. Only if I feared the meaning might be unclear have I inserted bracketed explanatory text, such as "40,000 Doll[ars]." I have also avoided the use of [sic] after the many grammatical and spelling "errors" found in the primary documents. In this era when Noah Webster was still alive, standardized spelling did not yet rule, so I consider most of these not to be errors but simply period use. The words "recieve," "blooddiest," and such, are not typos but the versions written in the source documents. I consider such odd spellings less distracting than interrupting the quotations constantly with [sic], and they offer more flavor than simply amending them to modern equivalents. In all quotations, italics for emphasis are from the original source.

BARBARY ENTANGLEMENTS

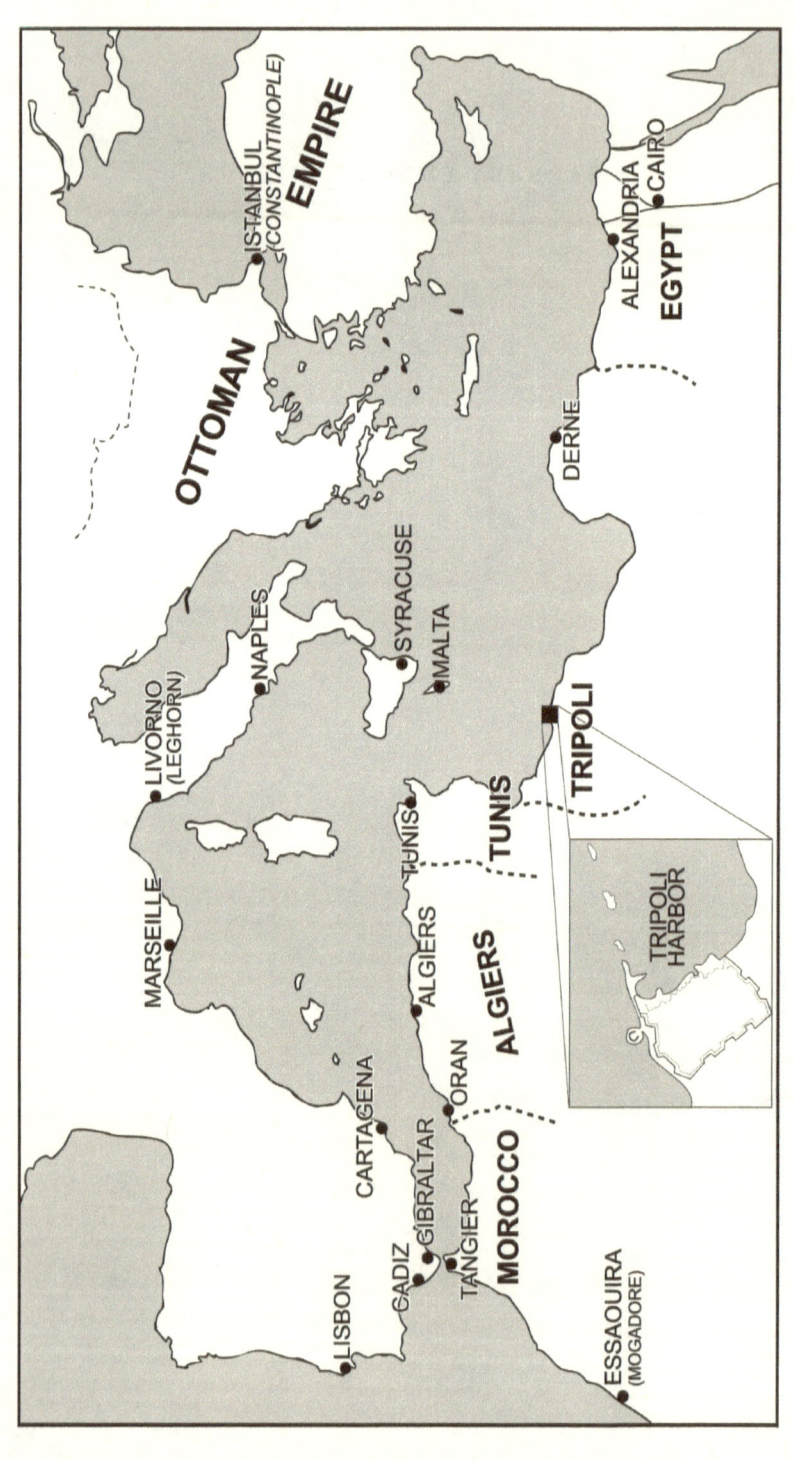

Introduction

ON 23 MARCH 1790 new Secretary of State Thomas Jefferson sat down with George Washington in the president's house in New York. They had time for a substantial conversation before the Tuesday afternoon levee, a semiformal weekly social reception to which President Washington welcomed gentlemen callers. It was Secretary Jefferson's second day on the job. On the first, he and President Washington had discussed what duties the newly formed cabinet position of secretary of state entailed. Today was the first opportunity to discuss foreign affairs, and the first order of business was that of fourteen American sailors still prisoners in Algiers almost five years after their capture. It was not Jefferson's first time taking on this nettlesome problem, and it would not be his last.[1]

Thomas Jefferson had been attempting to secure release for the crews of two American merchant vessels seized by Algerian corsairs since he received word of their capture in September 1785.[2] In addition to his role as minister to France, Congress had instructed Jefferson, along with John Adams and Benjamin Franklin, to treat with "Morocco and the Regencies of Algiers, Tunis and Tripoly."[3] This commission was envisioned as negotiating treaties that would allow American trade safe access to the Mediterranean. It soon extended to negotiating for prisoner release when Moroccan and Algerian corsairs captured three ships in the Gulf of Cadiz before the commissioners had even begun their diplomatic efforts. The Moroccan issue was soon solved, with the prisoners released and a treaty signed, but the Algerian issue remained a thorn in Jefferson's side for the remainder of his time in Europe.

Secretary Jefferson explained the issue of "our Captives in Algiers" to President Washington, "detailing their situation—the measures he had taken for their relief," and his efforts to obtain their release through the Mathurins, a French religious order which specialized in redeeming Christian captives in Muslim countries. Jefferson and Washington agreed that this effort "had better remain in that train a while longer." They determined to write a letter to William Short, Jefferson's replacement in France, asking him to look into how reasonable "expectations of redemption are at present" and to await further developments. This settled, they moved on to other topics and then to the afternoon's levee.[4]

Neither likely realized just how much time, effort, and money Barbary issues would require. Thomas Jefferson had stepped down as secretary of state before the prisoners were finally released in July 1796, at a cost for ransom and treaties that represented a fifth of the federal government's annual budget. Even then, Barbary challenges would continue throughout Jefferson's presidency and that of his successor, James Madison.

One of the newly independent United States' first external challenges was dealing with the North African "Barbary States" (Algiers, Tripoli, and Tunis, as regencies technically under the Ottoman Empire, and occasionally the independent Sultanate of Morocco), which based their economies largely on shipping predation or tributary treaties. Before the American Revolution, American ships were heavily involved in Mediterranean shipping, protected from North African corsairs as British subjects via Britain's treaties with those powers. While popularly imagined as pirates, the corsairs were under government control and are thus better understood as privateers, attacking shipping only of countries with which the Barbary powers were technically at war. Thus, the treaty protection was effective, and American ships crowded through the Strait of Gibraltar carrying a quarter of the colonies' fish exports, a sixth of their wheat and flour exports, and significant loads of rice. American shippers abandoned this trade during the revolution, more for fear of British than North African predation. After independence, the American government and merchant shippers were surprised to discover that Barbary powers considered any non-Muslim nation with whom they did not have an active treaty fair game for predation.[5] Moroccan corsairs captured the first American vessel in 1784, and fraught relations with North African powers continued through 1816, including several occasions during which Barbary powers considered themselves at war with the United States, and two during which the United States took offensive action. These conflicts challenged the new United States but also offered the opportunity to prove America's viability on the international stage. This book examines how the United States attempted to demonstrate that viability by acting on Barbary challenges as established European nations did.

This work provides the first examination of American interaction with the North African polities known in the eighteenth century as the Barbary States and with European countries on Barbary issues from the perspective of United States' efforts to assert viability and reliability as a sovereign nation within the European Westphalian nation-state system. This study shows the significance of these interactions in answering the question of how the United States became a player on the international stage. Barbary issues were central to the United States moving from Europe's periphery to becoming a power within the European international system. Independent America's initial interactions with North African powers were generally either ineffective or dependent on the intervention of one or more European states, but by the time of the Tripolitan War (1801–5), the United States was both acting and being treated as a minor power within the "republic of nations." By the time of the so-called Second Barbary War campaign of 1815, the United States was able to act as a significant player within that system.

In following this challenging and changing dynamic, the book seeks to explain what Barbary conflict and diplomacy meant to the newly independent United States and to bring nuance to a black-and-white imagined history of bloodthirsty Muslim pirates and virtuous American heroes. Some academic sources still present such images, supporting a "clash of civilizations" narrative and essentializing conflict between "The West" and "The Muslim World," though such voices have become increasingly rare.[6]

In popular history, such presentations continue to predominate. Fox News host Brian Kilmeade's *Thomas Jefferson and the Tripoli Pirates* (with Don Yaeger) typifies this approach, opening with the claim: "This is the story of how a new nation, saddled with war debt and desperate to establish credibility, was challenged by four Muslim powers. Our merchant ships were captured and the crews enslaved. Despite its youth, America would do what established western powers chose not to do: stand up to intimidation and lawlessness. Tired of Americans being captured and held for ransom, our third President decided to take on the Barbary powers in a war that is barely remembered today but is one that, in many ways, we are still fighting."[7]

While the notion that America's response to North African threats was in any way exceptional is not at all supported, Kilmeade's discussion of other Western powers brings up an important point, the meaning of America's actions to European powers—powers that the leaders of the early republic hoped would see America as a peer nation. In examining this issue, I follow Eliga Gould's argument that one of the early republic's greatest foreign policy goals was to win recognition as a free, independent, and "treaty-worthy" nation. Gould notes that the early American republic envisioned a "tripartite division" of its international relations, "starting with 'sister-nations' in Europe, as Thomas Jefferson wrote in his first address to Congress in 1801, followed by North Africa's Barbary States, and ending with what Jefferson called 'our Indian neighbors.'"[8] In fact, Jefferson's use of this tripartite division can be found in almost all his presidential addresses to Congress, and almost always in this order.[9] Jefferson's lack of any mention of Asian nations is not surprising. In this era, American diplomacy in Asia was limited to dealing with European colonial powers and to a single consul in Canton, China, who acted more as a commercial agent in his interactions with China and whose diplomacy was limited mostly to interactions with representatives of European "sister-nations." The mention and placement of the Barbary States is also unsurprising. Barbary affairs served as a bridge between what Americans saw as semi-sovereign Native American polities and fully sovereign European nations within the Westphalian system. While federal negotiators argued that the independent nations and tribes of Indians ought to be considered as foreign nations, not as subjects of any particular state, many, especially in state governments, contested this view. American negotiations with native polities regardless of the sovereignty they may have theoretically enjoyed, did little to impress European diplomats with America's ability to take part in the international system. That would require interaction with other powers in, or at least more connected to, the Westphalian system, an effort that proved more challenging than Americans anticipated.

The European network of independent sovereign states bound together by networks of treaties and generally agreed-upon principles of international law—including that of legal equality of states, regardless of size or power, and the principle of nonintervention in internal affairs—generally called the Westphalian system, may have existed more in theory than in practice. The treaties of Osnabruck and Münster, which made up the Peace of Westphalia ending the Thirty Years' War (1618–48), certainly did not include language making such broad guarantees. Likewise, interventions in other states' internal affairs did not cease after the peace and were to become endemic during the disruptions of the French Revolutionary (1792–1802) and Napoleonic Wars (1803–15). Nonetheless, American political and diplomatic leaders believed in Westphalia as underlying the normal order. John Adams, for example, wrote in 1784 that the Treaty of Münster "is the great Charter of Europe. it is the Basis of the publick Right of Europe."[10] Similarly, during the chaotic upheavals of 1803, Rufus King referred to the general war as taking the "Government of Europe" away from stability and security, which could not be restored until "another Compact like that of the great Treaty of Westphalia shall have reestablished the public Law, and national Guaranties that are essential to its political Existence."[11] The system owed more to networks of less known and often bilateral treaties and gradual acceptance of these principles as customary in treatises on international law than to the Peace of Westphalia, however. The writings of Samuel von Pufendorf, Hugo Grotius, and Emer de Vattel were particularly influential to American thought.

American leaders were drawn to Swiss jurist Vattel's approach, as it blended the humanist natural law with which they were enamored with the concept of voluntary law, created by agreements between theoretically equal partners in what he called the "republic of nations."[12] Thomas Jefferson was notably fond of Vattel, whom he called a leading light of the law of nations and noted that "on the constructions of treaties, Vattel has been most generally the guide."[13] Indeed, Jefferson used Vattelian arguments in multiple treaty negotiations and was even known to borrow his term "republic of nations."[14] Yet Jefferson was far from unique in his reliance on Vattel. From Edmond Randolph's arguments on relations between American states during the Confederation Period (1781–89) to Benjamin Franklin's overt efforts to include humanitarian principles in international treaties in an effort to thereby make international law recognize such principles, Vattel was the early republic's prime source on the law of nations.[15] In fact, so authoritative did these politicians and diplomats find Vattel's arguments that, instead of Westphalian, I generally refer to this system as Vattelian. Under whatever name, American leaders deeply desired the sister nations of Europe to acknowledge the United States as a partner within that international system.

Early American diplomacy in Europe was characterized by boundless optimism, epitomized by John Adams's Model Treaty and efforts by Adams and Jefferson to tie America into the Vattelian system through treaties based on Adams's model. European powers were less enthusiastic. As Peter and Nicholas Onuf noted, while France was happy to sign a Treaty of Amity and Commerce in 1778 as part of a war effort to weaken its great rival Britain, the end of the war removed the strategic impetus for other powers to tie themselves to America by treaties.[16] In order to interact with "the great theater of nations with advantage and glory," as Samuel Cooper put it in his 1780 sermon,[17] America had to show its ability to perform on that stage as more than just an irritant to Britain. This book shows that Barbary diplomacy played a significant and underappreciated role in demonstrating America's worthiness as an affiliate to the European community of nations. American diplomacy with the corsairing states built on experience garnered via what Leonard Sadowsky calls the "borderland diplomatic regime" of intra-American negotiation, which was key to solving disputes with North Africans and thus showing America as a capable international actor.[18] Further, diplomatic and military cooperation with

European powers on Barbary matters demonstrated that America could act as a partner nation within the European system rather than simply a peripheral pseudo-colony.

This work is largely a traditional international history, but my approach is also influenced by the transnational approach to American history. The interactions I examine were important to America not only in terms of direct issues of trade balance and diplomatic or military interaction with North African powers themselves but also in terms of signaling to, or even directly building ties with, European powers. Focusing on these concerns brings a new view of the Barbary Wars and of the notions Americans of the early republic had of their nation's place in the world. The study focuses on diplomatic and legal history. In terms of diplomatic history, it concentrates on exchanges not only between Americans and North Africans but also between Americans and Europeans on matters related to North African affairs. This diplomatic history is closely tied to legal historical issues in terms of European conceptions of the legitimacy of privateering and of North African and American approaches to international law. North Africans justified their predation internally by considering it legitimate jihad against non-Muslim enemies and externally by maintaining the forms of the European notions of the law of nations, such as prize courts. While European sources hint at this, examining North African records gives a much clearer picture of the law-bound nature of corsairing than do most previous studies that consider Barbary predation. This mutually accepted lawfulness was very important to the United States, which based its early foreign policy heavily on its notions of proper respect for the law of nations (particularly as presented by Vattel) and the recognition from sister nations that American politicians expected to flow from that legal respect. My approach also includes elements of military history, though less in terms of the details of operations and more in terms of foregrounding cooperation with European powers. For example, in chapter 4 I discuss joint operations with the Swedish navy during the Tripolitan War and how that cooperation showed American "treaty-worthiness."

Throughout, I argue that American interaction with Barbary powers was in no way exceptional; it was largely typical of European national approaches. That very typicality was important to realizing American independence in terms of national consolidation and of American efforts toward joining the community of nations that had previously been an exclusively European domain. This is largely an argument of continuity of approach to Barbary issues, vice the American exceptionalism, "new nation with a vigorous and different approach" argument seen in Kilmeade above. Nonetheless, my research does show significant change over time in terms of American capability to realize its goals of acting in the manner of and in concert with established European powers, both in diplomatic and military terms.

My approach to international history is influenced by the recent turn toward considering American history from a transnational perspective. Since the 1980s historians have responded to the lens of American exceptionalism by noting that American history is not, in fact, widely divergent from international trends and effects, through works such as Thomas Bender's *A Nation Among Nations,* which situates the American War of Independence as "part of a global war between great European powers" and as an expression of the "Age of Atlantic Revolutions." This book fits firmly in that tradition, though it focuses much more on traditional representatives of the state than is common in more recent transnational history.[19]

Several scholars of the early American republic have noted the new nation's fascination with Europe's views of the law of nations as a system of relations among sovereign states, though most consider that system as a model for the union of the American states, rather than a driver of foreign policy.[20] Eliga Gould's *Among the Powers of the Earth,* on the contrary, focuses on foreign policy as part of the early United States' efforts to join the European system. Gould argues convincingly that one of the early republic's greatest foreign policy goals was to win recognition as a free, independent, and treaty-worthy nation within the law-of-nations framework of Vattel's Europe, a "law-bound community of nations." Gould uses this frame to discuss relations with the countries holding colonial territory along United States borders: Spain, France, and England. He mentions the Barbary States only briefly, mostly in the context of the law of nations' recognition of the legality of slavery.[21] This book expands on Gould's lens of "seeking treaty-worthiness" to examine American interaction with the North African states, not only in bilateral terms but also in terms of the United States signaling viability and trustworthiness to European nations.

In contrast to the popular notion of Barbary piracy, all recent scholarly works explicitly or implicitly approach corsairing under "the Barbary System" as representing privateers under effective government control, such that peace treaties were meaningful and enforced. Nonetheless, many works continue to use the words *pirate* and *piracy*. This is perhaps apt, as American diplomats of the era had the same understanding of the legality of corsairing but nonetheless often used the term *pirate* in their writing even when speaking of legal predation, only carefully delineating piracy from privateering in cases when they were discussing both.[22] Most scholarship on early American interaction with North Africa focuses on bilateral relations with those powers, either diplomatically, militarily, or a combination of the two.[23] Other authors focus on the domestic impact of North African captivity and conflict on American politics and identity.[24] Europe is generally excluded from these studies, though several authors explore the influence, real and perceived, of European powers on the "Barbary System" in general and their desire to see American shipping targeted in particular. Lord Sheffield's 1783 *Observations on the Commerce of the American States* is particularly influential, with many authors highlighting Sheffield's observation "that the Barbary States are advantageous to the maritime powers is obvious."[25]

In terms of placing America's interactions in a broader international context, Frank Lambert's *The Barbary Wars* stands out. It discusses issues of American sovereignty and trade and sees Barbary contestation in terms of the struggle for free trade in the broader Atlantic world system. Recently, a handful of other scholars have followed that lead, looking at issues of international credit or military and diplomatic cooperation, most notably Abigail Mullen's recently published *To Fix a National Character: The United States in the First Barbary War, 1800–1805*. I recommend her work highly, as she foregrounds the daily challenges of American navy officers and consuls seeking to deal not only bilaterally with North African states but also in cooperation and contention with European counterparts, and offers a secondary focus on American efforts to secure its place in the

Mediterranean system during the Tripolitan War. This book expands on these scholars' insights and time frames, arguing that American interaction with Europe on Barbary affairs showed the United States' ability to live up to its obligations and highlighted the new nation as a potential partner rather than simply a supplicant, thus building treaty-worthiness. This partnership began with diplomatic cooperation and developed to coalition military operations by 1801. Though Mullen notes the frustration of some American officials in the Mediterranean that the United States was not considered a first-rate power at that time, America's status as an accepted minor power was a great step forward at the dawn of the nineteenth century, a step enabled largely by entangled interactions related to Barbary affairs.[26]

This book's focus on Barbary issues as part of a broader pattern of international relations in the early republic is not as much of a departure as it may, at first, appear. As Sadowsky has shown, diplomacy with Native American tribes and nations was closely tied to American efforts to join the European Westphalian regime, and Barbary affairs acted as a bridge between the two regimes.[27] Further, Lambert's focus on free trade implications of Barbary affairs is also strongly entangled with broader American foreign policy. As James Sofka has argued, from the 1780s through his presidency, Thomas Jefferson consistently championed a foreign policy with the goals of "securing the nation's trade routes, protecting its rights as a neutral power to undertake commerce between European belligerents, and build a naval force sufficient to defend and advance these commercial interests." His interactions with North African states as a diplomat and as president represent both continuity in American statecraft and confluence with European policies.[28] Additionally, Gould's discussion of seeking treaty-worthiness from European sister nations holding territory in North America covers diplomacy aimed at enabling trade as much as ensuring security. A major sticking point in treaty making with Spain, for example, was America's desire for a clause guaranteeing navigation rights on the Mississippi River for commercial traffic. Further, the American consular service, set up by Jefferson as secretary of state during the Washington administration, focused much more heavily on trade issues and dealing directly with merchants and sailors than on government-to-government diplomacy. Consuls were, for the most part, merchants themselves, who worked part-time on behalf of the United States government for no salary, instead receiving fees for services such as issuing passes and certifying documents. Consuls were appointed to important ports to deal with trade issues, whether the United States also had a minister accredited to the central government, as in several Spanish ports, or not, as in Canton, China, and Cap-Français, Saint-Domingue (modern Cap-Haïtien, Haiti).[29] Nonetheless, the intimate connection between trade and contestation in North Africa is well documented by Lambert. Though this work will not ignore the issue, as important as trade was to these interactions, I will focus more on "de-exceptionalizing" both North African practices and American responses to them, and on America's broader, but less tangible, foreign policy goal of being accepted as a sister nation in the Westphalian system.

Despite modern interpretations of lawless Barbary pirates and Americans who were shocked and refused to be enslaved or to be tributary, Barbary predation was neither lawless nor shocking. North African practices instead fell within recognized international bounds, and Americans had significant experience dealing with the supposedly exceptional issues of maritime predation, demands of ransom for prisoners, and the expectation of annuities as part of treaty making. Privateering, of course, was a completely normal part of warfare within European conceptions of international law, and Americans both practiced and fell prey to it during the American War of Independence. International law also sanctioned ransom for prisoners, though Americans were more familiar with the practice as part of intra-American conflicts with Indians. American diplomats were even experienced with the practice of needing to provide presents and annuities to make peace, though this practice was part of the borderland diplomatic regime, rather than negotiations with "fellow Europeans." Thus, American difficulty in dealing with these issues was more one of capacity than of unfamiliarity or unwillingness to engage with transgressive "pirate states."[30]

This study puts American interaction with North African states in the framework of completing the putative American independence of 1776 and entry into the Westphalian system via the 1778 treaties with France.

Though European powers all legally recognized the United States as a sovereign nation by 1783, in many ways it could not yet act like one. Furthermore, American identity was not yet well established among all its citizens, and its governing institutions were still in flux. The United States' actions in North Africa offered some of the new country's first opportunities to act on the international stage and build a national reputation, both among the European powers and among the American people. North African engagement was neither the beginning nor the end of this process, of course. On an international level, this venture included early cooperation via treaties of amity and commerce and contestation such as the Quasi-War with France and continued at least through the War of 1812 and the removal of British forts on United States–claimed territory and support to Native American groups living in the Old Northwest and Mississippi territories. Nonetheless, the Barbary Wars and associated diplomacy, in terms of interactions with both North African and European powers, played a much larger role in realizing American independence than usually presented.[31]

This book consists of five substantive chapters, bookended by this introduction and a short conclusion. Since the dynamics of American interaction with the Barbary powers followed the early republic's changing organization and power, the study is organized chronologically, with each chapter discussing the dynamics that characterized a given era.

Chapter 1, "The Barbary System: Mediterranean Corsairing at the Dawn of American Independence," examines Barbary corsairs and the legal framework of prize taking, both within the law of nations regime and as understood by Muslim jurists. This chapter is enriched by Algerian sources written in Arabic and translated into French by colonial archivists that are rarely considered by authors writing in English, which allows for a more nuanced understanding of the theory and practice of North African corsairing. Twenty-first-century scholars have generally understood that the vast majority of predatory North African ships were operating as legitimate privateers by the late seventeenth century. Few works, however, have concentrated on the implications of the difference between privateering and piracy except to note that since the vessels were regulated, negotiations with their regulating powers were meaningful. This chapter includes discussion of this legality, from both the European perspective and that of Islamic jurisprudence. It also addresses the debate among scholars who see corsairs as "holy warriors," those who see them as agents of the state, and those who see corsairs simply as economic extractors. The chapter argues for a synthesis of these views, showing economic motivation as primary but also noting that religious justification offered corsairs personal and public esteem. Chapter 1 further shows that there were two "Barbary Systems" at play in the era, though they operated within the same legal framework. Morocco's corsairs operated primarily as agents of the state, with captures aimed primarily toward foreign policy goals, while those of the Ottoman regencies operated primarily for profit, though under state control and with the state realizing some of the gains. Finally, the chapter examines North African captivity practices and argues that by the time of American independence, although European captives were still technically considered slaves, their treatment and ransoming practices far more closely resembled that of prisoners of war in Europe and of American captives of Indians, both before and after American independence, than the chattel slavery that victimized sub-Saharan Africans. The chapter clarifies that far from dealing with lawless pirates, early Americans were interacting with established members of the Vattelian system, so well accepted in the Mediterranean legal regime that Europeans and North Africans used each other's admiralty courts to adjudicate the status of captured vessels. If America wished to become part of this regime, it would need to do so within the accepted rules.[32]

Chapter 2, "American Sovereignty Checked: Diplomacy and Captivity in North Africa, 1776–1793," discusses the earliest captures of American vessels by North African corsairs and their results. After years of ignored diplomatic outreach to the United States, Morocco seized an American merchant ship in 1784 to evoke a diplomatic response, followed closely by two profit-motivated Algerian captures in 1785. The chapter examines the early attempts of American diplomats to secure the release of American prisoners, both through direct diplomacy with Barbary powers and through efforts to enlist European aid. Though there were notable similarities between diplomatic norms in North Africa and those Americans were familiar with in borderlands negotiation with American Indian groups, such as presents to facilitate talks and expectations of annuities, the power and resource imbalance did not favor American diplomats in North Africa. The crisis showed the new republic's limited ability to act as a sovereign nation, both in its supplicant relationship with European interlocutors and in its capacity to apply "neither Force nor Money" to solve issues with Algiers, where American prisoners would languish in captivity for over a decade.[33] Given Morocco's diplomatic goals and effective Spanish assistance, however, the United States was able to make peace with the only North African power with ports on the Atlantic. With Portugal closing the Strait of Gibraltar to the Ottoman regencies' ships, the humiliating situation in the Mediterranean was nonetheless stable. At home, American inability to secure the release of its captive citizens and safe passage for its Mediterranean trade served as a cipher for American weakness and ineffectiveness of government under the Articles of Confederation. Although fixing these failings was a large part of the argument in favor of the Constitution, even after it was ratified and the Washington administration seated, Barbary issues languished, since funds were short and prisoners few. In 1793 this changed when an abortive Algerian-Portuguese truce organized by the British to free up Portuguese naval assets to assist them in war with France had the side effect of allowing Algerian privateers through the Strait of Gibraltar to attack American shipping in the Atlantic. With dozens of new prisoners, the United States was under considerably more pressure to act.

Chapter 3, "A Minor Power: Diplomacy and American-European Cooperation in North Africa, 1793–1801," examines issues of diplomacy and law in American interactions with North African powers and with European partners on North African affairs. It explores the Washington administration and Congress's use of new constitutional powers both for treaty negotiations with North African powers and for building a small navy. The negotiations led to peace with Algiers and redemption of American prisoners in 1796, which not only opened the Mediterranean to American trade but also showed the new nation's commitment to its treaty responsibilities and ability to meet them. The chapter also introduces the larger international context in which these interactions took place, that of the disruptions of the French Revolutionary and Napoleonic Wars. These conflicts influenced smaller nations not only directly, via the great powers attempting to pull them in on one side or the other, but also tangentially. For example, European disruptions caused a hard-currency scarcity that threatened the United States' treaty with Algiers when diplomats had trouble redeeming letters of credit in order to pay the peace indemnity. Finally, chapter 3 examines the fraught, but not exceptional, relationships during the era from 1796 to 1801 when the United States, like other minor powers, paid annuities for peace with Barbary regencies, and American consuls built relationships and exchanged favors with other nations' diplomats in similar straits. It argues that the United States showed appropriate Western solidarity via its consuls' participation in what I have dubbed the "diplomatic commonwealth" in North Africa, thus building the republic's stature as a treaty-worthy partner. The ties were particularly strong between the United States, Denmark, and Sweden, all minor powers with a strong interest in neutral shipping rights. This culminated in a Swedish proposal in 1800 for an anti-Barbary military alliance. Though the United States demurred, owing to its determination to live up to all of its treaty obligations, even those with the Barbary States, the proposal showed that America had reached the stature of a credible partner nation.[34]

Chapter 4, "A Coalition of the Willing: The Multinational Tripolitan War, 1801–1805," focuses on the American-Tripolitan War (often called the First Barbary War) from a multinational perspective, arguing that it represented the United States' first overseas foray into coalition warfare via direct joint operations with Sweden, as well as support from the Kingdoms of Naples and Sicily in basing and loaning military resources, including personnel. The United States also cooperated militarily with the deposed former bey of Tripoli and governor of Derne province, Hamet Karamanli, in an overland expedition in 1805 facilitated by British and Ottoman officials in Egypt. During this conflict, the United States attempted to model its respect for the law of nations to both European and North African powers but also faced challenges from neutral North African nations with their own interpretations of international law. Additionally, like the diplomacy of the previous chapter, the Tripolitan War was also influenced by the larger context of the Napoleonic Wars. For example, the Kingdoms of Naples and Sicily withdrew from the coalition against Tripoli in 1804 as they got drawn into the War of the Third Coalition. Despite such challenges, respect for international norms and cooperation with other powers in warfare cemented the United States' position as a legitimate, if minor, power in the Vattelian system. The first American squadron commander in the Mediterranean, Commodore Richard Dale, pointed out this connection in 1801. Writing as cooperation with Sweden began, he pointed out not only the military advantages but also the value in being able to "empress on the minds of those people, also, the European Nations, what the Government of the United States can do," calling it an extremely favorable "opportunity for the U.S. to Establish a lasting reputation."[35] By 1805 European nations were suitably "empressed," and accepted the United States as a member of the sisterhood of nations, if not as the significant power that America imagined itself to be.

Chapter 5, "Changing Tides: Rising America and the Ebb of Corsairing, 1807–1825," shows the United States' development, mostly due to the War of 1812, from a decidedly minor power to, if not a great power, at least an established one. It also examines the long slow decline of North African corsairing, as power balances shifted and privateering lost legitimacy in Western eyes. The chapter discusses the difficulty in keeping peace with Barbary powers after the United States Navy withdrew from the Mediterranean in response to the *Chesapeake-Leopard* affair in 1807, in which a British warship fired on an American one. The year 1812 marked the start not only of the United States' war with Britain but also war with Algiers, though the second conflict was desultory until the first ended. The chapter discusses this lackluster contest and the surrounding issues' effects on American diplomatic efforts during the war and then contrasts this period with the short, sharp campaign of the so-called Second Barbary War in 1815 and America's imposition of treaties without peace indemnities or annuities. The United States sent two squadrons to respond to Algiers after the Treaty of Ghent was ratified, though the conflict was over before the second squadron arrived. The first squadron, under Commodore Stephen Decatur, defeated two Algerian warships—each caught alone in the Mediterranean by the entire squadron—and imposed a peace, all within two weeks of passing the Strait of Gibraltar. The chapter argues that, unlike the Tripolitan War, this conflict was less about trying to make a place in the European Vattelian system for America, and more about showing that the Vattelian system would now better be described as Western rather than European. The United States' response to this challenge demonstrated that it was no longer simply affiliated with the Vattelian system but was now an intrinsic part of it. The chapter further argues that neither the swift American campaign against Algiers nor the Anglo-Dutch bombardment of the following year represented the "defeat that broke the Barbary System." North African state-sponsored corsairing continued for at least another decade, though it gradually declined as power dynamics and norms of warfare changed following the end of the Napoleonic Wars. By 1825, rather than considering North African states a potential challenge, American diplomats considered them targets for European colonization.

The story of American challenges in Barbary is one of extensive change over time. The United States moved from being unable to meet the basic expectations of a sovereign nation after the captures of 1784–85 to functioning as a member of the Vattelian republic of nations by the end of the Tripolitan War. In 1785, as minister to France and one of the American peace commissioners to the Barbary powers, Thomas Jefferson had unsuccessfully petitioned for French assistance in gaining the release of American prisoners in Algiers. As president in 1804, he was mortified when current ministers made similar pleas regarding American prisoners in Tripoli, stating that they were making the United States appear like paupers "begging alms at every court in Europe." Jefferson felt that the young republic was no longer the incapable, peripheral, and disunified "pseudo-nation" that it had been during his ministry and had moved from needing alms to needing partners.[36] Although the United States still faced organizational challenges, Jefferson was in large measure correct, and experience and ties built via dealing with North African affairs played a significant role in bringing this change about. American relative power changed again during and following the War of 1812 with the military buildup that conflict engendered and the removal of serious challenges from Indian groups such as the Red Stick Creeks and Tecumseh's pan-Indian confederacy. The postwar United States was on much more solid footing in the international arena, and the Algerian conflict was the United States' opportunity to show its new status on the world stage. Yet, though this summary might give the impression that this steady development was somehow inevitable, as the American "Hercules in the cradle"[37] (as Alexander Hamilton put it) grew in strength, the change in American relative power actually depended on many external factors as well, from international assistance to pure fortune.

1

The Barbary System

MEDITERRANEAN CORSAIRING AT THE
DAWN OF AMERICAN INDEPENDENCE

AMERICAN INDEPENDENCE HAD SO far not been kind to James Leander Cathcart, an ambitious young man of education and pretentions to the status of gentleman. Though Cathcart had served as an officer aboard a privateer and/or in the Continental Navy during the Revolutionary War, he was only able to find work as a simple sailor aboard the merchant ship *Maria* after the conflict ended. On 25 July 1785 an armed ship of fourteen guns brought the *Maria* to just off the southwest coast of Portugal.[1] This itself was no surprise, as the area teemed with privateers who had the right to stop and inspect ships, seeking enemy shipping that could be considered a "good prize." During the War of Independence, American ships and sailors were subject to capture by the British and, if serving on naval vessels or privateers, also participated in the capture of British ships and sailors. Whether Cathcart had served as a regular or a privateer, he was definitely familiar with them. His uncle was a privateer, and Cathcart spent time on British prison ships during the war, where he doubtless interacted with many merchant sailor and privateer prisoners as well.[2] But the war was over now, and with America at peace, being stopped was simply an inconvenience—a matter of showing papers and submitting to an inspection.[3]

Cathcart's first hint that this inspection might not go well was when he realized that the ship that had stopped them was crewed by Muslims, or as he put it, "Mahomotans." Since Cathcart knew that Spain did not allow Algerian corsairs through the Strait of Gibraltar, he assumed that they must be Moroccans, and he had heard rumors that renegade Moroccan vessels had turned pirate and thus might not accept the fact that America and Morocco were at peace. As it turned out, this fear was unfounded. The corsairs were licensed and under government control. They were not Moroccans, however, but Algerians. Unbeknownst to Cathcart, Spain and Algiers had just made peace. Cathcart would later be convinced that Charles Logie, British consul to Algiers, had unleashed the Algerian corsairs on American shipping. In Cathcart's conception, as soon as Logie knew of the peace that removed Spanish blockage of the strait, he pointed out to Algiers that American ships would be lawful targets and were plentiful in the Gulf of Cadiz, as a form of revenge on Americans for rebelling against Britain. Though there is no evidence to support this, the Algerian corsairs had certainly taken quick advantage of the open strait, and the *Maria* was the first American vessel they found.

The corsairs examined the ship, demanding its flag and papers, including its Mediterranean pass. As Cathcart put it, "Of the first they had no knowledge and the papers they could not read and Mediterranean pass we had none."[4] One might think, then, that as lawful privateers of a country not at war with the United States, the corsairs would have released the *Maria* to go upon her way. But as America did not have a treaty with Algiers and came from non-Muslim lands (the *dar al-harb*, or "abode of war"), Algiers considered themselves at war by default. Thus, the *Maria* was a good prize, and the crew members the most valuable part of it. The corsairs took Cathcart and his shipmates to Algiers, where most of them spent over a decade in slavery.

But it was an odd sort of slavery from the American perspective. Although Cathcart considered himself a victim of "every scene of slavery," his new status offered him lucrative opportunities and was considerably less dangerous than his time on a British prison ship. On those ships, approximately half of American prisoners died in captivity, mostly of disease.[5] The plague threatened American captives in Algiers and killed several over the decade of captivity, but Algerian captivity was still safer than being held on British prison ships. Further, Algerian "ransom slaves" had privileges that were usually only available to Anglo-American prisoners of war if they were paroled. Prisoners in Algiers had the opportunity to earn money and engage in business, and even to buy their way out of mandatory labor. Cathcart took full advantage of these licenses, investing the earnings from his position as secretary lucratively, to the point that he was finally able to credibly style himself a gentleman. Upon his release in 1797, he had amassed a considerable fortune and purchased a ship that he sailed back to America, thus entitling him to the coveted title "Captain Cathcart" and enabling him to marry well.[6]

Before we examine American interaction with the "Barbary System" in detail, we need a clear view of what that system actually entailed. Understanding what sort of challenge Americans were facing is vital to analyzing how they dealt with it and what it meant to them. Three contending images of North African corsairing compete both in the public imagination and in scholarship: that of lawless piracy, that of religiously motivated "maritime jihad," and that of a capitalist enterprise motivated entirely by profit. The first of these remains current in popular conception but has fallen out of favor among scholars, as little research is required before one encounters the level of government and legal control over corsair activities. Still, some scholars who encounter North African corsairs tangentially to other research, or whose interest is in depicting Americans of the early republic as "standing up to lawlessness," sometimes perpetuate the stereotype of "Barbary pirates," often replacing the North African polities as the lawless actors, rather than the corsairs themselves.[7] Scholars who accept a "clash of civilizations" narrative emphasize essentialist notions of the continuation of religious clashes and present North African corsairing as a continuation of (alternately) endemic jihad, the Crusades, or the Spanish "Reconquista."[8] Most recent scholarship, however, focuses on economics and accepts the assessment of American prisoner in (and later United States consul to) Algiers Richard O'Brien, who coined the term "Barbary System" to describe the economically motivated corsairing and treaty making he observed, a term quickly picked up by other American diplomats in North Africa. O'Brien summed up corsairing motivations with the cynical statement "Money is the God of Algiers and Mahomet their prophet."[9] But the notion of corsair motivation as either economic or religious is a false dichotomy. The tradition of Islamic *ghazi* (literally "raiding" but also used for conquest of non-Islamic territory) includes no restrictions against "doing well by doing good." Within this tradition, all non-Muslims could be legitimate targets for raids unless they specifically made peace. Additionally, regardless of motivation, it is vital to understand the central place North African corsairs had in the Vattelian legal regime, as that regime constrained both their actions and America's response. If America wanted to be part of this international system, it would have to show its respect for the rules.[10]

This chapter argues that in addition to economic gain, North African leaders and corsairs derived prestige and legitimacy from their maritime predation against non-Muslims. In doing so, it traces the legal status of corsairing, both in Islamic jurisprudence and in that portion of the law of nations which came to be known as admiralty law. While Vattel's vision of international law was heavily Eurocentric, it included precedent based on North African practices. Additionally, the early modern treaties upon which Vattel's nonclassical legal arguments were based included extensive examples from bilateral agreements between "Christian" European powers and the Ottoman Empire. While the Ottomans are often thought of as Middle Eastern today, the "Sublime Porte" represented a vigorous European power long before it was the "sick man of Europe." Well-known precepts of maritime international law, such as the concept of sovereign territory extending from the shore for three nautical miles of territorial water, trace to international agreements between the Ottoman Empire and other European powers.[11]

North Africa's place in that network of agreements, and indeed within the Ottoman Empire itself, was far more contested. Though Morocco was never claimed by the Porte, the Regencies of Algiers, Tunis, and Tripoli were connected with varying strength to the Ottoman Empire from the mid-sixteenth century through at least 1830, and in some cases through World War I. These regencies were not regularized governorates within the Ottoman Empire but rather separate "hearths," a title also shared by the semi-independent Crimean Khanate. Such polities were appended to the empire under a level of control that varied widely, depending on international circumstances and on the power dynamics between the hearths and the Porte. In the 1620s many northern European powers gave up hope of the Ottoman Porte being able to control North African corsairing and began negotiating bilateral treaties directly with the regencies. These treaties framed the Barbary regencies as independent sovereign powers in the eyes of most European powers, as well as in the regencies' own eyes, further weakening Ottoman imperial control. The agreements also brought the North African regencies directly into the treaty-bound regime of international law.

Regardless of the religious perspective at play, by the mid-seventeenth century North African corsairing was a regularized and law-bound part of the Mediterranean international regime. While many authors, both of primary sources and of recent scholarship, use the terms pirate and corsair interchangeably (if they use the latter at all), the legal status of the two varied considerably. Pirates were those who preyed on commercial shipping or coastal communities without sanction from a recognized sovereign. Jurists of both international law based on the Roman tradition and of Islamic sharia considered unsanctioned pirates the "enemies of all mankind." Privateers and navies, of course, often committed the same acts, but as their actions were sanctioned by a sovereign as acts of war, jurists considered their actions legal. This simple clarification becomes more complicated when one considers controversies over who has sovereign right to license predation and the fact that many sea raiders committed both licit and illicit violence at different times, often even within the same voyage. In general, however, one can consider corsairing as a subtype of privateering, especially in the treaty-bound Mediterranean of the eighteenth and early nineteenth centuries. The primary difference between corsairing and other state-sponsored privateering lay in the assumption of hostility. While most nations and empires considered peace the default condition and only unleashed privateers on their enemies when they explicitly began hostilities, both Christian and Muslim corsairing polities retained earlier notions that nations of the other religion were valid targets unless peace was explicitly contracted.[12]

By the mid-eighteenth century, Barbary corsairs were heavily regulated by their respective governments. Indeed, many corsairing vessels were government owned, and those in private hands usually belonged to prominent and high-ranking officials in the regime acting in their private capacities but still very much under government control. Captains (*rais*) occasionally had an ownership interest in the vessel but were not private actors. Much of the regencies' budget came either directly from corsairing or, increasingly in the era examined, indirectly via indemnities paid for peace.

The popular image of low-slung Barbary galleys rowed by multitudes of Christian slaves was an anachronism by the time of American independence. Though Maltese corsairs sponsored by the Knights Hospitaller of Saint John continued to use rowed galleys well into the late eighteenth century, Barbary corsairs had moved on to sailing vessels capable of operating in much harsher sea conditions. References to North African galleys were extremely rare by the mid-eighteenth century, with the exceptions of occasional Moroccan vessels operating during good weather in the Strait of Gibraltar. Most corsairing vessels by this time were xebecs (slim ships with pronounced overhanging bow and stern and often augmented with a few oars for use in port and when becalmed), brigs (larger vessels with square-rigged sails also widely used in the Atlantic as both trade and light warships), and occasional frigates (purpose-built warships with a gundeck below the main deck).

With the reduced need for labor to power the galleys and the vast profits that could be realized from ransoms, North African captivity was very different from the "wretched galley slave" stereotype that Anglo-Americans still imagined in the 1780s. While captives were technically property, they were not slaves in the sense of chattel slavery practiced both in America and by North Africans on sub-Saharan Africans in the era. Instead, Christians and Muslims along the Ottoman frontier (and by the eighteenth century mostly within the Mediterranean) practiced what some scholars have taken to calling "ransom slavery" on each other, capturing prisoners primarily for their ransom value. Although individual prisoners might technically be the property of the owner of the ship that captured them, that did not mean that these private owners controlled the prisoners but only that they received the bulk of any ransom money. Far from being sent to "the slave markets" as some scholars envision, by the 1780s most prisoners were publicly held and most of their labor was used for public works. Prisoners also were granted extensive agency, able to do by right what chattel slaves could often only accomplish via resistance. Ransom slaves were allowed, for example, to hold property and improve their living conditions or even buy their way out of public labor with money remitted to them or that they earned themselves. Although his case is exceptional, James Cathcart had amassed a fortune of several thousand dollars by the time of his release from captivity in Algiers, and he returned to America in a ship he had purchased at public auction after its capture by Algerian corsairs.[13]

Jihad or Capitalism?

The notion of bloodthirsty and uncontrolled "Barbary pirates" is no longer found in scholarly history and has become rare even in popular history. If North African corsairing was not piracy then, what was it? Some scholars make the mistake of passing over this question entirely to focus on American interaction, without considering that interaction is entangled. One cannot interpret American responses without understanding what they were responding to, both in their perception and in the views of both North Africans and the international community. Most recent scholars do consider the question, however, and consider corsairing a form of extractive capitalism. Though the notion that corsairing represented a continuation of centuries-long religious warfare is still very common in popular histories, it has become exceptional in recent scholarship. I am only aware of two scholars who have published this century making that argument, neither of whom is primarily a historian of North Africa.[14] One scholar, on the other hand, argues that corsairs served as instruments of state policy on behalf of both the Ottoman Porte and the Tunisian *beylical* administration. In this conception, the North African regencies received an exemption from annual tax payments to Istanbul in exchange for "waging the corso against the Christian enemies of the Porte," and the regency used corsairing as a tool of control over elements of the *jund* (military) and as a source of revenue for the Tunisian treasury, enabling the administration to carry out its domestic policies.[15]

These few voices aside, most recent scholarship concurs that economics primarily motivated corsairs toward plunder and that corsairing was simply "cloaked as a Christian holy war or an Islamic jihad."[16] Frank Lambert, for example, calls North African corsairing (or piracy, as he calls it in this context) "a capitalist enterprise" and cites (as do many other authors) Richard O'Brien's bon mot that "Money is the God of Algiers." Lambert locates the genesis of North African economic dependence on corsairing in 1511, when Spain instituted a 50 percent surtax on Algiers's wool imports. In his estimation this unjust taxation led Algiers to "bolster its economy through piracy," as Spain's actions justified their efforts to "recoup their losses by any means."[17] Other scholars make similar economic arguments but tie corsairing to the effects of the so-called Northern Invasion of English, Dutch, and French shipping in the Mediterranean in the late sixteenth century.[18]

While corsairing was clearly not a continuation of unchanging and endemic holy war, recent repudiations of any religious component overstate the case. French scholar Daniel Panzac offers a vision that recognizes the primacy of economic motivation, while also considering the self-presentation of corsairs as religious warriors. As he puts it, "Although privateering had a recognized religious dimension and its political role was not negligible, its primary purpose was obviously an economic one." That said, he also asserts that corsairing was not simply cloaked in jihad, but that the corsairs "in the eyes of the population, were the *mudjahid*, fighters for the faith, *ghazis*, soldiers waging war against the Infidels."[19] How are we to reconcile this seemingly essentialized presentation with the notion of economic primacy? Panzac does not really try, simply presenting a source supporting these religious presentations and then changing the subject to economic matters. The issue need not be seen as a dichotomy however, as religion can be a motivating and justifying factor without making it determinative. Recent scholarship has begun to return to accepting *ghazi* self-presentation as more than simple rhetoric and that plunder and *ghazwa* are in no way contradictory impulses. Indeed, spoils were often seen as a sign of worthiness and God's favor, especially if some of the profits were used for religious endowments.[20]

This self-presentation was fully at play in late eighteenth-century North Africa. Part of the proceeds from corsairing were reserved for religious purposes, though it was a very small portion. Just enough, perhaps, to justify the use of the prestigious titles of *ghazi* and *mujahid*. The

Algerian Registry of Prizes from 1765 to 1827 generally only records the proceeds and the size of an individual share for each prize. A few records, however, indicate all the expenses taken from the gross value, from the state's one-eighth share to the wages paid to longshoremen who unloaded the prize. Of these itemized accounts, the majority include between a quarter and a half of a percent set aside for the maintenance of the tombs of holy men (*marabouts*). It is possible that all prizes in this era set aside such a portion and that it was simply not always recorded. As of 1702, a portion for *marabouts* was mandatory, and funds were distributed to six tomb sites. An undated administrative document that updated this policy added the tombs of twenty-eight *marabouts* (two of whom were women) to the list of supported holy sites and specified the procedures for collecting and distributing the funds during "our reign." From the format of the document, it appears to match several dated 1760, making it likely that this was the guidance of Dey Baba Ali, who reigned 1754–66.[21]

In addition to, and perhaps justified by, these small religious donations from corsairing's proceeds, the rulers of Algiers, Tunis, and Tripoli in the late eighteenth and early nineteenth centuries still consistently styled themselves as commanders of "frontier outposts of *jihad*,"[22] a presentation that apparently resonated even outside formal proclamations. For example, the memoirs of an Arab resident, Ahmad al-Zahhar (1781–1872), the chief Algerian descendant of the prophet, describe Mustafa Baba, dey of Algiers from 1799 to 1805, as "loving the *mujahidin* and *ghazi*." On the other hand, al-Zahhar's accounts simply highlight gains from raids and peace indemnities and spend little to no time discussing religious motivation or any damage done to putative religious enemies. For example, his entire entry entitled "War with Genoa" reads: "In the year 1209h [1794] the emir ordered seven *jihadi* ships prepared. As they were leaving, the emir ordered the captain to travel to the area of Genoa and Sardinia and take Genoese and Sardinian ships. They took ten Sardinian ships and some Genoese, and when the day of departure came, they headed to Algiers. In front of them came the prizes. And when they sold those prizes, they parceled out the money, which was eight sultanas each."[23]

The use of religious terminology while focusing on the spoils gained and examples of small donations of prize money to holy sites shows that religious motivation for corsairing resonated but did not predominate. While those scholars who see corsairing as a capitalist enterprise are largely correct, religion was nonetheless not simply a cynical cover for economic motivation; though religion provided justification more than motivation, it also offered corsairs personal and public esteem. This esteem was augmented by the legitimacy of their actions, not only in terms of religious rhetoric but in terms of internal and external legal frameworks.

Corsairing and Law

The legitimacy of raiding against non-Muslims was straightforward in Islamic jurisprudence, as was that of making peace. The Quran's ninth chapter, *surah at-tabah,* which calls for jihad against nonbelievers under certain conditions, specifically includes fellow "people of the book" (Jews and Christians) as legitimate targets "until they give the *jizyah* [a tax on non-Muslim residents] by hand and submit themselves."[24] Although the *jizyah* reference marks this passage as applying specifically to those living in Muslim lands and thus subject to taxation, both the Hanafi school of jurisprudence dominant in the Ottoman Empire and the Malaki school predominant in North Africa recognize the use of legal analogy (*qiyas*). Thus, peacemaking with Christians outside the *dar al-islam* was legitimate, especially if it included an indemnity that could be read as both a mark of submission and an analog to the *jizyah*. Though the law was clear, practice was less so. One of the most common problems of illicit violence in the Ottoman courts in the seventeenth century was that of Muslims raiding against protected communities that paid either the literal *jizyah,* such as Greek subjects of the empire, or the figurative one of having contracted a peace.[25]

Although legal systems based on Islamic jurisprudence did not maintain specific courts for maritime law issues, precedents and legal decrees (fatwas) developed in remarkable parallel with that of admiralty law in Europe. For example, salvage rights for recaptures were quite similar. Rulings from seventeenth-century chief muftis specified that if an "enemy infidel" takes a Muslim's ship out of Islamic territory and then sells it to a Muslim who returns to Islamic territory, the original owner must pay the new owner its value if he wishes it returned. If, however, the non-Muslims failed to complete a legal transfer of ownership by taking the ship out of the *dar al-islam* and simply sold it in place, the new owner would not have valid title and must return it to the original owner for free. Compare this to Grotius's 1625 statement that by the law of nations "things which, although seized by the enemy, have not yet been brought within his fortifications . . . have not yet changed ownership."[26] Vattel's 1758 guidance is even more similar, noting that a ship taken by the enemy does not count as "irrecoverably lost, until the ship be in a place of safety with regard to the enemy who has taken her, and entirely in his power," and therefore if retaken remains the original owner's property.[27]

It is unsurprising that these points of law compare so well. Both Grotius's and Vattel's visions of the law of nations were based heavily on international precedent. Though ancient practice played a large role, more recent precedent proved more convincing to both authors. For example, Grotius included a long chapter on the principle of "postliminy" (the doctrine that people and things taken in war reverted to their previous status and ownership once returned under the power of their original nation), which was based on his understanding of Roman law. He noted however that "to-day ships are not among the things which are recovered by postliminy," citing a 1620s case in France that held goods taken by Algerians had changed ownership by the law of war.[28] Treaties naturally made the best precedent, as they were not simply rulings within one country that considered international issues but binding international agreements. Many of those treaty agreements involved the Ottoman Empire, thus making it effectively a charter member of Vattel's imagined republic of nations and a prime builder of the laws that bound them.

Even issues not specified by treaty could be considered binding via customary international usage. The Vattelian notion of territorial waters extending a "cannon shot" from shore is an outstanding case in point. While he does not trace the origins of this precept, Michael Talbot's work on Ottoman maritime territorial claims shows its legal elaboration in the midst of an entangled diplomatic, military, and commercial regime in the seventeenth and eighteenth century. One of the great debates in international law in the seventeenth century was that between Grotius's "open sea" theory of the sea as a free resource to all, and Selden's "closed sea" theory, which held that if a nation held effectively controlled or "occupied" a sea, it could be possessed. The conventional history of this legal argument was that it was solved in 1703 when Dutch lawyer Cornelius van Bynkershoek proposed a compromise by which seas that were under actual threat of cannon fire from a fortified position on land were considered as part of the sovereign territory of the power owning the fortress. In actuality, this compromise did not settle the argument, which was still considered somewhat open by Vattel in 1758, nor was it a completely new concept.[29]

In the late seventeenth century, the British, Dutch, and French attacked each other's shipping in the Levant as part of the Nine Years' War (1688–97). The Ottoman Empire initially complained only about its neutrality being violated when hostilities occurred within range of one of its fortifications. When the Porte attempted to assert closed sea theory to declare a "hostility free zone" in the north Adriatic in 1696, the British ambassador to Istanbul protested that this was an "innovation contrary to the laws of the ocean" and that "it is not possible to give limits to any seaport beyond Canon shot without occasioning many undeterminable disputes."[30] It is thus clear that the notion was not exclusively an innovation of van Bynkershoek's. In fact, the basic precepts can be seen in Venetian-Ottoman treaties and diplomatic exchanges related to corsairing at least as early as the 1630s. Venice and the Porte pledged not to allow Maltese and Barbary corsairs, respectively, to use their ports to prey on the other, either as bases or as places to bring captured prizes. On the open ocean, enemy corsairs were fair game, but when Venice pursued Algerian and Tunisian ships into the port of Valona in 1638, it almost led to war as a violation of Ottoman sovereignty. Similarly, in 1644 when Maltese corsairs went ashore on Crete with a prize, the Porte held Venice responsible, though Venice argued that the Maltese had landed without their permission in a place where the Venetians had no fortification or cannons. The Ottoman Empire did not accept this as abrogating the Venetian treaty responsibility, and it led to the Cretan War of 1645–69. In these treaties and disputes lay the building blocks of the law of the sea.[31]

Many of the precepts of lawful and unlawful prize taking had roots in North African and European entanglement in the Mediterranean. The notion of privateering itself—that sovereigns could lawfully license private violence against their enemies—had been firmly entrenched since antiquity, but the specifics of the practice were often contested and negotiated through diplomatic channels. The disputes mentioned above, for example, fortified the notion that seizing an enemy ship within the territorial waters of a neutral power was a violation of that power's sovereignty and thus unlawful. While privateers often ignored this rule when they felt they might get away with it, courts often ordered the release of vessels so captured. North African powers fully recognized this precept. Thus, for example, an Algerian cruise of 1786 returned with eleven prizes, but three of them were released as unlawful. One Neapolitan vessel, an otherwise good prize, was released because it had been captured in Spanish waters. The other two were released as belonging to powers with whom Algiers was at peace, though one was particularly contentious in court, since although the vessel belonged to the Holy Roman Empire, it had no imperial subjects on board. The crew was entirely Genoan, a polity with which Algiers was at war.[32]

Such confused issues of a vessel's legitimate registry were extremely common in an era when crews and sometimes even ownership groups were often international, a problem that American-flagged ships or those with mixed crews that included American officers would later encounter. The commonly accepted usage of flying false flags and the less accepted but still rather common issues of unreadable (due to condition or to language barriers) or forged ships papers made this a difficult issue for would-be captors. Vessel nationality confusion was mitigated through the development of two-part passports. The consul representing the European power would provide a top cut to a special pattern, different for each treaty-bound nation (often scalloping through an illustration), that when matched up with the bottom that the protected ship kept among its papers would show an uninterrupted page. Thus, privateers could determine the ship's bona fides, even if they could not read the language of the passport. It is unclear when and with whom this style of Mediterranean pass originated. Treaties called for passports without specifying their format as early as the Dutch-Algerian treaty of 1712, and the two-part passes may have been used by then. It was clearly an established practice by 1736. In that year, the Danish Slave Fund Commission pointed out the need for two-part passports as part of the preparations for a proposed peace treaty between Denmark and Algiers.[33]

Such passes were in widespread use by the time of American independence, as illustrated by a proclamation from King George III of England in 1765 requiring the return of passes in a previous format in exchange for passes of a new form, as old ones "may have by accident or undue means fallen into the hands of foreigners."[34] Tunisian corsairs reportedly investigated and brought in a particularly bold example of such pass falsification in 1786. They stopped a large ship that presented papers and a Mediterranean pass for a British ship out of Waterford, Ireland. When an English-speaking member of the Tunisian crew tried to speak with the ship's crew, however, none of them spoke English. They claimed (in some mutually intelligible language, most likely Italian or the Mediterranean trade language based on it, "Lingua Franca") that the crew were all Irish speakers of Gaelic who knew no English. Upon investigation after the ship was sent in, however, the English consul discovered that the ship was from the Hanseatic League out of Lübeck and that the language they had claimed was Irish Gaelic was actually a dialect of German.[35] To avoid fraud and counterfeiting, European powers changed their passes regularly, often after complaints from North African powers about incidents like that above. These practices, created to regularize and limit maritime predation, led to a conventional maritime regime throughout the Mediterranean and indeed the broader Atlantic world.

By the time of American independence, international maritime law was standardized and generally accepted enough that it was common for captors to take their prizes to foreign admiralty courts. Captors were confident that if they proved it a "good prize," the court would condemn the vessel, which the captors could then keep as their own or, far more commonly, sell on the open market.[36] North African powers took full part in this international legal regime. Barbary corsairing was not just analogous to European systems of prize taking, it was an integral part of both its development and its practice. North African powers sometimes took their prizes to European courts rather than bringing them to their home ports for adjudication, most commonly when the prize would be difficult to get home owing either to its condition or to a shortage of available sailors for prize crews. In 1768, for example, Algerian corsairs had two prizes condemned in the British court at Port Mahon, Minorca, and sold them locally. While the Register of Prizes does not give a reason for these vessels not being brought into Algiers, other prizes from the same cruise were condemned and sold in Tunis, hinting that corsairs were choosing their venues primarily based on convenience during this particular cruise.[37] Similarly, one of the American ships Algiers captured in the Atlantic in 1793 was in bad enough shape that the captors decided to bring it in to the nearby port of Cadiz, Spain, where they sold it in place, as they were concerned about their prize crew getting it safely back to Algiers. Likewise, European privateers would sometimes bring their captures into North African ports for adjudication.[38] Though the origins of this practice are unknown, it was clearly normalized by the end of the eighteenth century. Far from lawless piracy, the "Barbary System" was part and parcel of the Vattelian international legal regime. European powers fully accepted the legitimacy of maritime predation as practiced by North African powers. Yet that acceptance was relatively recent, owing to disputes not about the practices themselves but rather about whether North African regencies had the sovereign power to authorize hostilities in their own right.

Barbary in the Ottoman Empire

Morocco's sovereign right to make war was clear-cut. Morocco had never been subordinated to the Ottoman Empire. Indeed, it was considered an empire in its own right, as it had consolidated several previously independent polities. Despite the creation or conquest of multiple European enclaves on its coasts throughout the early modern era, it was also never generally subordinated to a European power. Interestingly, the most well-known Moroccan corsairs, the famed "Salé Rovers" of the seventeenth century, were not under Moroccan imperial control at the time. Instead, Salé had declared itself a separate republic, though its lack of international recognition meant that its sovereignty was questionable. The Republic of Salé was short-lived, however, and by the mid-eighteenth century Moroccan corsairing was under central governmental control.

Seventeenth-century controversy about sovereignty largely centered on maritime predation in the Ottoman regencies of North Africa. Over the century, Ottoman imperial sovereignty in the regencies generally gave way to local de facto, and increasingly de jure, control over foreign policy. Maritime predation was not only an example of this change but also a prime driver of it. In the early seventeenth century, stout English, French, and Dutch vessels built for the harsher seas of the Atlantic became much more common in the already entangled Mediterranean regime of trade and conflict, a phenomenon that Fernand Braudel famously labeled the "Northern Invasion." While more recent scholarship has revised Braudel's notion of this process as sudden and dominating, the new players definitely had an impact on the diplomatic and legal regimes involving privateering. In addition to the issues of defining territorial water discussed above, these negotiations furthered the independent status of the North African regencies.[39]

As new Atlantic powers became players in the Mediterranean, they joined an existing diplomatic regime in Istanbul, a challenge the new United States would also have to face almost two centuries later. Initially, the newcomers worked together with established powers such as Venice on corsairing issues and made treaties with the Sublime Porte theoretically protecting their commerce. In 1617, however, the Dutch pioneered direct diplomacy in North Africa when they sent a mission to Algiers including both a Dutch and an Ottoman envoy in an attempt to win Algerian compliance with the treaty. Soon, France and England followed suit. Initially these efforts represented three-way diplomacy, but after witnessing Venice's abject failure to cow Algiers via invoking decrees from Istanbul in 1625, the northern powers turned to bilateral negotiations. That same year, England made a treaty with Algiers that, while referencing England's treaty with Istanbul as a basis, was nonetheless effectively a treaty between two sovereign powers. By 1676 English treaties with North African powers were no longer even mentioning Ottoman treaties and referred to Algiers, Tunis, and Tripoli as "kingdoms."[40] Based on these treaties, Irish jurist Charles

Molloy wrote in 1682 that the regencies had "acquired the reputation of a Government" and thus "cannot properly be esteemed Pirates."[41] The North African regimes had been welcomed into the republic of nations as sovereign powers largely on their willingness and ability to control corsairing after the Sublime Porte had shown the willingness but not the capacity. While the Ottomans continued to see the regencies as connected to the empire, their subordination became increasingly tenuous.

By the time of the American Revolution, that connection was limited mostly to the regencies' ethnic Turkish elites recruiting for their *jund* in Anatolia, giving periodic gifts to the Sublime Porte, and usually (but not always) sending their corsairing ships to join the Ottoman fleet when requested for a major campaign. While the Porte occasionally sent remonstrances against North African corsairs preying on powers at peace with the Ottoman Empire, mostly the Ottomans accepted separate foreign policies. For example, in 1754 the Ottoman courts prosecuted Ottoman subjects from Crete for participating in Tripoli's raids on Venetian shipping while the empire was at peace with Venice, but did not complain of Tripoli going to war with Venice. Instead, the Porte simply forbad Ottoman subjects from going to Tripoli to obtain a Tripolitan flag and participate in the corsairing, and sent a copy of this ruling to the bey of Tripoli. This decree both tacitly recognized that Tripolitans were not Ottoman subjects and that Tripoli had the right to make war outside Ottoman policy.[42]

The Ottoman Porte largely ignored affairs internal to or between the regencies as well. The Porte did not appoint judges and governors in the regencies, as it did in most parts of the empire. Even in cases of uprisings or interventions from one regency into another, the Porte would generally accept the outcome as a fait accompli, so long as the victors made formal submission and sent appropriate gifts, even if the violence was against a representative of the Ottoman regime. The fate of Ahmed (better known in America by the nickname Hamet) Karamanli, onetime bey of Tripoli and later ally of the United States during the Tripolitan War, serves as a case in point. When violence broke out in Tripoli in 1793 as part of a dynastic struggle, the Porte initially took no action. Then an Anatolian Ottoman officer named Ali Burghul was able to obtain a decree (*firman*) that he was empowered to restore order in Tripoli, for which he would be given its governorship if successful. While this could be interpreted as an act of good governance, it seems more a case of licensing a private adventure, especially given the Porte's response to following events. After Burghul successfully took Tripoli and drove Hamet Karamanli into exile, Bey Hammuda of Tunis intervened. In 1795 he sent armies into Tripoli, drove out Burghul, and installed a different Karamanli, Hamet's brother Yusuf, to the beyship. This direct contravention of Burghul's imperial *firman* was excused via an embassy with rich gifts, and Hammuda's ambassador returned with "the sultan's pardon, the present of a frigate and a firman of confirmation of investiture for Hammuda Pasha, as well as a robe of honor for the Qaramanli bey [Yusuf] in Tripoli."[43]

By the end of the eighteenth century, Algiers, Tunis, and Tripoli occupied a status between that of full independence and Ottoman possession. They were, perhaps, more analogous to franchises of the Ottoman state than to wholly owned subsidiaries. Tripoli was ruled by an Arabized dynasty of Turkish descent from Karaman in Anatolia, the Karamanlis. The Husayni dynasty of Tunis was similar, though descended from Cretan, rather than Anatolian, Turks. Algiers was governed by a dey chosen for life by election of the regency's Turkish *jund*, a practice that sometimes led it to be called a republic. All three regencies were considered sovereign by European powers, and all three had economies based largely on corsairing or the indemnities brought by peace treaties. If Americans wished to deal with corsairing powers, they would have to do so directly, as the Porte had little control over their activities. Further, Morocco's sovereign right to license predation was unquestionable. Surprisingly, though, the country from whence the most famous corsairs of the previous century had come had the smallest corsair fleet in North Africa and used it more for foreign policy leverage than for economic gain.

The Logistics and Practice of Corsairing

By the mid-eighteenth century, Morocco rarely had more than five seaworthy corsairing ships in commission. Although corsairing was no longer an economic staple, emperors began ordering their corsairs to make limited captures in preparation for opening negotiations over treaty disputes. To be sure, these negotiations often led to Morocco receiving peace indemnities, but they were quite small and clearly not a major portion of the country's economy. Instead, the goal was usually policy based. The case of the British ship *Ann* in 1756 is an illustrative example. Moroccan corsairs captured the *Ann* and imprisoned its crew and passengers (including Elizabeth Marsh, whose book *The Female Captive* became a classic of the captivity narrative genre) during a time of formal peace between Britain and Morocco. In 1755 British captains had traded munitions for fresh supplies from independent warlords on the Moroccan coast, angering the son (and effective regent) of Sultan Abdallah, Sidi Mohammed. This rupture gave Sidi Mohammed the opportunity to further one of his prime foreign policy goals. He ordered a British vessel captured and held the passengers and crew as hostages, looking not for ransoms but for Britain to establish a formal consulship in Morocco. After holding the captives for a few weeks, Sidi Mohammed effectively opened negotiations by sending the British governor of Gibraltar a letter permitting him to send a ship to retrieve the captives. The British ship's arrival led to several weeks of negotiations during which the release of the hostages was implicit but not guaranteed before other issues were settled. Sidi Mohammed made it clear that he expected Britain to appoint a formal consul within four months. If Britain refused, he would declare war, target British shipping with his corsairs generally rather than just this single object lesson, and cease selling supplies to the British garrison in Gibraltar. Though widespread corsairing served as a threat, Morocco used both that threat and the highly limited captures actually carried out as instruments of foreign policy. Independent America would experience similar "corsairing as diplomatic leverage" from Morocco in the decades to come.[44]

Yet Algiers, Tunis, and Tripoli would pose greater challenges in terms of both threats to American shipping and the expense of treaty making. In the regencies, corsairing was far more key to the economy, and leaders expected peace indemnities to substitute for corsairing income. As consuls came to realize, however, once legitimate targets became rare, peace with one power likely presaged a rupture with another. Even when indemnities were sufficiently lucrative, leaders had to keep some lawful targets for their corsairing fleets in order to keep them operational and because the corsairs themselves represented a powerful interest within the regencies. Since the gains of direct corsairing and indemnities paid to avoid it were distributed differently, corsairing interests sometimes diverged from that of leaders, particularly at the crew level, as most shipowners were also high officers of state, but most crew members' pay was based on the value of prizes seized.

Unsurprisingly, given these different foci, the regencies kept larger fleets of corsairing vessels than Morocco around the turn of the nineteenth century. In 1797 the Algerian Register of Prizes listed twenty-three vessels that had taken prizes. While it seems that not all these vessels were active at the same time (active fleet lists of this era seem to average eleven vessels, and several of the ships in the Register of Prizes had been lined through), they are particularly interesting, as the register includes the ownership of each vessel. Six were public property. Nine were owned by eminent individuals, most of whom were high officers of state acting in their private capacities, including two owned by the dey and four by the admiral of the fleet, one of which he also captained personally. Eight vessels were the property of ownership groups headed by the captain of the ship, including four who had other trades when not cruising: a watchmaker, a tanner, a weaver, and a blacksmith.[45]

The regencies of Tunis and Tripoli had similar, if smaller, corsairing fleets. An inventory prepared by an American observer (it seems to be William Eaton, but the document is unsigned) in Tunis in 1799 gives a fleet of thirteen vessels, one publicly owned, two each owned personally by the bey and the prime minister (*sahib at-tabb'a*, literally "keeper of the seal" and sometimes anglicized as "Sapitapa"), one owned by an ownership group, and the rest by three individuals whose names are given but who are not otherwise identified. Of those three, I was able to identify one as an officer of state with certainty and two provisionally. "Mah't [Mohamet] Galloulee" was the governor (*qa'id*) of Sfax, out of which his impressive five-ship squadron operated, and "Agi" is almost certainly a reference to Mohammed Hodja, the director of the arsenal (*amin at-tarsanah*). I was unable to find any further information on "Mah't Caiasci," but as his single ship was the only vessel operating out of Monastir, it is likely that he was the *qa'id* there. Though I could not to find an ownership registry or a fleet inventory for Tripoli in the 1790s to make a direct comparison, I was able to bracket the era. The French consul reported a fleet of fourteen ships in 1785, and in 1802 Commodore Dale's coordination with his Swedish counterpart included the intelligence that Tripoli had nine operational corsairing ships. Though it is likely that ownership distribution was similar to those of the other regencies, Tripoli's corsairing ships tended to be smaller, with several galliots (vessels with both sails and a bank of oars) that could be within economic reach of less eminent investors.[46]

The North African corsair fleets typically made three cruises a year, starting around March and returning from the last usually in December. Fitting out and crewing vessels was a major expense. Captures by public vessels and those owned by high officials were disproportionally high, likely because those ships received the resources they needed to cruise far more reliably. Algiers's 1797 cruises are particularly illustrative, as we have detailed information about ship ownership and a complete record of the prizes. Algerian corsairs made fifteen captures totaling twenty-two good prizes that year, almost all from various Italian states. Of those (counting shared captures proportionally), over half of the captures were made by publicly owned ships and those that were the private property of the dey. None of the other privately owned vessels made more than one capture, which four ships accomplished, and five vessels recorded only a half or one-third share in a capture.[47]

Once out on cruise, North African corsairs operated largely as did the many other privateers active in the Mediterranean, especially during time of war between the greater powers. The corsairs would congregate in the major shipping lanes. When the regencies were at peace with Spain, Portugal, and Britain, the Strait of Gibraltar was particularly lucrative grounds with many potential targets funneled into a small area. That same small area made it easy for any one of the above European powers to deny access to the strait, however. Except in times of easy access to the strait, most corsairs would operate on the routes into and out of major ports, especially enemy ports whose three-mile sovereignty did not need respecting and near which legitimate targets would predominate. These enemy port areas, while lucrative, were also riskier, as naval patrols were more likely, and if a chase got too near land it could get in range of shore batteries. Civilian status was no protection. Privateers could lawfully take any ship of enemy registry, though merchant ships were considered lawful combatants as well as targets and could thus contest the capture by force of arms.

Friendly or neutral ships had no such right to resort to combat. Privateers and regular naval vessels, North African and European alike, had the right to stop such shipping for inspection if they could bring the target within effective cannon range. This allowed for checking the actual registry of the vessel, as flying false flags was a common and accepted ruse. It also allowed the inspectors to check for violations of law or treaty. Predatory ships often "took in" friendly or neutral ships for violations. In the case of European navies and privateers, this was usually for attempting to deliver contraband of war to an enemy or to enter a blockaded port. When North African corsairs brought in ships belonging to countries at peace with the regency, it was usually for a treaty violation, such as not carrying the required Mediterranean pass, or for some other irregularity of the ship's papers. Inspecting crew members occasionally engaged in petty larceny, most commonly stealing watches or navigational equipment. This activity was not lawful, but it was also not limited to North African privateers. It was a common problem among profit-motivated maritime predators, and even regular navy members succumbed to temptation on occasion. For example, during the United States' undeclared "Quasi-War" with France (1798–1800) an American lieutenant was forced to resign his commission after admitting to permitting his subordinates to commit such pilfering. If an inspection found an irregularity, it was worth taking the ship to a prize court and potentially reaping large returns, but generally friendly ships were less likely to be considered good prizes unless the violation was blatant, and even if the cargo or the ship were condemned, crews of friendly ships were not subject to captivity. Captains tended to focus on enemy shipping as more reliably good prizes and more lucrative.[48]

Although American authors focus on the threat to American shipping (as do I for the majority of this work, with its interest in what these challenges meant to America), in practice the threat was mostly local. Of the twenty-two ships brought in by Algerian ships and condemned as good prizes in 1797, the Register of Prizes identifies twenty as belonging to Italian states with whom Algiers was at war. Only two were not so identified, and their nationality is not given at all. These twenty-two prizes and their cargos brought approximately 250,000 Spanish dollars (roughly equal to American dollars at the time) into the Algerian economy. This sum is exclusive of the captured passengers and crews, whose value, contrary to hyperbole (both contemporary and modern) about slave markets, could not be known until they were ransomed.[49]

Captivity vs. Slavery

Cross-Mediterranean slavery, as practiced by the mid-eighteenth century, bore little resemblance to the more familiar chattel slavery practiced by North Africans, Europeans, and Americans alike on sub-Saharan African victims. This difference loomed large in the lived experience of American captives, though they used the familiar rhetoric of slavery in presenting their plight in letters home. Rather than experiencing a life of chattel slavery, perhaps punctuated by multiple sales and raising children who were similarly enslaved, those captured by Mediterranean corsairs almost universally eventually returned to freedom if they avoided death (usually by illness or injury) before their release could be arranged.[50] The vast majority of these returnees were eventually ransomed, though a few were exchanged or set free, and even fewer—though highly publicized—would be freed when they converted to the religion of their captors. The ultimate fates of the 128 captives in Tunis at the beginning of Bey Hammuda's reign (1782–1814) are typical. Ninety-two of them were eventually ransomed, while twenty-eight died in captivity. Four were released, either as gestures of good will toward a foreign government or as pious acts, and two converted to Islam, becoming what Europeans called "renegades."[51]

Indeed, the practice of "ransom slavery" became so regularized that networks of private or religious ransom brokers took root, in addition to government diplomatic exchanges. Captives did not suffer the "social death" common to trans-Atlantic victims of slavery but rather remained in close contact with their home communities, as captors encouraged them to write to seek ransom payment either directly or at least via keeping connections alive and reminding family and community of their need. Daniel Hershenzon argues convincingly that communication from and about captives intensified cross-boundary contacts in the early modern Mediterranean as part of a complex interplay of market, religion, and social obligation, which formed a "transimperial political economy" of captivity and redemption.[52]

This system was well within the bounds of international law. While the idea that captured enemies could be enslaved was consistent with the law of nations, it was not the norm for inter-European conflict. In fact, Vattel stated that though enslavement was permitted in any case where the sovereign had a right to put a prisoner to death, "indeed that disgrace to humanity is happily banished from Europe."[53] This was either overstating the case or rested on a technical definition of slavery. It was certainly still normal for European powers to hold North Africans captive, require them to labor, and demand ransom for their release, just as the Barbary States did. To the North Africans, both circumstances were considered slavery. When American James Cathcart was captured by Algerian corsairs in 1785, he reported that the captain of the ship that took his had himself been a captive for several years in both Genoa and Spain. Cathcart quotes the captain as telling them, "Christians, be consoled. The world is full of vicissitudes. You shall be well used, I have been a slave myself and will treat you much better than I was treated." Cathcart also reported that the chief of the guards at Bagnio Belique, the main slave prison, had himself been a captive in Malta for fourteen years and "having been cruelly treated himself on board the Maltese Galleys, he was determined to retaliate on the slaves whom he had under his command."[54] Indeed, Malta held so many Muslim prisoners that in the seventeenth century it became standard practice to recognize an Ottoman jurist (*kadi*) among the captives as the representative of the central Ottoman legal system (though not those of North Africa) on the island. The "*Kadi* of Malta" predominately facilitated ransom agreements between captors, captives, ransom brokers, and lenders, binding together the laws of war as practiced by Maltese corsairs and the Ottoman legal regime.[55]

While this style of law-bound and ransom-focused captivity may not have been called slavery by the European captors, the North Africans saw no difference. They considered themselves slaves while captive and considered their captives to be slaves, though, as mentioned above, not in the sense of chattel slavery. By the time American citizens encountered North African captivity, almost all captives were publicly held, and those few who were not could be recalled by the government if their labor was needed for a public project or if the government had agreed to ransom terms. By the 1780s the regencies had regularized the general standard of captives being held by the public in various ways. A certain number of captives, always including the captain of the vessel, went to the public as a government share of corsairing profits. By 1788 Tunis had done away with its slave market for captives. Instead, the bey paid a fixed price of three hundred piastres (about eighty-five dollars) for each captive, which went into the overall value of the prize, which was then distributed by shares. Algiers had a similar system, though the slave market continued to technically exist. Any profits above sixty sequins (about seventy-five dollars) for a captive did not go to the prize shares but directly to the state treasury. This policy, combined with the power of recall mentioned above, led to almost all captives being purchased by the government at effectively fixed prices. I found no direct sources on the policy in Tripoli, but captivity narratives make it clear that most, if not all, captives were publicly held there as well.[56]

Captives were generally held in prisons (*bagnios*), whose conditions many authors sensationalize by cherry-picking from captivity narratives and eliding the fact that the conditions they are describing only applied to captives completely without resources. This is common in popular histories, but it can even be encountered in works by accredited scholars. The most egregious example of this I have encountered is Michael Oren's depiction of conditions for American seamen captured by Algerian corsairs in 1785. Oren uses an ellipsis-filled quote from Cathcart's *The Captives* to build a narrative that he was "cast into a dungeon 'perfectly dark . . . where slaves sleep four tier deep . . . many nearly naked, and few with more than an old blanket to cover them in the depth of winter.'"[57] This quote is blatantly misleading, as Cathcart reported being moved to the prison (Bagnio

Belique) well into his captivity when he had already accumulated resources, and the quotation comes from his much larger description of the building. The "perfectly dark" portion of the quote is taken from Cathcart's discussion of the windowless taverns on the first floor after they closed for the night, and the ellipsis elides over a page before the description of the rooms in which poor prisoners sleep. Here Oren also omits the fact that the "four tier" sleeping refers to cots "in square frames, one over the other" in the manner of bunk beds. Lastly, Oren fails to mention that this does not apply to Cathcart, as "those who have the means of subsistence either live in the tavern or little boxes called rooms," and that Cathcart himself was invited to stay in the dey's chief clerk's apartment.[58]

In reality, captives in North Africa had remarkable levels of agency, much of it inherent in the system, rather than the product of resistance, as was often the case for chattel slaves. While Barbary captives were only supplied basic food, shelter, and clothing and were required to labor on public works, money could mitigate all of these issues. Captives often received stipends from their governments, friends, and family. Additionally, captives could practice trades in the evenings (or all day if they could purchase the right not to appear for general work), and many Christian captives kept taverns, as it was forbidden to Muslims—many of whom nonetheless patronized them. Cathcart estimated that twenty-seven to thirty taverns were active in Algiers at any given time, most of them in the *bagnios*. It was even possible to live outside the *bagnios* with an appropriate payment and a local guarantor. This privilege was common for ship captains, who often resided in the homes of European consuls. Consuls also occasionally hired prisoners, with part of their wages going to the payments required to obtain permission and the rest going to the prisoner, who was usually saving toward their ransom. Captives had a surprising amount of property rights, though all property was liable to seizure for misdeeds, and in case of a captive's death his property went to the regency, leaving any debts uncollectable. Thus, it was difficult for captives to obtain loans, but once they had capital, they could amass considerable wealth. Cathcart is an exceptional case, as he obtained clerk positions that came with significant perquisites, but he estimated his net worth as of his release at $10,000, including a prize ship that he had purchased and three taverns. Less exceptionally, his fellow prisoner Richard O'Brien, who had no such ventures, had nonetheless managed to amass a savings of about $300 as of his release.[59]

Although American captives used the term "slavery" in their letters to evoke sympathy, most Americans who were familiar with Barbary captivity conditions would likely have seen them as more analogous to Indian captivity than to the chattel slavery the term evoked in the United States. For example, the captivity narrative of O. M. Spencer, contemporary with the Algerian captivity of O'Brien and Cathcart, mentions an American couple captured by the Miami in 1791 who were held under remarkably similar conditions. They worked to earn their ransom fee (the man as a boatman and the woman as a washer and seamstress) and lived in the meantime in a mixed Indian community along the Auglaize River in the Old Northwest, alongside several free Europeans. While I found no examples of Americans making this analogy overtly, American leaders never used the term "slave" to refer to Americans held in Barbary, calling them instead captives or prisoners. Indeed, the term's only appearances in the records are when the captives were urging action on their behalf or when captives or diplomats translated North African statements directly.[60]

This then was the "Barbary System" of the late eighteenth century—a law-bound and profit-motivated system of maritime predation and imprisonment for ransom, justified and elevated on religious grounds. This system, far from the "piracy" it is so frequently depicted as, was fully lawful, under both Islamic and international law. Most European governments found North African motivations for making war distasteful but accepted their methods during war as legitimate privateering, going so far as to share the use of prize courts. Even captivity practices were largely common, for all that the terminology differed. Europeans usually did not require fellow European prisoners to labor or to pay ransoms, but they could do so lawfully and sometimes did.[61] When it came to the Muslim captives of European corsairs and the European captives of North African corsairs, the systems were almost identical. If America wished to be accepted as a European-style nation within the Vattelian system, it would also have to accept the Barbary System that was part of it.

In truth, there were actually two Barbary Systems at play by this era: the capitalist privateering and for-profit treaty-making system of Algiers, Tunis, and Tripoli, and the foreign policy-driven hostage-taking system used by Morocco. American sailors and diplomats would get the chance to experience both shortly after American independence was won but would start with Morocco's less known, and less difficult, hostage diplomacy.

2

American Sovereignty Checked

DIPLOMACY AND CAPTIVITY IN NORTH AFRICA, 1776–1793

O N 4 OCTOBER 1784 Moroccan frigate captain Hamet Turqui seized the American ship *Betsey* in the Gulf of Cadiz. Four days later, he brought the ship into Tangiers and sent the crew to the court of Emperor Mohammed III in Marrakesh.[1] This capture was followed only nine months later by Algerian ships seizing the *Maria* of Boston and the *Dauphin* of Philadelphia and holding their crews in "ransom slavery." Thus began a decade of American captivity and frustration in diplomatic relations with North African polities and with European powers on Barbary affairs. Surprisingly, however, the *Betsey* incident represented a rare bright spot in this otherwise unproductive interaction. Emperor Mohammed III had ordered her capture for diplomatic reasons, rather than financial gain, and America did well both in direct negotiations with Morocco and from relations built with Spanish statesmen during the process. This early success raised American hopes, only to see interaction with Algiers uncover American feebleness and European disinterest in furthering American interests.

When previous historians have focused on Europe's role in America's dealings with Barbary, it is usually in the competitive, rather than cooperative, sphere.[2] This is unsurprising, as mercantilist theories of the time saw trade as something of a zero-sum game, and American gains in the Mediterranean would be viewed as coming necessarily at other nations' loss. For the carrying trade (ships hired to transport other countries' cargos), this theory had validity. Mercantilist theory held that this applied to the exchange of goods and specie as well. In 1783 John Holbrook, Earl of Sheffield, defended this theory vigorously in his book-length pamphlet *Observations on the Commerce of the American States*. Sheffield argued strenuously that an independent America must be treated as a foreign competitor and that the Acts of Navigation should be applied rigorously to American trade. As he put it, "By asserting their independence, the Americans have at once renounced the privileges, as well as the duties, of British subjects—they are become foreign states; and if in some instances, such as the loss of carrying-trade, they should feel the inconvenience of their choice, they should not, nor ought they to, complain."[3]

The role that the Barbary threat played in this system was clear to Sheffield. He argued that England would be a natural gathering point of trade items to be packaged together and sent on to America, as American vessels would be unable to trade directly in the Mediterranean owing to the corsair threat. Sheffield noted that Americans could not protect themselves from this hazard as "they cannot pretend to a navy," and that it was not in the interest of any of the great maritime powers to offer protection. Indeed, Sheffield argued, "that the Barbary States are advantageous to the maritime powers is certain. If they were suppressed, the little States of Italy, &c. would have much more of the carrying trade."[4] This view of North African corsairs was widespread. In 1783 Benjamin Franklin stated his concern that Britain might actively encourage Barbary corsairs to target American shipping to discourage competition. He noted, "I have in London heard it as a Maxim among the Merchants, that *if there were no Algiers it would be worth Englands while to build one*."[5]

Benjamin Franklin had already suffered a disappointment related to seeking foreign protections from North African corsairs. He had departed for France in October 1776 with a draft Treaty of Commerce and Amity, written by John Adams, which included an article calling for France to protect American vessels and people from Barbary predation exactly as Britain had before the War of Independence. Congress realized that this was a lot to ask and sent instructions to Franklin and his fellow commissioners, Silas Dean and Lea Arthur, that the article should be retained if possible but should be waived if it would disrupt treaty agreement. They were to settle for French leverage in obtaining Mediterranean passes from the Barbary States for American vessels if French officials considered active protection an unreasonable request. Even that proved more than France was willing to offer. After much negotiation, the commissioners signed the finalized treaty on 6 February 1778. By this time the Barbary article had been watered down to France offering simply to employ "good Offices and Interposition" with Barbary powers in case of difficulty.[6]

This chapter follows the early republic's generally ineffective diplomatic response to North African issues and European powers on Barbary issues, from Franklin's negotiation on Barbary protection and an initial Moroccan trade invitation in 1777, to more formal outreach in 1779 and the captures of 1784–85, through the second round of Algerian captures in 1793. It shows that, though America had been recognized as an independent nation by France in 1778 and even by Great Britain in 1783, in many ways the new Confederation, and even the early Federal Republic, could not uphold its sovereignty. The fledgling United States was slow to establish normal diplomatic relations outside of Western Europe and depended heavily on those powers to help with North African issues. This dependence worked out well once the United States engaged with Morocco through Spanish channels, both in terms of settling affairs with Morocco and of building diplomatic ties with Spain. The fitful attempts to deal with Algiers through French good offices, however, went nowhere.

In 1779 Morocco began its attempts to form ties with the new nation of the United States as part of Emperor Mohammed III's policy of establishing Western trade connections. After years of American unresponsiveness, some due to actual exigencies of the War of Independence and some due to fear of what formal diplomacy might cost the impoverished new government, Morocco forced an American response by seizing a single American merchant ship in 1784. American diplomats engaged Spain to assist, which was so successful that the crew was released before America's envoy was even chosen. The United States was not only able to complete an advantageous treaty with Morocco at a minimal cost but also to build diplomatic relationships with Spain that enabled treaty negotiations. In the end, the two nations were not able to reach a mutually acceptable agreement, as Spain was unwilling to allow American navigation of the Mississippi and the Southern states were unwilling to sign a treaty without that right, but it was a good start.

The next year Algerian corsairs also captured American ships, but their goal was gain, not diplomacy—or potentially gain by means of diplomacy, but financial gain came first. Neither Congress nor the American peace commissioners, John Adams and Thomas Jefferson, had the expertise or the budget required to deal with this issue. Furthermore, Adams and Jefferson's hopes for the effects of the French good offices obligated by the Franco-American treaty came to nothing. In fact, French diplomats secretly instructed their subordinates not to help, as allowing American merchant shipping free access to the Mediterranean was considered threatening to French interests. As Jefferson and Adams worked through other possible solutions without success, it quickly became obvious that the new American republic did not have the capacity to act as a fully sovereign and independent nation, and American captives remained in captivity for over a decade.

This failure served as a cipher of American weakness throughout the Confederation era. Algerian captivity became a powerful tool of social and political critique. It was used as an argument against the practice of slavery and to critique American sectarianism and social practices. But most of all it was used as an argument for the need for a more powerful central government and the ratification of the United States Constitution. Ratification advocates paired Algerian captivity and Algiers's ability to deny American shipping the use of the Mediterranean with British restrictions on shipping and occupation of military posts within the Ohio Territory to argue that America had not yet realized the free and independent status that the revolution had been fought for but rather languished as a dependent pseudo-colony. This argument was highly effective, and anti-Federalists generally chose not to engage it at all but instead to limit their attacks on the Constitution to the amount and types of power it authorized.

After ratification, Federal era America found itself no more ready to deal with Barbary affairs than the Confederation era government had been. The Washington administration did not succeed in engaging Algiers at all during its first term. The administration's first formal diplomatic contact was abandoned in late 1793, as conditions had changed so much since its authorization that David Humphreys's commission was a dead letter. Between the time the mission was finally organized in September of that year and his arrival in a nearby port to request a diplomatic passport for a visit to Algiers, Algerian corsairs had captured over one hundred additional Americans.

For all this futility, however, American interactions with both North Africans and Europeans on North African issues did bear some fruit.

Stalling Morocco

By 1784 Moroccan Emperor Mohammed III was tired of waiting for American response to his diplomatic outreach efforts and revisited the strategy he had used to get Britain to appoint a consul in 1756 when, as acting sovereign, he had ordered the capture of the British ship *Ann*. Mohammed ascended to his father's throne in 1757 and had long since consolidated his rule by the time of American independence. Though his often quoted "recognition of American independence" in 1777 was not a formal diplomatic act, he had been actively attempting to form ties with the United State since 1779. In an effort to connect his country to the bourgeoning Atlantic trade, Emperor Mohammed founded the trade city of Essaouira in 1760 on the ruins of an abandoned Portuguese outpost in southwestern Morocco known to Europeans as Mogadore. This gave him a port close to the royal city of Marrakesh that was also convenient to trans-Atlantic trade routes to go with his principal Mediterranean-facing port of Tangiers. European merchants and consuls operating in Morocco primarily set up headquarters in one of these two ports, making them also cities of diplomacy. The famed 1777 proclamation that referenced America was an attempt to bolster trade in Morocco's ports rather than the world's first formal recognition of American independence, as it is often cited. Emperor Mohammed sent a letter to the various consuls and merchant houses in Tangier on 20 December 1777, asking them to pass on the information that Morocco allowed free entry to its ports to unrepresented "nations," a list of which included "the Americans." The fact that this list also included Leghorn (Livorno), which at the time was appended to the Holy Roman Empire, makes it clear that this document is not an attempt to assert formal recognition of sovereignty but rather an attempt to attract merchants.[7]

Emperor Mohammed expanded on his efforts to develop trade and diplomatic ties when, in 1779, he appointed French merchant Etienne Caille as "consul" for all nations not separately represented in Morocco. The previous year, Caille had written as a private citizen to the American commissioners in France (then still Benjamin Franklin, Silas Dean, and Arthur Lee) to offer his good offices to negotiate a peace between the United States and Morocco. Now that Caille had a formal position, he immediately wrote to Congress, via both Benjamin Franklin and John Jay, to renew the offer.[8] John Jay sent a friendly, but noncommittal, reply and referred the matter to Congress, which responded similarly. With the press of affairs and slow post across the Atlantic, it was more than a year after Caille's letter that Congress responded, and longer yet before any response was received. In November 1780 congressional instructions to Benjamin Franklin focused on obtaining war loans from France, but they appended a paragraph noting Caille's correspondence and instructing Franklin to correspond with Caille "if you shall have no objection to the contrary" and "assure him in terms most respectful to the emperor that the United States . . . shall embrace a favorable opportunity" to negotiate in the future.[9] In December, Congress wrote a letter to Emperor Mohammed that made negotiations seem much more imminent, claiming that the United States had instructed its minister in France to choose a delegate to open negotiations.[10]

Here matters stalled completely until the end of the American War of Independence, and when they restarted it was at the instigation of a private citizen. Robert Montgomery, an American merchant living in Alicante, Spain, struck up a "friendly Intimacy" with Mustapha Belznachi, a Moroccan diplomat returning from an embassy to Algiers in early 1783, who encouraged him to write to Emperor Mohammed to propose treaty negotiations.[11] Montgomery took it on himself to do so in a manner that implied that he was writing on behalf of the United States Congress. This letter caused no end of consternation among American political elites. Upon hearing of it, Congress instructed its ministers in France (now John

Adams, Benjamin Franklin, and Thomas Jefferson) to "enquire on what grounds Mr. Montgomery has undertaken to write in the name of the United States, to the Emperor of Morocco, a letter by which their characters and interests may be so materially affected."[12] As it turns out, John Adams had already done so, and his response shows that the issue was not simply one of indignation over private diplomacy. Indeed, Adams's concerns hint that America had been intentionally putting off formal response to Moroccan outreach out of fear of potential cost. As he wrote, "It is the Custom among the African & Asiatic Nations to send and recieve Presents with Ambassadors, and Congress has never to my knowledge made Provision for any Presents, or given Authority to any Man to go to the Emperor or write to him."[13] Montgomery replied that he was sorry if he had erred in taking advantage of "So favourable An Opertunity" without consulting with officials owing to time constraints but assured Adams that Morocco was interested in establishing commercial ties, and as to presents, "Nothing of that Kind would be Expected from Congress being an Infant State." Montgomery seemed convinced that although he may have technically overstepped his authority, with the diplomatic ball in motion "a thing So Esential to Our Commerce As Good friendship And Harmoney with the Moores will be Seriously thought of."[14] In this assessment, he seriously underestimated the inertia of diplomacy under the Confederation Congress.

Emperor Mohammed certainly considered Montgomery's letter a formal beginning to discussions and assigned his foreign minister, Eliaho Leve, to respond. Leve wrote Montgomery in April 1783 that the emperor wished to negotiate a treaty of peace and commerce and had tasked Etienne Caille's secretary, Giacomo Crocco, to travel to Paris and escort one of the American ministers or their designated representative to the Moroccan court for negotiations. This appointment alarmed the ministers. John Adams, apparently not understanding the difference between the regencies and Morocco and having heard that Holland paid $100,000 annually for peace with Algiers, feared that American finances would not allow for treaties with North African powers. When Benjamin Franklin received a letter from Crocco in July 1783 asking for travel expenses for his trip to Paris, it seems to have confirmed the ministers' fear that peace would be unbearably expensive, and Franklin left the letter unanswered.[15] In November, Crocco, who was in Madrid at the time, tried again, specifying his expense request as "fifteen hundred hard Dollars" and noting that if he had to return to Morocco empty-handed, it would upset Emperor Mohammed and "may forever indispose him against the United Provinces [States]."[16]

This letter was a hint that the ministers' fiscal fears may have been overblown, but they nonetheless felt that Franklin's three-year-old authorization to correspond with Caille did not extend to formal treaty negotiations and continued to stall. Franklin wrote back to Crocco, explaining that he was awaiting direction from Congress and that "as soon as their Affairs are a little settled, which by so severe a War carried on in the Bowels of their Country by one of the most powerful Nations of Europe, have necessarily been much deranged, they will readily manifest equally good Dispositions; and take all the proper Steps to cultivate and secure the Friendship" of Morocco and its emperor.[17]

Benjamin Franklin's letter bought the United States another six-month delay in considering Moroccan matters, during which Congress acted, though the commissioners were not yet aware of it. On 12 May 1784 Congress authorized Adams, Franklin, and Jefferson to negotiate treaties with the North African powers, allowing a budget of $80,000 to reach treaties with all four states. This was not a novel way of diplomacy for the Confederation Congress, which was well accustomed to present- and annuity-based diplomacy with Indian nations, especially when seeking land cessations. Indeed, just two months before, Congress had acted on a report written by Thomas Jefferson before his departure for France and authorized $15,000 for commissioners negotiating with Indians in the Ohio Valley to purchase "a quantity of goods, to be disposed of to the Indians at the opening of the proposed treaty."[18] Setting aside similar funds for dealing with North African powers may have made them seem analogous to Indian nations, rather than European sister nations, but the notion of disbursement-based diplomacy was not seen as new or transgressive. Unfortunately for Adams, Franklin, and Jefferson, word of congressional funding had not yet reached them when Consul Caille, in Paris on personal business, visited Franklin in July to discuss Moroccan affairs. There is no record of how the discussion proceeded, other than

Caille's explanations of the Barbary System, but whatever Franklin said on America's behalf was insufficient to mollify Moroccan frustration. Instead, it came across as yet another example of the United States failing to seriously engage with Morocco. When Caille reported to Mohammed III, the emperor's patience ran out, and he fell back on his favorite tool of coercive diplomacy. Having succeeded in pressuring Denmark into making peace via taking in (and later releasing) two Danish ships in the year's early cruise, Moroccan corsairs went hunting for an American vessel.[19]

Engaging Morocco (and Spain)

Among the several Moroccan vessels at sea, Hamet Turqui's frigate was the first to find an American ship. Though Americans would rarely risk passing through the Strait of Gibraltar now that they no longer carried valid Mediterranean passes, they carried on extensive trade into and out of Atlantic ports of southern Portugal and Spain. Cruising in the shipping lanes of the Gulf of Cadiz, Turqui quickly came upon the *Betsey*, which had just sailed out of Cadiz on her way to Philadelphia with a load of salt.[20] Captain Irwin and his crew were not, as one author imagined, "locked in the hold as human cargo, headed for the slave markets of Morocco."[21] Rather, they were brought into Tangier aboard their own ship and then departed overland, headed for an audience with Emperor Mohammed in Marrakesh. The emperor informed them that, though he was at peace with America, they "would remain prisoners till Congress may think proper to send an ambassador." He then dispatched them to his prized Atlantic port city of Essaouira (Mogadore), where they lived at liberty and with a weekly allowance.[22] Emperor Mohammed made it very clear that this capture was intended to compel American diplomatic engagement, which it quickly did.

Rather than simple bilateral diplomacy, however, America's response centered on Spanish relations almost as much as those with Morocco. The commissioners, for their part, had barely heard news of their new mandate before they were faced with the *Betsey* crisis. Their official commissions had not yet arrived, and they had not had the opportunity to do more than ask for advice, such as how European powers negotiated in North Africa and what gifts were expected. William Carmichael, chargé d'affaires to Spain, was the first American diplomat to pass on word of the incident. In his letter informing Jefferson of the seizure, he also informed him that the Spanish foreign minister, the Count de Floridablanca, had offered Spanish assistance. Floridablanca instructed Juan Salmon, the Spanish consul general in Morocco, to press for the release of the *Betsey* and her crew. With his point made and an established regional power vouching for formal American response, Emperor Mohammed released Captain Irwin and his crew to Francisco Salinas y Monfiño, a Spanish diplomat and nephew of Floridablanca, who had come to Morocco on a separate mission. The crew was released in June and returned to Cadiz with Salinas y Monfiño in July 1785, before the newly appointed American commissioners had even selected a representative to go to Morocco.[23] Carmichael reported that between the cooperation on Morocco and the positive reception of Spanish Ambassador Don Diego de Gardoqui in Philadelphia, Spanish-American relations were greatly improved. He envisioned quick treaty negotiations between the United States and Spain, and "a solid and permanent connection between the respective Countries."[24] This interpretation of American-Spanish relations built on Moroccan cooperation also appeared in print in the influential *Pennsylvania Packet* newspaper, which published an extract of a letter on the subject which may have been written by Carmichael himself, though the author is not cited.[25]

Carmichael was correct that the negotiations with Spain would be quick, but they did not lead to a lasting connection. They led instead to the ill-fated Jay-Gardoqui Treaty of 1786, which was not ratified by Congress owing to its leaving intact Spain's right to bar American navigation on the Mississippi River. America had reached treaty-worthiness in Spain's eyes, but Spain was not willing to agree to terms the Southern states demanded. This abortive treaty represented a step toward acceptance as a sister nation but was hardly a triumph. Spanish intercession did, however, lead to quick and fruitful American negotiations with Morocco.

In September 1785 Adams and Jefferson as the remaining commissioners (Benjamin Franklin being aboard the ship *London Packet* on his way back to the United States),[26] determined to divide their budgeted $80,000 for North African treaties by allocating $40,000 toward Algiers, as "they certainly possess more than half of the whole power of the pyratical states"; $20,000 for peace with Morocco; and $10,000 each for Tunis and Tripoli.[27] This fractional sea power–based division of their budget shows once again that the commissioners did not understand the difference between Morocco's use of corsairing as an instrument of diplomacy and the regencies' corsairing as an economic staple. Adams and Jefferson also selected representatives to negotiate peace. John Lamb, a captain during the revolution with experience trading in North Africa as a purchaser of donkeys, would be sent to the regencies, while Morocco would receive a representative with more diplomatic experience, the United States consul general in France, Thomas Barclay.[28]

Barclay immediately sought council from his diplomatic contacts in Paris and obtained a letter of recommendation to the Moroccan court from French Naval Secretary Marachel de Castries and advice on appropriate presents for various members of the court. He wrote Jefferson and Adams that he expected presents to come to about 40,000 livres (approximately $6,000). Barclay departed Paris in January 1786 (apparently overland, judging by the locations in the headings of letters he wrote along the way) and arrived in Madrid in March, where he met with Spanish Foreign Minister Floridablanca and received a letter from the king of Spain to the emperor of Morocco in support of the peace mission.[29]

Barclay arrived in Essaouira, Morocco, in early June, and by the end of the month, with the help of Moroccan enthusiasm and European diplomatic backing, he had successfully negotiated a treaty almost identical to the proposal that Benjamin Franklin had drafted before his return to America. The treaty included trade arrangements and a stipulation that in case of war between the two countries prisoners would not be enslaved. Instead, they would be exchanged one for one via cartels during the conflict or at the close of hostilities, with any additional prisoners being released at a fixed price of one hundred dollars each. At his first audience with Mohammed III, the emperor presented Barclay with a young American sailor named James Mercier. Mercier had apparently been shipwrecked along the Saharan coast south of Morocco and held by nomadic tribesmen (a common spot for shipwrecks and fate for their victims, including the later famous case of James Riley) until the emperor ransomed him. Barclay reported that there were no European slaves in Morocco except a handful of similar captives whom the emperor regularly ransomed from their captors and turned over to their countries' diplomats. Barclay spent two more months in Morocco waiting for signatures and investigating port facilities and the potential for future trade.[30]

Barclay's mission was highly successful, though it also built unwarranted confidence among negotiators who were unaware of the different systems at play in Morocco and the Ottoman regencies. In September, Thomas Barclay left Tangier for Cadiz, leaving the hulk of the *Betsey* on the beach. Morocco had released the vessel long since, but with the ship and its cargo damaged because of neglect, and Barclay ignorant of the owners' and insurers' intent, he felt it best to let it remain. Instead, he returned with treasures far more valuable—a freed American prisoner, a breakthrough treaty, and a plethora of diplomatic ties and goodwill with France and Spain. He also raised Adams and Jefferson's expectations unrealistically in regard to dealing with the regencies. In Morocco, European sponsorship was highly effective, and costs were low. Barclay made peace without any indemnity and only minimal presents. Even including his salary and expenses over his nine-month mission, peace with Morocco came in under budget at 4,000 pounds sterling (approximately $18,000). Treating with Algiers, which had captured two American ships just as the commissioners were organizing Barclay's and Lamb's missions, would prove a completely different experience.[31]

Attempting Algerian Engagement

America's time without captives in North Africa was remarkably short. Just weeks after the *Betsey*'s crew arrived in Cadiz in July 1785, Algerian corsairs seized the *Maria* and the *Dauphin* off the coast of Portugal. Although corsairs from the regencies had in the past extended their cruises into the Atlantic, a long-running war between Spain and Algiers had included Spanish patrols closing the Strait of Gibraltar to corsairs since 1775. Contrary to popular narratives that the later American war with Tripoli was exceptional and an example to European powers that did not dare stand up to Barbary aggression, Spain was one of many European powers that found itself at war with the regencies in this era. Spain prosecuted the war vigorously, including repeated bombardments of Algiers and even an attempt at an amphibious invasion. The attempted invasion in 1775 was an abject disaster, however, simply supplying Algiers with a large number of prisoners to be ransomed, and Spain turned to naval patrols and occasional bombardments. In 1785 Spain gave up the conflict and paid a staggering sum for peace, reportedly $2.5 million. That sum not only drove up the price of peace for other countries but also opened the strait. While Portugal soon closed the strait again, the captures that Algiers made during its window of opportunity made Lamb's mission to Algiers significantly more complicated. Instead of seeking a treaty with regencies that had no previous interaction with the United States, he was now attempting to make a peace after actual hostilities and secure the release of twenty-one American prisoners.[32]

Among those prisoners was James Cathcart, whose captivity narrative informs this study, and Captain Richard O'Brien of the *Dauphin*, who during his captivity would become the spokesman for the American prisoners and source of information on Algerian affairs for the United States for American diplomats, and even an informal diplomat in his own right. Captain O'Brien thus became the first American sailor in Barbary to engage in North African diplomacy. Many more would follow, including several serving navy officers. But O'Brien's navy days were behind him. Like Cathcart, he had served as a naval officer during the War of Independence, holding the position of first lieutenant on the Virginia State Navy fourteen-gun brig *Jefferson*. On 27 April 1781 O'Brien was in command owing to the captain's absence during the Battle of Osborne's Landing. During this action, the *Jefferson* was captured and burned, along with almost the entirety of the Virginia State Navy's small fleet, and he served thereafter on a privateer.[33] O'Brien, an almost stereotypical sea captain, had no difficulty finding a merchant command after the war. Even when not sailing, he was known for peppering his communication with nautical allusions, such as warning diplomats of "lee shores" or "mistaking eddies for the main current." His use of such language became a running joke in Philadelphia in his later life, with newspapers noting, for example, that events in Haiti or Europe, looked, as O'Brien would say, "squally."[34]

O'Brien was joined in captivity by the *Maria*'s captain, Isaac Stephens of Boston, and a captain without a ship, Zacheus Coffin of Nantucket. Coffin was a passenger on the *Dauphin*, returning to the United States. No reason for his taking passage is recorded, and it is possible that he had lost his ship to accident or confiscation, but that would likely have been worthy of mention. It is more likely that he had captained a ship built in America and delivered to a customer in Europe, as was relatively common. As captains, the three men became part of the European consular community. Since each country's consul was generally expelled from Algiers before hostilities began, it was part of the traditional diplomatic exchange of favors for other consuls to look after the interests of captives from the expelled consul's country. For example, European ships' officers in captivity were generally not held in prisons but instead released to the surety of one of the consuls, who would host them at the consular residence. In spite of potential British resentment toward independent America, the British consul to Algiers, Charles Logie, initially proffered that traditional aid to the American captives. He took O'Brien, Stephens, and Coffin into his home and offered a small allowance to the common sailors that provided them, for example, better accommodations than the tiered bunks in the Bagnio Belique. Logie seems to have done so somewhat reluctantly, and his charity was apparently not within cultural norms. Perhaps because of resentment toward American shippers, he expected manual labor from the captains in return for his sponsorship, a sight that shocked captive American sailors when they visited their captains during a liberty from their own work. Still, the captains were part of the Western expatriate community and communicated freely.[35]

The captains' first duty was to write home in an effort to get ransom negotiations started. They wrote both to their shipowners and to the American agent in Cadiz, Richard Harrison. He, in turn, copied William Carmichael in Madrid, who informed Thomas Jefferson in Paris. By the time this chain of correspondence came to fruition in October 1785, Jefferson and Adams were already organizing Lamb's originally envisioned peace mission. By late August, O'Brien had received information about Adams and Jefferson's roles and written to them directly, hinting to them that not only the captives' condition but also American standing among other nations required succor. As O'Brien put it, it was "the Method of all Christian powers whose Subjects falls in the Hands of Those Savages to Make Some provision for them, untill they are redeemed." He also pushed for a speedy redemption, as the more prisoners were taken, the more peace would cost. Finally, he warned that if all other powers made peace with Algiers, America would be unable to, as "they Must Be at war with Some."[36] Based on the dates of responses, these letters seem to have arrived at about the same time as the news from Carmichael. It was far too late to consult with Congress or seek additional funding. The commissioners had few resources with which to work. The most they could do was to authorize Lamb to treat for the prisoners' release "if it can be obtained for sums within our power."[37] Even here they had to warn that if Congress did not approve of their initiative, there was the possibility that the government might require released prisoners to reimburse the public treasury for the cost of their ransoms.[38]

Aside from the remaining funds authorized by Congress, the commissioners' most valuable resource was diplomatic assistance from the established powers. Carmichael once again spoke to Foreign Minister Floridablanca, who passed word to Spain's Algerian peace negotiator, the Count de Expilly. This intervention did nothing for redeeming the prisoners or making a peace treaty, as Spain was too wrapped up in its own fraught negotiations with Algiers to get deeply involved in America's, but it did get the captains out of their tense lodging with British Consul Logie. By December 1785 they were living in the house of a French merchant, the Spanish consul having posted a bond of 560 pounds sterling against their escape. The captains paid two dollars a month for their liberty and were even allowed to dine aboard visiting American ships. Once no longer dependent on his charity, O'Brien felt comfortable complaining of Logie, who "treated us with indifference." In a sign of the entangled nature of Mediterranean shipping and corsairing, and of how American sailors normalized these issues, much of this information was reported by Captain Johan Lagerholm, who met with the captive captains in Algiers while in port there. Lagerholm had been first mate on the *Betsey* when she was taken into Morocco in 1784 and had stayed in the Mediterranean as captain of a ship "manned by *Algerines* and partly owned by a merchant in Gibraltar."[39]

Adams and Jefferson had much higher hopes for French assistance than simply improving the prisoners' treatment in captivity. After all, America had a treaty claim to French "good Offices and Interposition" in case of Barbary difficulties. They wrote to French Foreign Minister Vergennes, invoking Article 8 of the Treaty of Amity and requesting French influence and support for their agent, John Lamb. All that they were able to obtain was a letter from Navy Minister de Castries to the French consul in Algiers instructing him to support American efforts. Mercantile policy won out over even such minor assistance, however. It is highly unlikely that Lamb would have been able to reach an agreement with Algiers in any case, given the extreme disparity between Algerian demands and Lamb's budget. Even so, he was certainly not helped by the coded addendum to de Castries letter to French Consul de Kercy, which countermanded the open instructions to help the Americans conclude a treaty, stating that "there is no advantage to us in procuring for them a tranquil navigation in the Mediterranean."[40]

Armed with this unhelpful letter, a few thousand dollars in specie, and instructions to make treaties his first priority but also to ransom the prisoners if possible (aiming to pay no more than one hundred dollars apiece), Lamb departed Paris in January 1786. He traveled overland to Madrid and then Barcelona and arrived in Algiers on 25 March, "after maney little Disapointments." Whatever these little disappointments may have been, they paled in comparison to the disappointment the American prisoners found in him and his mission. Lamb had three interviews with Dey Baba Mohammed and reported that "he would not speake of Peace" at all and "set the Slaves a most Exorbitent price" of $60,000, or the entire remaining budget for peace with all three regencies. According to Lamb, the prime minister (*sahib at-tabba'*) told him that this price would likely come down once Algiers's peace with Spain was finalized, as "the price that was set on our people was [only] to Put a more modest face on the Price that they intend to make the Spaniard pay." Lamb further reported that the prime minister recommended that America pause negotiations until the Spanish business was concluded. Lamb then deposited a few hundred dollars with an Irish merchant in Algiers for distribution to the prisoners and departed for Madrid, theoretically to await the completion of the Spanish negotiations but in fact washing his hands of the matter entirely.[41]

Lamb's reports of his negotiations were very different than what the prisoners had heard. Local sources told them that Lamb had agreed to a price for ransom and left claiming he was going to obtain the money and would be back within four months. Further, the prisoners had no kind words to say about Lamb himself, being surprised that he spoke only English and considering him credulously led by British Consul Logie, who was actually acting against American interests. While their impression of Lamb was likely colored by their disappointment in the mission's failure, their judgment was unequivocal: "We are much surprized at Mr. Lamb's ungentleman like behaviour whilst he was in Algiers and could hardly believe Congress would [have] sent such a man to negotiate so important an affair as the making a peace with the Algerines where it required the most able Statesman and Politician."[42] By this time, the most able statesmen with local contacts and expertise that America could muster were the captives themselves.

Though O'Brien likely did not see himself in this light, in the same letter in which he complained of Lamb, he also offered detailed information about the diplomatic landscape in Algiers, among both the locals and the European diplomats and expatriates. The captive mariner O'Brien showed a deep understanding of both structural and personal dynamics in the regency. It was clear that the senior prisoners, most of them the officers of captured ships, not only had significant agency but were also well connected in the community. By then, the first mates had also gained their freedom of the town, and the American community had spread, with one officer staying with the Swedish consul. How Swedish Consul General Mathias Skjoldebrand came to host Americans is unknown, but the connection was to grow into a close and lasting relationship, both between the captives and the Skjoldebrands and, more generally, between America and Sweden on Barbary issues. Given their local expertise and contacts, the prisoners could likely have negotiated effectively for their own release had they the two resources that the commissioners also lacked in sufficiency—money and congressional authority.

Grasping at Straws

By July 1786 Thomas Jefferson was frustrated with the continued captivity of American sailors and the high price demanded by Algiers for ransom and peace. While he acknowledged that Congress had specified in their instructions that he and Adams seek peace through negotiations, he felt it more appropriate to "effect a peace thro' the medium of war." Jefferson acknowledged that this was simply a private opinion that he wished to discuss with Adams, and not policy within their purview. Nonetheless, he argued it strongly and in terms that would look familiar as descriptors of his policy once he became president. Jefferson argued that war with Algiers would likely not be any more expensive than the cost of peace, would be more honorable, and, perhaps most importantly, would earn America respect in Europe. Jefferson argued that this could be accomplished with a fleet of "150 guns" (approximately six frigates). Further, he was convinced that Portugal and Naples would join in a coalition, and he envisioned other nations that were not significant maritime powers joining as well. He even thought that Spain would enroll if their peace with Algiers fell through.[43]

There were some very tentative hints that some of the smaller powers, at least, would be interested in a coalition. Just weeks after Jefferson's letter above, Carmichael reported that "it might be possible to draw in the Italian Powers in case that hostile measures should be adopted by the States."[44] Both Carmichael and John Lamb's secretary during the Algiers mission reported receiving hints from Portuguese diplomats that Portugal was interested in forming a confederacy against the Barbary States.[45] But this was simply discussion, not actual planning. Aside from being beyond the scope of Adams and Jefferson's instructions, this notion of a military coalition foundered on one very important deficiency—America had no navy. The entire Continental Navy had been decommissioned at the end of the War of Independence, and there was no prospect of a new one. Adams agreed with Jefferson about the value in creating a small United States Navy, whether it was used to fight Algiers or not, but predicted cynically "that neither Force nor Money will be applied. Our States are so backward that they will do nothing for some years."[46]

This prediction was borne out, as after the disappointment of the Lamb mission the United States did not engage Algiers again during the Confederation period. Many different initiatives were discussed, but none led to action. There was some consideration of attempting to get the Ottoman Porte to intervene, but the commissioners soon abandoned the idea. The information they received from European diplomats, from John Lamb's report on his discussions with the Algerian prime minister, and from the interview they had with Tripolitan Ambassador ʿAbd ar-Rahman al-Ajar (with whom they met while he was in London on other business) all agreed that the regencies made their own decisions about peace and war. Jefferson also floated the notions of getting the Mathurin Order, a Catholic brotherhood that specialized in redeeming captives, involved in negotiations but never got authorization or funding for that initiative.[47] The only active diplomatic activity was represented by Congress writing two letters in July 1787, one to Spain thanking them for their help with Morocco and the other to Emperor Mohammed of Morocco to "request your favorable imposition to incline Algiers, Tunis, and Tripoli, to peace with us on such terms as may consist with our honor and the circumstances of our new and distant States." No response is recorded.[48]

That same month, Congress explored Thomas Jefferson's idea of a coalition against the regencies. William Grayson of Virginia moved that Jefferson be "directed to form a Confederacy of the powers of Europe now at War" or willing to go to war with the regencies. This confederacy's charter would include an article dividing responsibilities and forbidding any members making peace with the regencies separately. Grayson envisioned that the United States' contribution would be limited to one frigate and two sloops of war, though this clause was deleted from the resolution.[49] After debate, the motion was referred to Secretary of Foreign Affairs John Jay to report. Jay replied that while he thought it was a good idea and referred Congress back to his report of October 1785 in which he had recommended the foundation of a five-frigate navy in response to the earliest reports of Algerian hostilities, the motion was "rendered unseasonable by the present State of our Affairs." Owing to "the Inefficiency of our national Government," Jay considered the sad state of both merchant shipping and government revenue insufficient to support a navy.[50] The motion was apparently tabled and never taken back up. But the frustration over an inefficient government that could not meet the obligations of such a treaty, much less spearhead it, continued to grow. Indeed, inability to deal with Barbary affairs became a potent argument for those advocating for moving from the Confederation to a federal government.

Throughout this period, the American prisoners waited for relief. Instead, they found some of their existing sources of relief dry up. Jefferson stopped their monthly stipend in order to give the impression that the government had lost interest in them, as he believed that this would lower their ransom price. He realized that this was harsh but thought it temporary, as "the moment I have money, the business shall be set into motion."[51] That moment never came during his tenure as minister to France. In the meantime, the captives suffered their first death. Captain Zacheus Coffin died of consumption (tuberculosis) in November 1787, leaving behind a wife and eleven children in Nantucket. Though consumption was a threat everywhere, the following year saw plague, the great dread of North Africa, take two of the prisoners. Each time the plague returned, O'Brien would write another letter reminding the government of their condition and offering advice for negotiating a peace and their redemption.[52] In September 1788 the captives heard news of the new United States Constitution and immediately submitted a new petition to Congress. They understood that "untill Such time as affairs So important was adjusted at home nothing Could be done abroad" but pled that "now that the new Constitution of a Fut[u]re Government is Ratafied we hope you will Honourd Sirs, Give Such powers to your Ministers in Europe So as, finally to Extricate your unfortunate petitioners & Countrymen from thire wretched & unfortunate Lot of Slavery."[53] Simple ratification of the Constitution was not sufficient for their cause to draw federal efforts, however, and it was not until the Washington administration was consolidated that Jefferson took up the Algiers question again, now as secretary of state.

The Home Front

The notion that American inability to meet the North African challenge could be solved by a federal government with real power over the states was not limited to a few political elites and the captives in Algiers. It was, in fact, the most common rhetorical use of ongoing Algerian captivity in the American public sphere, narrowly edging out that of critiquing the American practice of slavery. Many scholars have written ably on the domestic effects of North African predation in the early American republic. Nonetheless, the issue of American futility in Algiers as an argument for the need for a more powerful central government, and especially for ratifying the United States Constitution, deserves a bit more development. This issue was not only important to domestic affairs but, as O'Brien argued, vital in enabling a unified response to international issues, so that America would be perceived both as treaty-worthy and as capable of ratifying and enforcing those treaties, once made. While some scholars' interpretations that the American public feared the appearance of corsairs on the coast does not stand up to further investigation, the claim of such fears was an effective tool for critiquing American society, including the need for national unity and military preparedness.

Many scholars, most notably Lawrence Peskin, have explored the role of Barbary conflict and captivity on the development of American national identity.[54] One of the largest factors in that dynamic is the interpretation that the conflict was a continuation of the War of Independence, with Britain using North African corsairs as proxies to keep America from its rightful place as a sister nation, such as Charles Logie's alleged role in encouraging Algerian corsairing against American targets. It was a common assumption that Barbary corsairs, like Native American raiders, were "unleashed" by Britain, rather than simply acting in their own interest. This assumption found expression from casual mention in newspaper articles to analysis from political pamphleteers. As just one of many examples, Sylvanus Bourn's essays "A Sketch of the Political State of America" published under the pseudonym "Americanus" claimed that Britain urged Barbary corsairs "to continual depredations on our vessels, travelling the seas in [quest?] of lawful gain" and fabricated stories of captures to drive up insurance rates and thus ruin the American shipping economy.[55]

The other great factor in building American identity was that the idea of the captives as "fellow Americans" rather than Virginians, Pennsylvanians, and so on. The vicissitudes of "our suffering brethren" (as prisoners in Tripoli were referenced in countless Fourth of July toasts during the Tripolitan War) helped expand the bounds of the "in-group" and thus national identity. Though this effect was even more notable later, it began in the 1780s with the publication of Richard O'Brien's letters throughout the thirteen states.[56] In August 1786 a pseudonymous Benevolus referred to the captives as "fellow citizens now groaning in slavery," belittled the American government for not living up to the example of European countries in redeeming them, and said that "our national character" required setting up a public subscription to achieve their redemption if the government could not do so. This letter summed up the critique of America as unable to act as a sovereign nation and showed captivity's effect on Americans' self-identity. With its discussion of the horrors of slavery, it also invited comparisons to American practice. That point would be made in the same paper two weeks later.[57]

The suffering of American captives in Algiers was technically slavery, and the captives so presented themselves, especially when petitioning for relief. Thus, as many scholars have noted, their plight served as a valuable rhetorical foil to the American practice of importing enslaved Africans and enslaving their descendants.[58] While this issue is not directly related to the focus of this book, it is worth noting as a counterpoint to the national unity that Algerian comparisons were often used to build. Instead, these critiques were highly divisive. North African settings were particularly apt for criticizing American society, as Americans had long become accustomed to considering Islamic society and practices as tyrannical and barbaric. If North Africans held slaves, how could Americans justify it in themselves? If Americans could be held *as* slaves, how could one argue that slavery showed that black Africans were inherently inferior? None of these points were lost on one reader of Benevolus's letter who responded as Humanus and noted that "every remark of his is applicable to the oppressed Africans, who are held bondage in a *land of liberty*." This began a tradition of what Timothy Marr calls "comparative orientalism" on the issue of slavery that lasted until the United States Civil War. Ironically, Humanus's letter was printed opposite an advertisement from an individual seeking to purchase "a Negro BOY from 10 to 12 years old."[59]

The rhetorical technique of criticizing American slavery via a North African mirror endured because it was highly visceral and difficult for supporters of slavery to counter. The story of Benjamin Franklin's last published essay is a case in point. After Franklin submitted a petition to Congress in 1790 calling for an end to the slave trade, a pro-slavery congressman from Georgia made a speech defending the practice, which was published in the *Federal Gazette.* In the speech, Congressman James Jackson argued that slavery was a positive force. As Robert Allison presents it, Jackson claimed that slavery "lifted the slaves out of barbarism and taught them Christian virtues." If the slaves were freed, Jackson said, it would ruin Georgia's economy, since no one would work in the rice fields, and freed slaves would be prey to Indian attacks. Franklin responded with cutting satire, claiming to like the speech very much, as it reminded him of one he had heard from a dey of Algiers. He then proceeded to put all of Jackson's arguments in the mouth of his fictional dey and referring to Christian slaves instead of Africans. Although traditionally in the honor culture of print wars during the early republic this would likely have led to a response, there is no record of Jackson replying. It is likely that he realized that he would only open himself and his position up to further ridicule and make himself seem a bully, especially as Franklin was in failing health.[60]

The use of comparative orientalism was not limited to the issue of slavery of course. North African settings or putative North African correspondents were used to critique multiple aspects of American society, from gender roles to obsessive "pursuit of wealth and pleasure" and military complacency.[61] Scholars who believe that Americans feared Barbary invasion of the American mainland in the Confederation era have misinterpreted a source that was, in fact, just such an example of comparative orientalism. There was no such panic. Almost all accounts of such fears trace back to a putative letter from a dey of Algiers demanding tribute from Philadelphia on threat of invasion, or to sources that mention fear of Algerine depredations but only in the context of corsairing's effect on the shipping industry, not a fear of invasion. An examination of the famed letter printed in the 3 May 1785 edition of the *Pennsylvania Packet*, purportedly written by "Al Koraschi Ebnallad, Sovereign and Supreme Dey of Algiers," from the standpoint of comparative orientalism clearly shows that this document was meant as a piece of satirical American social commentary. It is also clear that, aside from the social critiques, the letter is also aimed at lampooning America's lack of military preparedness, showing America's inability to fulfill the expectations of a functional sovereign nation and acting as a spur toward correcting the problem.[62]

The fact that this letter is a farce is obvious. Not only is the name of the dey incorrect, but it is not even an actual Arabic or Turkish name. Further, the letter is dated to the year 1163 Hijri, which if accurate would have made the letter almost thirty-five years old as of its printing. Additionally, it is written in a parody of the style of an Anglo-American legal document. While one scholar acknowledges that the letter is not genuine, she maintains that it reflects a widespread belief in the potential for corsair raids on American shores. Another scholar goes further yet, presenting the letter as a legitimate threat and portent of future Algerian captures, though he does acknowledge in an endnote that "there is some question as to the authenticity of the letter." He nonetheless argues that its widespread re-publication in other newspapers shows its impact.[63]

I would argue that this author is correct that this letter was impactful, but not because it was so "unsettling," nor because of its re-publication. Early American papers reprinted almost everything from other newspapers that they thought their readers might find interesting, in a sort of unspoken "Associated Press" arrangement. They usually did so without comment. The impact of the Al Koraschi Ebnallad letter was not due to anything it said about North Africans but because of what it said about North Americans, specifically Philadelphians.[64]

The Ebnallad letter was submitted to the *Pennsylvania Packet* by a pseudonymous "Y.Z." as commentary on Philadelphia society, which the author portrayed as overly sectarian and complacent, particularly in terms of paying for needed defenses. His literary device was that the letter was a translation of Algerian threats and demands. The "dey" threatened that he would send two ships to the Delaware River to anchor outside Philadelphia and "reduce it instantly to ashes" unless his demands were met. The demands included money, manufactured goods, and "40 of their most beautiful and virtuous damsels." The author mocked Christian sectarianism by having Ebnallad demand one "fair and unblemished virgin" and one zealous priest of each sect so that "we can decide the difference of each mode of belief, by its effects, as well as on the bodies as the souls of the sectaries," after which he would inform them of his decision, so that they could live "peaceably and serene," "laying aside all controversies and disputes, which are fit for women only." Lest anyone miss the commentary implied, the "translator" noted that the threat highlighted the city's defenselessness due to legislative neglect, such that "any paltry pirate" would be able to "lay Philadelphia under contribution." Further, he emphasized his commentary on wealth and virtue, noting that if such a demand came to pass, "whatever volunteers there might be among the ladies, I fancy most of our rich men would carry their wealth away as precipitously as possible."[65]

While it must remain conjectural, I suggest that this letter may have been written by Francis Hopkinson, a signatory of the Declaration of Independence and a noted political satirist who held the position of judge of the Philadelphia Admiralty Court at the time of the letter's publication. (For the full text of this letter and discussion of its author, see appendix 1.) Regardless of the authorship, it is clear that, aside from his mockery of Philadelphia society, the author's main point was the state's pitiful military readiness, such that anyone (Algerine or not) with a "sloop of twenty guns" could wreak havoc at will. This was an issue that would resonate in many of the United States under the Articles of Confederation.[66]

Indeed, inability to resolve Barbary threats and captivity became a standard reference for Confederation era weakness and futility, and a common trope for arguing the need for a federal system that would allow America to act effectively on the international stage. On 13 March 1786, just weeks after the first confirmed news of the Algerine captures reached the United States, Charles Pinkney argued in Congress that a "wise and well concerted system of federal policy" was needed to rescue American commerce from the predatory Barbary States, as well as dealing with the "hostile conduct of the savages on our frontiers" and the British "holding our posts contrary to the treaty."[67] This speech set the rhetorical trinity of American inability to act as a sovereign nation and not being seen as treaty-worthy by Britain, even in terms of compliance with the peace treaty already signed.

This rhetoric resonated strongly and spread quickly. The following month, the *Pennsylvania Gazette* used it in editorial comments on trade restrictions in the West Indies. The editor compared French and British trade restrictions to "the Mediterranean trade shut to America by the depredations of the Barbary corsairs." He then bemoaned congressional inability to enforce "any commercial treaty they make" and stated that "the union of the Thirteen States is much too weak, even to combat the machinations of any petty Prince, however contemptible, who shall chuse to insult the American flag."[68] By early July the argument had reached the Boston papers. A pseudonymous Seneca urged action in response to these national failings, which made the union "a rope of sand" and kept America from treaty-worthiness, as "our Ministers in foreign Courts are treated as Ministers of power without a head."[69] From the news of the Algerian captures through the ratification of the Constitution, Confederation futility in Barbary affairs was a common argument for a more powerful federal government. Moreover, this issue was almost always joined with British issues (either navigation restrictions, the refusal to cede the frontier posts, or both) and often to Native American conflict, as dolorous examples of American failure.

The connection between the Algiers crisis and the Constitution was emphasized in a book published anonymously (and now attributed to Peter Markoe) during the Constitutional Convention. In yet another example of comparative orientalism, the book presented itself as a series of letters explaining America from the perspective of an Algerian spy, appropriately titled the *Algerine Spy in Pennsylvania*, and purporting to describe events from 1783 until the convention itself. Along with his general social commentary, Markoe mocked the State of Rhode Island for failing to send a delegation to the convention. He had his main character suggest invading the state (potentially via bribing Daniel Shays to lead an insurrection) if it failed to ratify, so that the Ottoman Empire might have an island base for corsairing near the enemy coast, much like the Christians had in Malta.[70]

Once the Constitutional Convention ended, advocates employed the same arguments in favor of ratification. In February 1788, for example, Reverend Mister Thacher of the Massachusetts Convention urged ratification with an address that started with an excoriation of Rhode Island and seemingly responding to each of Seneca's 1786 points about American weakness. As well as British and Algerian challenges, he added another major treaty concern, that "the haughty Spaniard has deprived us of the navigation of the Mississippi." America needed a federal government, as decentralization had left America open to "every species of infamy abroad, and poverty at home."[71] John Jay also made the traditional Algerian arguments as part of his remarks on how the Constitution would rationalize foreign affairs in his "federalist-like" pamphlet *An Address to the People of New-York, on the Subject of the Constitution* in April 1788, which was also reprinted in newspapers throughout the country.[72] Foreign weakness, including the inability to deal with Barbary affairs, was a common and effective argument for the Constitution's stronger federal union. By 21 June 1788 that effort came to fruition when New Hampshire became the ninth state to ratify the Constitution. But it would take almost a year for the new Congress and the Washington administration to be selected and sworn in, and it would be almost a year after that before this new government would turn to Barbary affairs.

Abortive Engagement

When the new federal government did begin to consider the question of North African treaties and ransom of the captives in Algiers, it did not move quickly, and when it first did, the United States remained unable to meet its implied obligations. In December 1790 Thomas Jefferson, now secretary of state, presented options for dealing with the ongoing Algiers captivity. He enumerated the potential costs of a negotiated treaty, which various sources estimated between $320,000 and $1 million, but also offered the option "to repel Force by Force." This would, of course, require a navy. As part of his argument that such a navy could be kept small, however, Jefferson revisited his call for international cooperation, saying that the various nations at war with Algiers could rotate blockade duty so that each navy would only tie down ships for a portion of the year. Congress discussed this option but felt that the problem could be solved much more cheaply than Jefferson's estimates. In February 1791 the Senate consented to ransoming the prisoners in Algiers "provided the expence shall not exceed 40,000 Doll[ars]."[73]

This resolution did not lead to opening negotiations, however, but instead to a long delay and a thorny constitutional debate. President Washington initially responded with his intent to "take measures for the ransom of our citizens in captivity at Algiers . . . so soon as the monies necessary shall be appropriated by the legislature."[74] That did not happen during the first Congress, which ended its third and final session on 3 May 1791. While Congress was on recess, O'Brien wrote from Algiers, warning of the threat of a peace with Portugal that could once again open the Strait of Gibraltar to Algerian corsairs. Additionally, Dey Baba Mohammed died and was replaced by Hassan, who had been prime minister (*sahib at-tabba'*) most recently and had been the minister of the marine (*wakil al-hodj*) at the time of the capture of the *Dauphin* and *Maria*. Hassan had a reputation for goodwill toward the American prisoners, so this may have been an auspicious time for negotiations, but it was not to be. The second Congress also did not take up the issue until near the end of its first session (24 October 1791 to 8 May 1792).[75]

In March 1792 the Senate committee on Mediterranean issues finally explained their concern in a discussion with the administration: that since congressional deliberations were public and printed in the newspapers, mercantile European nations would be forewarned and would take steps to block American efforts to make a peace that would open the Mediterranean to American shipping. The committee asked the president if he would be amenable to spending money on a treaty with Algiers without an appropriation. President Washington was unsure of the constitutional ramifications of the question and referred it to Secretary of State Jefferson. Jefferson opined that though the administration had to respect

Congress's power of the purse, letting the House of Representatives vote on a treaty appropriation in advance would give them unconstitutional power over treaty making. Thus, there was no requirement to have an advance appropriation, and the administration could negotiate a provisional treaty that would not be binding until ratified and funded by the Senate and the House, respectively. He also argued, however, that experience showed that one must negotiate with Algiers with "cash in hand." Therefore, the administration asked for, and on 8 May received, an appropriation of $50,000 not specified as related to a treaty but instead "to defray any expense which may be incurred in relation to the intercourse between the United States and foreign nations." With constitutional and fiscal questions finally sorted out, the administration was ready to act.[76]

The Washington administration chose the most eminent American then in Europe without a position, Revolutionary War hero John Paul Jones, who was living in Paris. Jones had spent some time in Russian service after the Continental Navy's decommissioning and had moved to Paris in 1790 while between positions. On 1 June 1792 Jefferson wrote him with his commission and instructions for treaty and ransom negotiations with Algiers. Jones was authorized to offer up to $25,000 annually for peace, and up to $27,000 to ransom the remaining thirteen prisoners who had not been privately ransomed or died in captivity. Jefferson advised Jones to follow the guidance of Richard O'Brien, noting "you will find him intimately acquainted with the manner in which and characters with whom business is to be done there," in terms of both the Algerians and the European consuls.[77] Whether or not this negotiation would have succeeded, given Jones's budget, it was at least put on a better footing than Lamb's mission. Jones had government authority and funding, along with local American diplomatic expertise in place to guide him. The question of funding sufficiency was moot, however, as Jones died suddenly in July 1792, never having heard of his selection for the mission, much less having received his commission and instructions.

Having learned the lessons of long delays in communication hindering diplomatic missions, however, the Washington administration had already arranged a Plan B. America had, in Thomas Barclay, an experienced and successful North African negotiator, though he was already engaged when Jones was chosen. Barclay was on a mission to Morocco to reconfirm the previous treaty with the new emperor, Mohammed III having died in 1790. On 11 June 1792 President Washington wrote Barclay, explaining the planned Algerian negotiations and noting that "it is sometime however since we have heard of Admiral Jones, and as, in the event of any accident to him, it might occasion an injurious delay." Washington asked Barclay to take up Jones's commission and instructions in that case and move on to Algiers as soon as his business in Morocco was completed.[78] As it happened, dynastic affairs in Morocco were still unsettled after Mohammed III's death, so Barclay was unable to accomplish his primary mission, making him available to go to Algiers. Coordination still took considerable time, however. Barclay received the papers originally planned for Jones on Christmas Eve 1792. He immediately accepted the commission and set out to Lisbon to draw funds for the Algiers mission from David Humphreys, minister to Portugal and Washington's former military aide. Shortly after his arrival in Lisbon, however, Barclay too died suddenly, on 19 January 1793. Humphreys wrote to Jefferson to inform him of the setback and offer his assistance to whatever new commissioner to Algiers might be appointed. There was no Plan C. Jefferson received the bad news on 16 March. Included in the packet was another letter from O'Brien warning of a potential peace between Portugal and Algiers, which could once again allow corsairs out of the Mediterranean to threaten American shipping.[79]

The Washington administration acted as quickly as possible, though not quickly enough to arrange a peace before the Algerian corsairs reached the Atlantic. Within a week of receiving the packet, the administration had chosen Humphreys to handle the Algiers matter personally and dispatched his instructions. Humphreys received word of his new assignment two months later and immediately accepted but had to await instructions that Jefferson had informed him would come via a Captain Cutting. Cutting did not arrive in Lisbon until the first of September 1793, after which Humphreys immediately chartered a Swedish ship and set out for Algiers. But it was too late. By the time he departed on 17 September, the long-feared Portuguese-Algiers truce had come to pass. By the time he arrived in Alicante and wrote to Algiers seeking a diplomatic passport, Algerian corsairs had already captured ten more American ships and 105 additional prisoners. Though Portugal repudiated the truce in November and closed the Strait of Gibraltar again, Humphrey's mission had suddenly become much more urgent but also impossible to even consider under the funding limits set. Humphreys returned to Lisbon without having ever made it to Algiers.[80]

America's first attempts at engaging Europe on Barbary matters were rather supplicant, as American diplomats sought aid and protection from the great European powers of France, England, and Spain. This proved somewhat effective in terms of engaging Spain for help with Morocco. Not only did Spanish efforts lead to quick release of the *Betsey* and her crew, but they also helped lay the groundwork for America's first treaty outside Europe. This engagement also helped convince Spain that the United States was at least treaty-worthy enough to engage in negotiations, though it did not lead to such a close relationship that Spain was willing to offer a major mercantile advantage by opening the Mississippi to American trade. The commissioners quickly learned that absent anything to offer, all the great powers were more interested in their mercantile advantage than in offering the fledgling United States aid. The disappointment of French "assistance" with the Lamb mission to Algiers and the perceived British encouragement of Barbary predation of American shipping made that abundantly clear. Nor could the American government's limited authority and revenue collection capability during the Confederation era afford the new nation the power to coerce or induce in foreign affairs. The inability to deal with Algerian captivity and closure of the Mediterranean was a powerful example of the need for central government and helped convince Americans to ratify the United States Constitution.

But the Constitution was no panacea. America was still not strong enough to coerce or induce North African powers. Federal America probably also still lacked the ability to garner European diplomatic assistance on the issue, but flush with perceived power and feeling burned by previous experience, the new State Department did not even try. Jefferson warned John Paul Jones in the same instructions that eventually fell to

David Humphreys that though Richard O'Brien could help him with the character of the European consuls in Algiers, "you will probably not think it prudent to repose confidence in any of them."[81] Far from being a mission that showed American capacity to the would-be sister nations of Europe, the Jones/Barclay/Humphreys mission instead exposed continued diplomatic weakness. After the captures of 1793, the new nation could no longer dismiss its imprisoned citizens as a mere handful of Americans involved in a minor matter. The expanded Algerian challenge would require far greater effort and considerably more money. It would also make clear, as the efforts continued, that America's natural partners were not the great maritime powers of Europe but the small neutral ones.

3

A Minor Power

DIPLOMACY AND AMERICAN-EUROPEAN COOPERATION IN NORTH AFRICA, 1793–1801

IN AUGUST 1796 Captain Richard O'Brien was captured by Barbary corsairs. Again. O'Brien had been paroled from Algerian captivity to accompany (and later command) the brig *Sophia* and exchange American letters of credit for cash to pay for his own ransom, as well as that of his fellow prisoners and the indemnity promised to Algiers as part of the peace negotiations of September 1795. Owing to disruptions caused by the French Revolutionary Wars (1792–1802), specie was hard to come by. O'Brien went from European banking center to banking center, leaving empty-handed or managing only a fractional exchange each time. After months of delays, O'Brien sailed the *Sophia* out of Lisbon on 4 August 1796 to return to Algiers with partial payment, $200,000 in hard currency. On the voyage he was stopped by Tripolitan corsairs who were not willing to accept the *Sophia*'s Algerian passport at face value. Either suspecting some irregularity or simply unwilling to give up such a lucrative prize so easily, the corsairs took the *Sophia* into Tripoli for adjudication. After investigating the Algerian papers and some preliminary peace discussions (which Tripolitan officials would later claim included O'Brien promising the *Sophia* once it was no longer needed for the Algerian mission), Bey Yusuf Karamanli released O'Brien to return to Algiers.[1]

Finally arriving in Algiers on 1 October 1796, O'Brien reported to Joel Barlow, the newly assigned American agent in Algiers for peace negotiations. Barlow was almost finished securing peace with Algiers, needing only the remainder of the promised cash, and had plans to negotiate similar treaties with Tunis and Tripoli, which would open the Mediterranean to American shipping. O'Brien's new-made connections in Tripoli were serendipitous, and Barlow sent him back to Tripoli with $40,000 in cash, gifts worth about $4,000, and a draft treaty. Just a month later, Bey Yusuf signed a treaty negotiated by O'Brien with the assistance of Spanish Consul de Souza. The Arabic and English texts of this treaty did not match. Most of the translation issues were minor, but ironically, and apparently unnoticed until 1930, the most famous article of the treaty does not have an Arabic equivalent at all. Joel Barlow was an ardent proponent of the separation of church and state (and often accused of personal deism or atheism). He undoubtedly felt great satisfaction when he heard the news that the United States ratified the treaty in June 1797, not only because of his role in securing access to the Mediterranean for American shipping but also because of how the treaty reinforced secular government in the United States' legal system. Via the Tripoli treaty, Barlow had successfully added the phrase "the government of the United States of America is not in any sense founded on the Christian Religion" to the supreme laws of the country.[2]

One of the greatest complaints about the central government under the Articles of Confederation was that even when Congress could successfully conclude a treaty, it could not enforce it if any of the states should object. If America were to be a reliable partner nation, this inability would have to go. The framers of the Constitution tackled treaty-worthiness in Article VI, first reassuring all partners that any engagements and debts the United States had entered into previously would remain binding after ratification. Further, the article put all international treaties to which the country is party on equal footing with the Constitution itself as "supreme law of the land," superseding any state laws or constitutions.[3]

This chapter covers American diplomacy in North Africa in terms of both making and keeping peace with the regencies of Algiers, Tunis, and Tripoli and of interacting with the European diplomatic community on Barbary issues. It argues that American interactions with the regencies were governed by American understanding of international law and were driven by the desire to demonstrate the United States as a reliable partner both to the regencies themselves and to Europe. As such, American diplomats and politicians accepted the most onerous parts of the Barbary System, corsairing itself and the indemnities required to make peace and thus avoid it, as legitimate. The law of the sea sanctioned privateering, and the indemnities were legitimized by treaty. American officials reserved their chief outrage for any demands not so codified, which they considered "illegitimate exactions," though the regencies considered them customary usage. American diplomats would often acquiesce to these exactions out of considerations of cost versus benefit in keeping the peace but felt free to resist them without damaging America's reputation as a reliable treaty-worthy partner.

The chapter further argues that American interactions with the regencies were far from exceptional. They were, instead, very much in line with, and sometimes coordinated with, those of European nations, especially the smaller powers such as Sweden and Denmark. Indeed, this very normalcy and the practice of diplomatic cooperation among the Western diplomatic communities in the regencies played a major role in regularizing America's place in the European diplomatic regime. While these interactions occurred at a low diplomatic level (most countries, including the United States, had only consular offices in North Africa, not embassies), they made America a known factor in the diplomatic milieu. The regular exchange of favors built ties, particularly with other small powers who found Barbary challenges particularly vexing, forming a Western "diplomatic commonwealth" in the regencies, of which American representatives were an integral part.

These ties were first forged not by formal American diplomats but by American sailors held captive in Algiers, who formed strong connections within the European expatriate community, especially with Swedish Consul General Mathias Skjoldebrand and his brother Pierre Eric, with American captives sharing their home as early as 1786. By the time Joseph Donaldson, the first credentialed American diplomat since John Lamb, arrived in Algiers in 1795, the relationship had grown very close indeed. Early in 1793 the Swedish brothers had gone so far as to ransom an American seaman who would have been in danger if he remained in Algiers. After the captures of 1793, the Skjoldebrands were the primary sponsors of prisoners and a major conduit of information to David Humphreys, in his role as commissioner plenipotentiary for negotiations with Algiers.[4] Humphreys's designated representative Donaldson arrived in Algiers well informed and able to draw on local expertise both from the Swedish consul and from prisoners O'Brien and Cathcart, who were well placed in the expatriate community and the Algerian bureaucracy, respectively. He was also armed with far more governmental authority than Lamb had enjoyed. With these resources, Donaldson was quickly able to make a provisional peace.

The resource that Donaldson most lacked was money. Although he had the authority to pledge American funds, he did not have considerable cash in hand. His partner agent, Joel Barlow, faced great challenges keeping the agreement together in the face of interminable delays in meeting its stipulations. His and O'Brien's efforts and frustration in trying to gather specie were important not just in terms of freeing the prisoners and opening the Mediterranean trade. As Hannah Farber has demonstrated, this saga was also critical in demonstrating America's creditworthiness and commercial reputation in Europe.[5] It was at least as important, however, in establishing America's treaty-worthiness and diplomatic reputation in Europe. Having taken on the treaty obligation to pay Algiers, failure to consummate the payment would have been failure to respect what America claimed was its own supreme law. O'Brien and Barlow both had to act creatively to avoid this disaster. While working on the funding for the Algiers treaty, they also completed the Tripoli treaty that brought up the interesting constitutional issues mentioned above, and (via correspondence and a local proxy) a treaty with Tunis.

Because of the high potential of ruptures with the regencies, which were known to abrogate treaties based on questionable casus belli when in need of legitimate targets for predation, the Adams administration appointed the State Department's first salaried resident diplomats outside Europe as consuls for the regencies. The administration found two local experts to take on the responsibilities. Former prisoner and ad hoc diplomat Richard O'Brien was appointed consul general in Algiers, with supervisory power over the consuls in Tunis and Tripoli. Fellow former prisoner and chief Christian secretary to the dey of Algiers, James Cathcart, became consul to Tripoli. The third consulship fell to Secretary of State Pickering's protégé and erstwhile captain in the post–War of Independence United States Army, William Eaton. Despite their limited resources and support, as well as their dysfunctional interpersonal relationships, these consuls successfully kept the peace for several years, dealing with issues considered legitimate, such as deficiencies in delivering treaty-obligated annuities, and illegitimate, such as demands for donations of military stores not specified by treaty.

In addition to keeping the peace and administrating American affairs in the regencies, the consuls were active in the Western diplomatic commonwealth. Their part in the normal exchange of favors built diplomatic ties. Just as the American prisoners had enjoyed the sponsorship of the Swedish consul, for example, William Eaton handled Danish affairs in Tunis when their consul was expelled during a conflict in 1800, sponsoring the captains of several captured Danish vessels, even to the point of helping them buy back their ships. Further, much as the Skjoldebrands stepped in to ransom an American sailor in extremis, Eaton did the same for Maria Anna Porcile, the captive daughter of a minor Sardinian noble. These sorts of interactions built webs of friendship and obligation that not only raised America's standing as a sister nation but also paid direct dividends, such as when Denmark returned Eaton's representation of their prisoners in Tunis by representing American interests in Tripoli.[6]

It was not long before these consular-level ties illuminated a continuity of interest among Denmark, Sweden, and the United States and led to ministerial-level engagement on potential cooperation on Barbary affairs, culminating in 1800 in Sweden proposing a coalition among the three to protect each other's commerce in the Mediterranean. Their central shared interest was that of free trade. Indeed, that same year Sweden and Denmark joined with other neutral nations in the Second League of Armed Neutrality, also known as the League of the North, to defend the rights of neutral shipping, a move that Britain considered a form of participation in the War of the Second Coalition and led to the British destruction of much of Denmark's fleet in the 1801 Battle of Copenhagen. The United States was also participating in the fringes of the War of the Second Coalition as a defender of neutral shipping in its Quasi-War conflict with

France. In the Mediterranean, the three countries faced not only interference from great powers as a limit of their neutral trade but also the threat of the Barbary corsairs. Although such a partnership would be aligned with their free trade interests, it would not align with the United States' efforts to show its reliability as a treaty partner. The Adams administration felt it must decline Sweden's proposal, noting that even toward the Barbary powers "the engagements of the United States, tho' unreasonably burthensome, ought to be performed." Nonetheless, the proposal was a valuable recognition of America as an actor in the European milieu, and the administration was interested in revisiting it in the case that North African powers should "break their treaties with us," at which time "the United States will be at perfect liberty" to join such a coalition. That liberty would come within a year.[7]

Engaging Algiers

The captures of 1793 drastically increased the priority that the Washington administration and Congress gave to Algerian affairs. Their response reversed the lack of a navy that had mooted Thomas Jefferson's proposed anti-Barbary alliance and left the United States unable to participate fully within the Vattelian international regime. In December 1790 Secretary of State Jefferson had presented options for dealing with the ongoing Algiers captivity. He had enumerated the potential costs of a negotiated treaty but also offered the option "to repel Force by Force." This would, of course, require a navy. As part of his argument that such a navy could be kept small, however, he had revisited his call for international cooperation, saying that the various nations at war with Algiers could rotate blockade duty so that each navy would only tie down ships for a portion of the year.[8] This proposal had not gone far, as the assumed price of a peace was far lower than the cost of even a small navy. In March 1794, just months after news of the new captures arrived, Congress changed its position and passed "An Act to provide a Naval Armament." The act called for building a six-ship navy of 248 guns, remarkably parallel to that called for in Jefferson's first musings to Adams on the subject in 1785. The notion of a navy was popular among Federalists but controversial among the newly developing Democratic-Republican opposition. While some felt that a navy could not, like a standing army, be used to oppress the citizens, others argued that it was an unwarranted expense that would promote office seeking and burden the public. As a compromise measure, the naval act also called for cancellation of the program "if a peace shall take place between the United States and the Regency of Algiers."[9]

Congress also prioritized the resources needed to realize such a peace, the making of which would not only open the Mediterranean for American commerce and return the suffering captives but also model European practice and showcase the United States as a viable nation. A week before the navy bill passed, Congress authorized $1 million to "defray any expenses which may be incurred, in relation to the intercourse between the United States and foreign nations."[10] There seems to have been a misapprehension within the Washington administration that these funds were intended to pay for the naval armament, but by mid-July this had been straightened out. Jefferson's replacement as secretary of state, Edmund Randolph, wrote to David Humphreys advising him of the new budget and renewing his commission and instructions to ransom American prisoners and make peace with Algiers. Humphreys reached out to his best source of Algerian information, Richard O'Brien, who informed him that the dey was asking almost $2.5 million for peace and recommended a counteroffer of $600,000. Sure enough, a formal demand for the former amount followed in December 1794, under the hand of the dey's chief Christian secretary, James Cathcart. Humphreys was at the same time charged with finalizing the renewal of America's treaty with Morocco (the succession issues that had kept Barclay from accomplishing it having finally been resolved) and his regular ministerial duties in Portugal. He thus delegated his Algerian mission to Joseph Donaldson (an otherwise obscure gentleman whom the Washington administration planned to appoint as consul to either Tunis or Tripoli) and Joel Barlow. While Donaldson, who arrived first, was advised to seek the assistance of the French consul, he found more value in the assistance of the American prisoners and the Skjoldebrands.[11]

The relationship between the Americans and Swedish Consul General Mathias Skjoldebrand and his brother Pierre Eric had become quite close over the years of American captivity. As well as hosting prisoners in the consular house, the Skjoldebrands had loaned money to individual prisoners on occasion, once as much as $5,000 to James Cathcart to buy a prize loaded with wine. Early in 1793 the brothers had ransomed American seaman George Smith, who had been captured in 1785, at the very high sum of $2,696 (more than was usually expected to ransom a captain), because he had somehow displeased Dey Hassan sufficiently that he would have been executed if not ransomed. The United States government, after a considerable delay for internal coordination, reimbursed the brothers for this expense in 1795. In the same letter in which Humphreys was authorized to appoint Donaldson as his agent, Secretary of State Randolph also informed him that the administration had appointed Pierre Eric Skjoldebrand as United States consul to Algiers. Pierre Eric took this responsibility seriously, coordinating for Donaldson while he was in Alicante, negotiating via correspondence, and chartering a ship to bring Donaldson to Algiers once the dey issued a passport. Donaldson finally arrived in Algiers on 3 September 1795, a decade after the first captures.[12]

Based on O'Brien's and Cathcart's descriptions of the peace negotiations, Donaldson did not seem any more temperamentally suited to North African diplomacy than Lamb had been. What he had that Lamb had lacked, though, was authority, funding, and local assistance that was reliably aligned with American interests. Though Cathcart often seemed to exaggerate his importance to various affairs, his expertise in court traditions does seem to have smoothed over Donaldson's abrupt manner. During the negotiations, Donaldson complained, "If you want an Algerine Turk to be your friend, he must be bought. Their language is how can you be my friend when you give me nothing."[13] Cathcart, on the other hand, claimed that Donaldson failed to understand the customary distributions that greased North African diplomacy and that only by Cathcart's arranging the funds to please all parties was America able to procure peace. This seems somewhat just, as the specifications included such arcana as $247 worth of gifts for each of the dey's two chief cooks. Although this was probably not key to the negotiations, it certainly sped them. With the resources at his command, Donaldson was able to reach an agreement for ransoming the prisoners and for peace just two days after his arrival, at a price of $624,500 in specie, as well as agreeing to furnish an annual shipment of 12,000 sequins (about $21,000) worth of naval stores.[14]

This agreement came so quickly that it was signed before Donaldson's fellow agent Joel Barlow even received his instructions. But it was not operative until paid. Donaldson had only $60,000 in specie, just enough to cover the peace presents and his expenses. To secure the release of the prisoners and American access to the Mediterranean, Donaldson needed to convert his credit to cash. After the experience with Lamb, neither the Algerian council of ministers (*diwan*) nor the American prisoners were comfortable with the idea of Donaldson departing to gather funds. Instead, O'Brien was dispatched to Lisbon to meet with Humphreys, and then to London, where he expected to pick up specie from America's merchant banker, Sir Francis Baring. England was suffering a cash shortage at the time, likely related to its role bankrolling the anti-French First Coalition, and Baring was only able to offer a credit for redemption at Cadiz. O'Brien feared that Spain would also be unwilling to let such a large sum be exported from their territory during the conflict, which proved accurate. He then crossed the Atlantic to seek specie or guidance in Philadelphia, returned to Lisbon once again, and finally sailed for Algiers in late July with a partial payment, five months after his departure.[15]

In the midst of O'Brien's peregrinations, Joel Barlow's arrival in Algiers freed Joseph Donaldson to travel to Livorno, where he expected to be able to gather the remaining specie. Instead, his efforts were also impeded by the War of the First Coalition, as French forces occupied Livorno in July 1796 and the British navy blockaded the port. Barlow made multiple partial payments of the ransom and indemnity and eventually offered Dey Hassan an American-built frigate as an additional compensation for tolerating the delays.[16] A payment of $200,000 (borrowed in Algiers from the trading house of Bacri for repayment to their branch in Livorno) in July 1796 covered the ransoms, and the American prisoners were released, leaving Barlow, as he colorfully put it in a letter to his wife, Ruth, "the last American slave in Algiers."[17] In October, O'Brien finally arrived in Algiers after his detour to Tripoli, with the partial payment from Lisbon. The following January, the specie from Livorno arrived, finalizing the agreement that had been signed sixteen months earlier.[18] This unexpectedly difficult fund transfer illustrates the dislocations of the Wars of the French Revolution on even seemingly unrelated affairs. It was also key to establishing not only American creditworthiness, as Hannah Farber has argued, but also America's willingness and capacity to live up to treaty obligations. The persistent and creative efforts of American agents demonstrated American treaty-worthiness both to Algiers and to the European diplomatic community stationed there.

Matters of Law

Further American treaty making in North Africa not only showed American capacity to Europeans but directly involved European interlocutors. Barlow negotiated treaties with Tunis and Tripoli during his time in Algiers, but he did so remotely, relying on agents in the regencies. In the case of Tunis, negotiations were carried on via correspondence, with American interests represented by a local French merchant, Joseph Famin. In Tripoli, Barlow was represented by an American agent with North African experience, Richard O'Brien. O'Brien depended heavily on local expertise and assistance from the Spanish Consul General de Souza, who witnessed both the treaty and the distribution of the peace presents and indemnity. Both of these negotiations went relatively smoothly, but each included a complication that illustrated the early republic's approach to international law. The first of these was the famous Article 11 of the Tripoli treaty.[19]

Article 11 refutes any religious enmity between the Unites States and Tripoli, noting that America has no legal or historical animosity toward Islam and its government "is not in any sense founded on the Christian Religion." The treaty's ratification made that statement part of America's "supreme law of the land." Although the Constitution already forbad any religious test for public office and kept Congress from making any "law respecting an establishment of religion, or prohibiting the free exercise thereof," Article 11 goes further in asserting America's secular foundation. It is not clear that Barlow included this clause specifically to do so. On the one hand, he seemed to legitimately believe that the absence of religious motivation for conflict would improve the chances of a lasting peace. He wrote in 1796 that he believed that America would have an easier time keeping a lasting peace with Algiers than other European powers, with whom peace rarely lasted, because Algerine Turks "do not consider us as Christians" and would thus not have a religious motivation for hostilities. Article 11 could simply be Barlow's effort to formalize that understanding in order to make future ruptures less likely.[20]

There is circumstantial evidence for the notion that this article was intended as much for an international legal audience as a Tripolitan one, however. Barlow was a noted freethinker, a dabbler in French politics, and a strong advocate of the total separation of church and state. In his pro–French Revolution 1792 work *Advice to the Privileged Classes,* Barlow warned that "nations are cruel in proportion as they are guided by priests" and trumpeted America's lack of an established church as ensuring "the continuation of public instruction, in the science of liberty and happiness, and promises a long duration to a representative government."[21] His utopian epic poem *The Columbiad* (still in progress at the time) extolled secularism to the point that it drew attacks as being "aethiestical."[22] It seems likely that Barlow's intent was both to strengthen the United States' legal basis for excluding religion from government and to add ammunition to his arguments against a state religion in the First French Republic.

Although Barlow never claimed Article 11 as a blow for secularism, if he thought it would curb potential ruptures with Tripoli, he miscalculated. The article does not even appear in the Arabic text of the treaty. Neither O'Brien, who was present for the negotiations, nor Barlow, who received the completed treaty in Algiers and signed it there, read Arabic, so it is not clear that they were even aware of the discrepancy. The fact that Hunter Miller refers to the English text of the treaty as the "Barlow translation" has misled some commenters to assume that Barlow inserted the controversial text personally and post facto, but it was actually included in the original document drawn up in Tripoli. The original treaty is written in pamphlet form, with one folio showing an article in English and its facing folio showing it in Arabic. The folio opposite Article 11, however, is not an article of the treaty at all but rather a note that the dey of Algiers recommends that Tripoli assent to a treaty, seemingly in order to imply Algiers's sponsorship and perhaps senior status over Tripoli. (For a discussion of both folios, see appendix 2.) Why Article 11 is left out of the Arabic text of the treaty is unclear, but it seems likely that, as well as being unimpressed by the argument, the leadership of Tripoli did not want to open themselves up to any potential religious ruling (*fatwa*) against future hostilities with the United States.[23]

When the treaty came before the United States Senate, the clause was not particularly controversial. The ratification was unanimous, and there is no record that Article 11 was formally debated, though when it was noted in the *Aurora* three years later, Secretary of War McHenry wrote to a friend that he had objected at the time. McHenry, commenting on the newspaper article, wrote that "the Senate, my good friend, and I said so at the time, ought never to have ratified the treaty alluded to, with the declaration that 'the government of the United States is not, *in any sense*, founded on the Christian religion.' What else is it founded on?"[24] The treaty's declaration was cited in the *Aurora* during the run-up to the election of 1800 as precedent for Thomas Jefferson's government secularism, with the correspondent noting that this principle was already recognized in "*the supreme laws of the land.*" McHenry responded that "this act always appeared to me like *trampling upon the cross*. I do not recollect that Barlow was even reprimanded for this outrage upon the government and religion." If Barlow had indeed been attempting to surreptitiously bolster the legal case for American secular government, he succeeded. In doing so, he inserted himself into one of the great controversies of the age of revolution, in Europe as well as in America.[25]

The complication in Tunisian negotiations was less thorny as a question of law but more of a diplomatic challenge and a strong example of America's acceptance of privateering as a normal and law-bound issue. During Donaldson's stay in Algiers, he arranged an eight-month truce with Tunis on 8 November 1795 via the regency's local chargé d'affaires, al-Haj Ali. Donaldson sought to cover time for negotiations, in case any American ships heard of the Algerian peace and assumed that the Mediterranean was now safe.[26] Barlow shared Donaldson's concern, noting in a letter to minister to France James Monroe that, in an evocative turn of phrase, American merchant shippers "would sail into the mouth of hell, if the Devil was to turn Catholic so as to make a good market for codfish."[27] As the truce was nearing expiration, Barlow began his correspondence with Joseph Famin to conclude a treaty. Tunisian Bey Hammuda responded that he had never heard of the referenced truce, but that he was willing to grant one for six months, beginning immediately. Unfortunately, as Donaldson and Barlow had feared might happen, Edward Rand, the owner aboard the American ship *Eliza*, had heard in Gibraltar that "peace was made with all Mahometan powers" and proceeded on a voyage to Barcelona and then Sète, France. Two days out of Sète, the *Eliza* was taken by a Tunisian cruiser. When the ships arrived in Tunis, the parties found out about the truce, but also that the capture was apparently made one day before the truce had gone into effect. The *Eliza* was thus condemned as a good prize, and her crew and owner imprisoned.[28]

When Barlow received this news, he was furious—not with Tunis but with Rand. There was no doubt that the *Eliza* was a good prize. Since peace negotiations were ongoing, Tunis added the status of the ship, its cargo, and its crew to the negotiations. Barlow redeemed all three but was not pleased about it and considered the vessel and its cargo United States property, since he had effectively bought the prize with government funds. He wrote to Rand complaining that his capture would add at least $30,000 to the price of peace and that Barlow would not have consented to the redemption of the ship itself "were it not for the sake of facilitating the negotiation with the Bey and to favour your return & that of the crew to America." Barlow was also finalizing the release of the Algerian prisoners at the time and thought that the newly United States–owned *Eliza* might serve to take them back to America as well. He therefore ordered the ship to Livorno and made the redemption contingent on Rand's compliance and on signing a receipt for the ship as public property.[29]

The *Eliza* did not end up transferring former captives (other than her own crew) back to America but nonetheless remained government property. The former owner petitioned Congress for return or restitution on the grounds that the original truce (unrecognized by Tunis, though that is not mentioned in the petition) was still in effect on the date of capture, and therefore the ship was not a good prize but rather an illegal taking, which would not change the right of ownership. Rand's attorney apparently recognized the weakness of this argument, likely as the ship had been condemned by a valid prize court. He added a secondary plea that "if the legal property may be considered to have been acquired by the seizure ... it cannot be supposed that the United States would negotiate with the Bey for a vessell and sixteen Pipes Brandy for their own benefit ... no other rational idea seems to present itself but a ransom for the benefit of the original owners."[30] There is no evidence that this argument swayed Congress. A year after the petition was filed, Secretary of State Pickering informed the consul in Algiers that the *Eliza* (now renamed the *Maria*) had been sold at Boston for a small sum, noting that "the loss sustained in this case having arisen from the fraud or folly of the American master we must be content to bear," so it seems unlikely that any compensation was forthcoming to Rand.[31]

The law-bound nature of privateering was not always so clear-cut as in the *Eliza* case, however. While many principles, such as the right to capture one's enemies, were universal, some issues of international maritime law were contested. One of these elements, that of the rights of friendly and neutral ships carrying enemy cargo, was one that America, the neutral states of Europe, and the North African regencies largely agreed on. There were two competing traditions on this issue in international law: that of "harm your enemy" and that of "free ships make free goods." The older of these traditions, based on the 1495 Barcelonan legal treatise *Consolato del Mare*, held that enemy goods in neutral ships were liable to confiscation, but the ship was not, or at least not solely for carrying enemy goods. This was the principle held firmly by the British. Thus, for example, in 1793 when two American ships were taken with French goods, both cargos were condemned as French, but one vessel was released, while the other was condemned not for carrying French goods but for making an illegal "false declaration" of its cargo.[32]

While the great naval powers were relatively constant in applying the *Consolato* interpretation, the Dutch principle of "free ships make free goods" was making strong inroads. By this principle, enemy goods were not good prizes in friendly or neutral ships unless they were contraband, or the ship was taken attempting to run a blockade. This principle was not universally accepted in international law and was usually set by bilateral treaty. It was very popular between countries who were usually neutral and had significant merchant marines. Thomas Jefferson referred to it as "the great question of the Maritime law of nations, which at present agitates Europe, that is to say, Whether free ships shall make free goods?" and made a natural law argument that they should. He also pointed out that America worked to include it in every treaty of amity and commerce and to encourage it as the general usage, but that it was not worth a war.[33]

The controversy over "free ships, free goods" not only led to the famed Leagues of Armed Neutrality (1780–83 and 1800–1801), which attempted to resist Britain's maximal assertation of *Consolato* principles during wars with France, but also led to one of the first examples of American diplomats in North Africa acting in concert with those of other nations. Shortly before Barlow's departure from Algiers in the spring of 1797, the new French consul to Algiers, Jean Bon St. Andre, took advantage of the opportunity provided by the British Navy's withdrawal from the Mediterranean in the early days of the Anglo-Spanish War (1796–1802, with the British fleet absent from the Mediterranean from 1797 to April 1798) to commission a privateer. In a policy foreshadowing that which would shortly lead to the "Quasi-War" between France and the United States, St. Andre instructed the crew to take neutral ships and send them in to Algiers for adjudication. Joel Barlow was fine with extensive privateering in the Mediterranean in 1797 among "the states of Europe, at war with each other. There is no harm in that." He was concerned, however, when St. Andre ordered his privateer to "take every neutral he could find . . . and send them to this port." Barlow explained that "it has been the general rule not to send a friend's vessel here, though loaded with enemy's goods," even for those countries dedicated to the *Consolato* model of forfeiture. The concern was that the Barbary powers might abandon the "free ships, free goods" principle once they saw the *Consolato* model in action, since it would open up so many potential prizes. Barlow and the Swedish and Danish consuls remonstrated with St. Andre that "goods on a neutral vessel under capture should not be discharged in this place." When that argument failed, the group petitioned the dey to shut his port to all such vessels.[34] This represented the first example of American diplomats cooperating with those of other European nations on Barbary issues and becoming part of the regular diplomatic community as more than recipients of aid.

Algiers's response also stands in sharp contrast to American diplomats' experience in China (the other location of consuls not accredited to either European or colonial governments in this era), highlighting North Africa's involvement in the Vattelian system. China did not acknowledge Europe's theoretically universal law of nations and refused to get involved in disputes between foreign nations, even when the complaint involved violations of Chinese neutrality. Consuls Samuel Snow and his successor Edward Carrington tried fruitlessly for several years in the early 1800s, for example, to convince China to interfere in Britain's practice of impressing sailors off American ships in Chinese harbors. The local authorities in Canton consistently declined to interfere or even to forward the request to higher authorities. Algiers, on the other hand, was concerned about both precedent and potential disruption to local shipping. The dey responded to Barlow and his colleagues' complaint immediately and forbad St. Andre to bring in neutral ships.[35]

Barlow wrote to the United States minister at Paris warning of the complaint likely coming soon from the French government and explaining that though he had no wish to produce a rupture with France, he felt that he had to act. "If by our folly they [the corsairing states] should be taught the contrary principle, the carrying trade is at an end."[36] It is unlikely, however, that just seeing this principle in action would have changed North African usage, as the *Consolato* model had already been the most common legal tradition in the Mediterranean for centuries. The bigger problem for America was that Barbary practice went beyond free ships freeing the cargo to that cargo becoming the responsibility of the carrying country. O'Brien explained that the convention was that "free colours make both goods and passengers free" and if taken "those colours, on board which vessels these goods or passengers were, must make all damages good to the Algerians and the other Barbary States." He further explained that the then ongoing war between Tunis and Venice was due to two Tunisian cargos on board Venetian vessels that had been seized by a third party and for which Venice had refused to offer compensation.[37]

North African usage that the carrying country was responsible for damages contrasted with the general European understanding that the dispute in such a case was between the losing party and the seizing party.

It proved a costly policy when the "American" ship *Fortune* was condemned of a cargo of wheat belonging to Algerian subjects. The case of the *Fortune*, which was originally chartered simply to take the former American prisoners from Algiers to Livorno, demonstrates the entangled nature of maritime ownership and of different conventions regarding cargo seizure. The *Fortune* was a former British transport (the *Bridget* of London) that St. Andre's privateer had captured and brought into Algiers. The capture of a vessel belonging to a country at war with France was not, as the targeting of neutrals had been, in any way controversial. The trading house of Bacri (which had financed the prisoners' ransom) purchased the former *Bridget* after it was condemned. It then became "American" via a theoretical sale and, when captured, was crewed by former American prisoners in Algiers and carrying cargo belonging to the Bacris. The Bacris had "sold" the *Fortune* to Barlow in July of 1796 in order to let it fly a United States flag while the former prisoners were taken to Livorno. The American flag would protect the ship from being targeted by Genoa or Tuscany, with whom Algiers was at war. Barlow planned that this would get the prisoners safely to Livorno, where the sale would be canceled and the ship would return to its prior owners. Instead, the Bacris apparently made out a similarly theoretical bill of sale to Joseph Donaldson in Livorno and then "hired" the ship from him to ship wheat under an American flag. The ship remained crewed by former prisoners, who were hired for the voyage. Donaldson denied any knowledge of the scheme, which he blamed on either the Bacris, the *Fortune*'s American Captain William Smith, or both, having falsely testified to the American consul to Marseilles that Smith was acting as Donaldson's agent in order to procure papers. The *Fortune* was then detained by the British, as it was apparently delivering wheat to France, and not to Genoa, as its papers claimed. While Barlow protested that the ship belonged to the Bacris, who had apparently admitted that they had not been paid for it, the dey ruled that as it sailed under American colors and papers, the cargo was America's responsibility.[38]

The *Fortune* incident had long-lasting effects and demonstrated the complexity that lay behind seemingly straightforward issues such as a ship's nationality or differences in maritime law. It took several years to settle the claim. Barlow left the Bacris an IOU when he departed Algiers, leaving the issue in his successor's hands. After several letters seeking clarification and instructions, the claim was finally paid in 1800. When James Madison took over as secretary of state in 1801, he referenced the incident in his letters of instruction to the United States consuls in North Africa as showing "the disadvantage of employing our vessels in the freight of Algerine property." He instructed the consuls to "discourage that branch of trade" and to attempt, as far as possible, to repress expectation or claims of indemnification for loss of property in American bottoms.[39]

Though there were some frustrations in the details, the issue of privateering and the North African notions of the laws thereof were, for the most part, in agreement with American practice and views of the law of nations. While modern eyes may expect to see this "policy of piracy" as inherently incompatible with diplomacy, it was a normal part of diplomatic practice in the era, and mitigating it was exactly what was expected of these early diplomats and what they expected of the position. Soon, America would appoint full-time diplomats to the regencies. Two of them would arrive with extensive experience with the region, having spent over a decade in Algiers already, albeit involuntarily.

Consuls in Barbary

Generally, American consuls were private merchants based in a given location who were given limited diplomatic credentials and received fees for services but no salary. This model would not work for the regencies, both because no American merchant houses were based in their principal ports and because there was a higher level of diplomatic effort and expertise expected. Thus, Adams decided "to vest the Consul at Algiers with a degree of discretionary power which can be requisite in no other situation," and argued that "to encourage a person deserving the Public confidence to accept so expensive and responsible a station, it appears indispensable to allow him a handsome salary." Adams gave the consul general at Algiers supervisory power over the consuls at Tunis and Tripoli and the authority to commit public funds. This position's "handsome salary" was $4,000 a year, with the consuls at Tunis and Tripoli each to receive $2,000.[40]

There really was no question about whom to choose as consul general, if he would accept the position. Richard O'Brien had taken a commission from Dey Hassan, who was impressed with the quality of American-built ships and had ordered two ships at Algerian expense in addition to the frigate offered as compensation for slow payment of the peace indemnity. Barlow strongly recommended O'Brien as his successor, and O'Brien's position as construction and procurement agent for the Algerian ships took him to Philadelphia, where he was able to demonstrate his expertise directly to the Adams administration. O'Brien wrote an extensive document on Barbary affairs for Secretary of State Pickering that informed American policy, and showed that Barlow's recommendation was well-founded.[41]

Fellow former captive and aspiring diplomat James Cathcart came less well recommended. In fact, Barlow wrote to Secretary of State Pickering from Algiers in May 1796, "I am told that Mr. Cathcart has hopes of obtaining the consulate to this place. He has neither the talents nor the dignity of character necessary for the purpose." Barlow nonetheless suggested that he be hired as an agent for gathering the naval stores specified by the Algiers treaty.[42] Dey Hassan had released Cathcart during the long wait for delivery of the peace indemnity in order to encourage the American government to meet its commitment, but by the time he arrived in Philadelphia, the other prisoners had already been released, and most of the specie had been delivered to Algiers. The administration accepted Barlow's recommendation and employed Cathcart in procuring peace presents and the annual "tribute." Pickering appreciated Cathcart's regional expertise and apparently felt comfortable with him taking the subordinate role of consul to Tripoli.[43]

Joseph Donaldson was no longer under consideration for a consular post, perhaps because of his role in the *Fortune* affair, leaving the position of consul to Tunis open with no suitable candidates with experience in North Africa. Pickering turned to his protégé William Eaton. Eaton was a former captain in the Legion of the United States, recently renamed the United States Army. After serving in the Northwest Indian War under General Wayne, Eaton had been dispatched to southern Georgia to garrison the border with Spanish Florida and Seminole and Creek territory. There he built and commanded Fort Pickering, named after the former secretary of war, who had recently moved to head the State Department. After less than a year in command, Eaton was court-martialed for abuse of authority and improper financial dealings in what he described as an attempt to punish him for objecting to his superior Lieutenant Colonel Gaither's improper land speculation. Based on Eaton's later actions and on Gaither's later cashiering, it seems likely that both of these interpretations had merit. Though he was sentenced to only a two-month suspension of command, his superior sent him to Philadelphia to report to the new secretary of war, James McHenry, who neither confirmed nor overturned the court-martial. Eaton stayed in Philadelphia, serving as an aide to Pickering, who, after sending him to arrest a suspect in the Blount Conspiracy, then appointed him as consul to Tunis.[44]

On 18 January 1798 O'Brien departed for Algiers, with instructions giving him broad discretionary powers, aboard the promised frigate, which was dubbed the *Crescent* in a nod to the symbol of Islam. They sailed in company with the Algiers-ordered schooner *Hamdullah,* similarly named in honor of its recipients' faith. While some were surprised that America would help arm Algiers, O'Brien argued that this was actually a positive, as Algiers was likely to use the ships against France, whom he saw as a mutual enemy, given the deteriorating relationship that would soon break out into the "Quasi-War" between the United States and France. As Abigail Mullen argues, this, at least theoretically, put American policy in line with the previous European strategy of using Barbary powers as proxies in wider conflicts. O'Brien delivered the ships and took up his position as consul general on 26 February.[45] Just under a year later, Eaton and Cathcart followed. Cathcart's instructions specified the importance of cooperating with "the Consuls of any nation who shall manifest a sincere disposition to serve us."[46] Though Pickering unsurprisingly (given the outbreak of the Quasi-War that summer) recommended working with British diplomats and warned against those of France, it was a sign of America's more natural partners in North Africa that Eaton and Cathcart sailed in company with the third ship commissioned for Algiers, which grateful Americans had named the *Skjoldebrand.*

As semipermanent residents rather than individuals on a specific mission, European consuls usually brought their families with them to North

Africa. These family members are rarely discussed in the diplomatic record but were not entirely restricted to the private sphere. Private and public spheres frequently intersected via social engagement among the diplomatic expatriate community, particularly the hosting of dinners at which adult family members (mostly consuls' wives) shared the table. O'Brien was a bachelor, and Eaton had left his wife, Elizabeth (Eliza), at home in Brimfield, Massachusetts, as was his regular habit. Since his marriage in 1792, Eaton had lived in Brimfield for only a few months, when on leave of absence from the army in early 1795. Nor had he taken Eliza along on any of his assignments, instead only visiting for a few weeks at a time as his duties allowed.[47] Cathcart, on the other hand, had married during his stay in Philadelphia and brought his new wife, Jane (née Woodside), to his posting in Tripoli. The Cathcarts also brought along a servant by the name of Elizabeth (Betsy) Robeson, who is one of the very few women in the Western diplomatic communities in North Africa whose agency has made it into the public record. When Elizabeth arrived with the Cathcarts and Eaton in Algiers, the flotilla's first stop, she refused to continue on to Tripoli and accused James Cathcart of improper behavior, reportedly stating that she had assumed that a diplomat would be "at least civilized, if not refined." Though the nature of Cathcart's impropriety was left unspoken, the subtext of unwanted sexual advances was clear.[48]

Richard O'Brien hosted Elizabeth Robeson at the next American expatriate dinner, which offended Cathcart, who left the dinner early with his wife. Cathcart and O'Brien fell out over the issue, with Cathcart complaining that O'Brien had "seduced his maid away from him."[49] Two months later, O'Brien and Robeson married. According to William Eaton, who kept up a correspondence with Elizabeth from his post in Tunis (she was at pains to clarify to him that her husband was completely aware of their correspondence and did not consider it inappropriate), this distressed Jane Cathcart, as her servant had suddenly surpassed her in social precedence. Mid-twentieth-century historians Wright and Macleod took this as a formal change in rank, claiming that Jane was upset that Elizabeth had "stepped a notch ahead of her in the diplomatic protocol." This comment is rather anachronistic, as there is no evidence of a rigid protocol within the State Department at the time, particularly at the consular level.[50]

Fortunately for the American consuls in North Africa and their families, their service was removed from the scrupulous precedence expected in European diplomatic circles, which Sadosky describes as "the polite world outside of, but adjacent to, the formal world of the court."[51] There, American ministers operated at a disadvantage, owing to their title being less eminent than that of "ambassador" and to the lack of a prestigious monarch as their superior. In North Africa, European consuls were of the merchant class (usually their primary profession) and only just qualified to gentle status. Though Elizabeth O'Brien's husband, as consul general, held a slightly higher position than James Cathcart's, that did not extend to formal primacy for her over Jane Cathcart. Nonetheless, Eaton may have been correct about Jane's resistance to her maid's sudden change in relative status. Though class barriers were more permeable in America than in much of Europe, upper classes still tended to resent those perceived as parvenues.[52] O'Brien announced his nuptials in his dispatches in his typical bluff manner, appending to his monthly report to the secretary of state the simple note: "O'Brien got married the 25th of March."[53] Elizabeth does not show up often in the diplomatic correspondence from then on, but judging from the more detailed notes of O'Brien's eventual successor, Tobias Lear, about his wife Frances's role, it is likely that Elizabeth also played a role as hostess within the community and as a "representative of the American fair" to merchant and naval officers in the Mediterranean.

In the same dispatch in which O'Brien announced his marriage, he likened himself, Eaton, and Cathcart to "light houses erected on 3 dangerous shoals, said light houses erected to prevent Valuable commerce running thereon."[54] This simile accurately reflects the consuls' primary role. The consuls had two main lines of effort: keeping the peace in place in order to keep the Mediterranean safe for American shipping, and protecting that shipping from predation during times of peace by dealing with legal issues, issuing passes, and generally administering to the needs of Americans in the Mediterranean. The first of these may have been more impactful, but smaller issues were more common.

While peace removed a nation's shipping from indiscriminate capture, ships could still be sent in for judgment owing to perceived irregularities. While planning for the post-peace influx of American shipping into the

Mediterranean, both Joel Barlow and Richard O'Brien pointed out potential issues that could get ships sent in. Even if they were not condemned, being sent in for judgment incurred a large time cost and a risk of petty plunder, and if further irregularities were found, it could be worse. Barlow and O'Brien were particularly concerned about the multiple versions of American flags flown by ships, some with eagles or Irish harps over the stripes, etc.[55] They recommended that Congress specify one flag for merchant shipping, as "a variance in the flag from the one deposited [with the Algiers government] will always expose the ship to be brought in."[56] As well as variety within the national standard, O'Brien expressed concern with ships flying state flags, stating that Algerians "will declare the[y] made a peace with one nation & one flag, not with 16 nations & 16 flags." Further, O'Brien suggested that passports needed to be reprinted in a pattern that would make it easier to ensure a good match between top and bottom. To combat counterfeiting, passports were cut with distinctive scallops and a top given to the corsairs to check for a match. O'Brien brought this issue up multiple times, both before his consulship and during it, as a mismatch could lead to a claim of a forged passport and forfeiture of cargo. As he colorfully put it in his 1796 memo on Barbary affairs, "The passport Mediterranean should be cut with that nicety of a Bank Note . . . if the top does not agree with the bottom, adieu Cargo."[57] As late as 1801 he complained that it had still not been fixed and that "this Circumstance I have fully stated to The late administration."[58] This issue was finally addressed in 1803.[59]

American vessels were indeed sent into Barbary ports even during times of peace. James Cathcart wrote looking for instructions on how to deal with cases in which Tripoli should "capture any of our vessels on any pretense whatever & that I should find it impossible to clear them by fair means" and on whether he should resort to bribery or "wait the determination of the [Tripolitan] government." He mentioned that he had written to O'Brien on the same subject and would follow his advice until he heard from the secretary of state.[60] O'Brien had already dealt with such an instance and had no scruples about using bribery and subterfuge. Several months earlier, while Cathcart was still en route to Tripoli, Algerian corsairs had brought in the Philadelphia brig *Mary* for not having a Mediterranean passport after the deadline for acquiring one had passed. O'Brien was unwilling to let the crew suffer the consequences, particularly that of captivity, as America would have had to pay at least $42,000 to redeem them. He claimed (in an apparently completely fabricated story) that the ship's papers had been disordered by both French and British inspection parties and that a document (which fortunately for him, the Algerian inspectors could not read) that was actually the vessel's bill of sale was instead a temporary passport (*pass avant*) and explanatory note from another consul to be used until the ship could get back to America and get a new Mediterranean passport. Three thousand dollars and the newness of the peace convinced the dey to rule that, though the vessel was a legal prize, he would clear it as a one-time favor.[61]

Fortunately for Cathcart, the only American vessel sent into Tripoli during his consulship was quickly cleared and released. There seems to be subtext that the ship was brought in as a show of power and a negotiation ploy, though Bey Yusuf claimed that he had given no orders for American vessels to be brought in, and its papers were all in order. The captain who brought her in was reportedly dismissed from the regency's service.[62]

A far more common problem was petty plunder, most often by the boat crew that boarded a vessel to check papers, even if everything was in order and the vessel was free to go on. For example, O'Brien was plundered of his savings of $300 and some stores when he was detained by Tripoli on his way to pay the Algiers prisoner ransom.[63] While the losses were relatively minor, diplomats protested such action heartily, as this practice was extra-legal and considered unjust and insulting. When protesting a similar action, Cathcart referred to it as "demanding satisfaction for the insult our flag had suffer'd."[64] Cathcart experienced this type of plunder himself when his ship was stopped for inspection by a Tunisian corsair while on a voyage between Malta and Sicily. Although all papers were in order, the Tunisian boarding party stole some provisions from him and the "Captains Octant, Chart, & only Compass."[65] Such petty plunder was not restricted to North Africans. In May of 1802 crew members of an American schooner plundered a Tripolitan ship of a total of $257.49 worth of valuables, for which Eaton arranged for restitution.[66]

While the consuls felt it their duty to do their best to protect or, if necessary, redeem American shipping, they had no qualms that prizes condemned by North African prize courts conveyed legal transfer of ownership. In fact, Eaton, O'Brien, and Cathcart all purchased prizes during their time as consuls. There was no restriction on consuls being involved in personal trade at the time. Eaton and Cathcart both purchased multiple vessels and went into business in 1799, separately and together, in the carrying trade and in buying and reselling condemned cargos. Eaton argued that the ties of trade that he was forming would help stabilize American peace with Tunis. Eaton and Cathcart had both fallen out with O'Brien by that time and did not participate in business with him. Cathcart was jealous of O'Brien receiving the more prestigious post and upset that he had married Cathcart's former maid. Eaton, on the other hand, distrusted O'Brien's pragmatic streak in dealing with the regencies, considering him accommodationist. Both Cathcart and Eaton found O'Brien's willingness to deal with the Jewish house of Bacri (or, as they referred to it, the "Jewish Directory") as a source of credit for the United States distasteful, and possibly compromising. Although scholars often overstate the disfunction of the relationship among the consuls, which was mostly limited to scornful journal entries and letters to each other, if it did not prevent them from serving effectively, it made business partnership out of the question. Nonetheless, O'Brien also purchased at least one vessel from the Regency of Algiers for use in returning the American crews of ships built in America and delivered to Algiers. He also used his ship, which he imaginatively named the *O'Brien,* as a packet to deliver diplomatic messages.[67]

If the act of privateering itself was accepted as legitimate and normal by American diplomats, the Barbary traditions of going to war were much more problematic. The consuls warned frequently that the regencies had to always be at war with at least one nation to give valid targets to their cruisers and, therefore, often made war on very little pretext. The consuls complained regularly of late annuities, as that could be used to claim that the United States had abrogated the treaty and could thus be warred upon. The regular refrain was that the "regalia," as it was called, should be complete and prompt and should be accompanied by armed vessels to give second thoughts about America as an easy target. The secretary of state often instructed the consuls to attempt to get the requirement for an annual regalia of naval stores converted to the equivalent in cash, which would obviate this risk, but none of the Barbary powers were interested in such an exchange, perhaps partly for that very reason.[68] The likelihood of eventual declaration of war frustrated the consuls, leading O'Brien to remark that he was "liveing in hopes of reliefe like unto a mariner on a wreck," largely owing to the Algiers regalia "not arriveing we being 2½ years in arrears and the dey has declared to me that our friendship entirely depended on this Event."[69] The requirement for regalia was onerous, and problems with quality or delivery could open America to predation, but United States officials nonetheless accepted it as a legitimate treaty requirement.

A much thornier issue was that of requests and demands not covered by treaty. These came in two types, customary payments (such as the presents for the dey's cooks included as part of the peace negotiations or presents distributed when a new consul took office) and simple requests or demands for money or presents. Cathcart and O'Brien generally accepted the first of these after learning the norms during their captivity, whereas other diplomats did not necessarily even differentiate between them. Eaton found them odious but negotiated them fairly successfully. Eaton had spent time as a subordinate to General Anthony Wayne in the Northwest Indian War (1786–95) and as the installation commander of a small fort in southern Georgia, dealing with disputes between Americans and Cherokees. He was thus familiar with the gifts that were a customary part of American borderland diplomacy, but in North Africa, at least, he considered them uncouth, if not transgressive. They were among the sources of his frequent comparisons of North Africans to Native Americans, both of whom he sometimes called "savages," but he was willing to participate when the event was well-established custom.[70]

All the consuls had trouble with superiors in Philadelphia (and later "Washington City") questioning their accounts. While it seems reasonable that in the atmosphere of the XYZ Affair, the State Department would want receipts for money spent to influence foreign agents, the consuls were offended. Eaton noted rather simply, "These people never give receipts for presents. I could not prevail on the Bey nor his minister to receipt the articles delivered him as the conditions of peace."[71] The usually patient O'Brien, on the other hand, responded bluntly, with his agitation showing in his writing, which took irregular punctuation and capitalization to new heights. "This whole business Must depend On the Honour Honesty & Patriotism of The Consul, and if his nation Cannot put This required And necessary Confidence in him, They Should Send A person or persons whom they Could More fully depend and rely on. you will observe that the Customs of this Country is prior to our Laws whom cannot alter algerine Customs & Usages."[72]

More annoying than these customary quid pro quos was the culture of requesting or demanding gifts or bribes. Most consuls were willing to apply an effective bribe—and account it as such, though obviously without a receipt—when there was a return to be had. Eaton, for example, bribed a surveyor to accept American powder that had been "somewhat damaged" in transit.[73] Demands for gifts that were not a payment for something or part of a negotiation, however, frustrated them greatly. One of the few times Cathcart, who usually presented himself as a cultural interlocutor, belittled the local culture was when he was explaining his accounts. After stating that "the small expences charged in my acct. are impositions which the Consuls of every nation at Peace with this Regency puts up with & many of them to a much greater extent than I have or ever will; exclusive of which the Bashaws family who are numerous, poor, proud & mean to excess, are continually troubling the Consuls for trifles," he went on to tell how two pigs that had been demanded of him were used as attempted medical cures and then added, "I mention the above merely to inform you of the absurdity of these peoples ideas."[74]

Personal bribes or requests for gifts frustrated the consuls somewhat, but demands for military equipment not covered by treaty specifications caused much stronger responses. For example, in 1801 a fire destroyed fifty thousand stands of small arms in the bey of Tunis's palace. Tunis demanded ten thousand muskets from America to help make up the loss. Eaton was incensed, telling an unspecified minister sent to make the demand that that Tunis "will never recieve a Single musket from the United States," as such donations were not stipulated by treaty. The minister argued that gifts above those owed as a condition of peace were "an established custom" that "we recieve from all friendly nations once every two or three years." When Eaton rejected this argument and insisted that "the discharge of our treaty obligations will put an end to our contributions here," the minister reportedly replied, "Your peace depends on your compliance with this demand of my Master." Although the consuls would often comply with demands they felt illegitimate, when a cost-benefit analysis showed that peace was more economically beneficial than conflict, this was not one of those times. Eaton simply retorted, "If so said I, on me be the responsibility of breaking the peace. I wish you a good morning."[75]

Demands for ships also caused friction. Desperate to save the peace treaty with Algiers when American attempts to gather specie for payment was significantly delayed, Barlow and Donaldson had sweetened the deal by offering an American ship of thirty-six guns in exchange for six months' leeway for payment. This was not an exaction, of course, but it set a precedent. When he arrived at Tripoli, Cathcart was told that during treaty negotiations O'Brien too had promised Tripoli a ship, a claim that O'Brien challenged as completely fabricated. Nonetheless, Cathcart was forced to pay $8,000 in lieu of the allegedly promised ship.[76] Tunis then demanded an American ship as well. Eventually a minister demanded that Eaton write a letter to the president requesting a thirty-six-gun frigate because "we must have this expression of *friendship*, as you have given the Dey of Algiers. My master is afflicted that your Prince does not show him as much friendship as he does the Dey!" Eaton refused to write, much as he had in the muskets incident, stating that "their arrogance increases in proportion to the moderation of the nations they dare insult, and their exactions to our manifestations of a desire to cultivate their friendship."[77]

The issue that eventually led to a rupture with Tripoli was a similar demand not stipulated by treaty. Bey Yusuf was apparently dissatisfied that Tripoli did not receive an annual regalia from the United States as Algiers and Tunis did. He began demanding a regalia or an unspecified "present" to make up for its lack as early as May 1800. In October he renewed this demand while the American brig *Catherine* was in port, having been brought in (purportedly without authorization) by Rais Amr Shelli. Although Cathcart issued a formal protest of these demands, he was also willing to offer additional payments to keep the peace. In February 1801 Bey Yusuf abrogated the existing treaty with the United States and demanded a $225,000 indemnity and an annual regalia of $20,000 for a new peace. Cathcart responded with an offer of $20,000 for an eighteen-month truce to allow for negotiations. When the bey rejected Cathcart's offer, and immediately before Tripoli formally declared war on the United States, Cathcart extended his offer to $30,000 and reduced the proposed length of the truce to ten months. While Cathcart found Tripoli's demands completely unjust, he also felt a responsibility to do all he could to avoid or delay a rupture that would be even more costly.[78]

European-American Diplomatic Engagement in North Africa

In addition to directly protecting American interests, the consuls in North Africa also integrated America into the European diplomatic network. The European communities in the North African capitols were tight-knit, often exchanging social calls, particularly dinners. Although the consuls in North Africa mention these gatherings only in passing, their counterpart in Canton, a similar expatriate community of diplomats and merchants, explained this exchange as part of the community's diplomatic norm. Consul Samuel Shaw reported "national civilities" such as the exchange of "invitation[s] to table," and weekly concerts "performed by Gentlemen of the several Nations," hosted by the British and the Danes.[79] While the consuls in North Africa did not mention concerts, dinner gatherings were established custom.[80] In fact, Eaton argued that the expectation of hosting dinners implied either that consuls should be paid more or that the cost of such semiofficial gatherings should be reimbursable expenses, citing as an example the cost of ninety dollars to host a dinner in honor of a visiting British admiral.[81]

As well as social and cultural ties, the types of diplomatic challenges the various nations experienced were often similar. For example, in January 1800 Algiers imprisoned and chained the Spanish consul after a dispute between Algiers and Spain over the Spanish seizure of an Algerian brig in which the consul was not directly involved. The diplomatic community was concerned about the precedent this set, so the Swedish, Danish, Dutch, and American consuls all went together to the minister of the marine and "fully remonstrated against the regency for setting the Spanish Consul in

Chains." They further offered to stand surety for the Spanish consul, and each of them but the Dutch consul donated $400 to the senior imam in exchange for his reminding the dey of the Quranic injunction "not to persicute Christians at peace with them."[82] This sort of collective action among the consuls tied America into the diplomatic commonwealth.

Another norm binding the Western diplomatic commonwealth in the regencies was exchanging favors in terms of handling each other's interests when a consul was away, whether traveling for personal or official reasons or having been expelled at the beginning of hostilities. As we have seen before, it was customary for consuls to host prisoners from other countries and sometimes even to ransom them when in extremis, such as the Skjoldebrands' ransoming (later reimbursed) of George Smith in 1793. The American consuls were a regular part of this exchange of favors. Eaton, for example, hosted Sardinian captives and even spent 17,000 Tunisian piasters (approximately $1,900) to redeem Maria Anna Porcile, daughter of the Sardinian Chevalier Don Antonio Porcile, from Tunisian captivity. Maria Anna came from the island of San Pietro, almost the entire population of which Tunisian corsairs under Rais Mohammed Roumaili had captured in 1799. Maria Anna's grandfather, the Count Porcile, was assigned as the negotiator for their redemption. He reached an agreement for ransoms in June of 1800, though they apparently remained unpaid until at least 1802, when a new negotiator was named. Eaton had previously paid Maria Anna's ransom because she was in distress, with the implication that she faced sexual exploitation. Eaton had assumed that he would be reimbursed either when the general redemption was paid or directly by Don Porcile. He was less fortunate than the Skjoldebrands, however, as Sardinia considered this arrangement a private matter, and the chevalier claimed destitution and wrote to Thomas Jefferson asking the United States to forgive the cost. Eaton later made a contentious claim on the federal government for the amount. Regardless of the accounting, these sorts of redemptions and assistance to captives were part of normal European diplomacy in North Africa, and American participation showed appropriate Western solidarity.[83]

One incident that is usually interpreted as an emasculating sign of American weakness (in both modern analysis and by Americans at the time) also offered America some diplomatic advantages. In late 1800 Algiers was visited for the first time by a United States naval vessel, the USS *George Washington*. America now had a navy, in part in response to the Algerian captures of the previous decade. While the March 1794 law "An Act to provide a Naval Armament" had included a cancellation clause in case of peace with Algiers, by the time that treaty was signed, three of the six frigates called for by the act were nearing completion, which Congress permitted. In 1797 the United States Navy launched its three-frigate fleet. This fleet was to expand significantly with the outbreak of the Quasi-War with France. One of the first additions was the "frigate" *George Washington*, which had originally been built as an East India freighter and had been purchased and converted to a warship in 1798. While the Quasi-War was still ongoing, by 1800 America was far behind on Algiers's annual regalia, owing in part to the conflict and in part to the travails of the freighter *Hero*, which usually delivered stores to North Africa. Therefore, the *George Washington* was chosen to make the overdue delivery. With its merchant origins, it had a large cargo capacity, and it also carried sufficient armament to protect itself from French privateers or even smaller navy vessels. The *George Washington* arrived in Algiers on 17 September 1800, but instead of returning to the United States as planned, it was compelled to take an Algerian ambassador and tribute to Istanbul.[84]

The impressment of the *George Washington* is often, and erroneously, seen as a sign of singular American powerlessness; other Western nations faced similar demands. In fact, it was apparently common for Britain to undertake such missions, and Denmark had ships sent to Rhodes on Algiers's behalf at the same time as the *George Washington* incident and also to Istanbul upon the *George Washington*'s return.[85] Nonetheless, Americans did not feel honored to be forced on such a voyage, nor did they consider it a "great mark of the dey's favour," as they were told they should.[86] O'Brien and the *George Washington*'s captain, William Bainbridge, resisted the dey's demand until it came to the point of compliance or immediate war, which would include attack on the anchored *George Washington* and enslavement of the crew. Considering that Algiers already had a casus belli in the American arrears in treaty stipulations and the likely consequences of refusal, they acquiesced.[87] The ship's crew and the American consuls considered the incident an extreme humiliation, especially the mounting of an Algerian flag on the mainmast. Captain Bainbridge noted in his log, "We must be the porters of savage Tygers & more Savage Algerines Ambassadors . . . the pendant of the United States was struck and the Algerine Flag hoisted at the Main top Gallant royal mast head. 7 guns were fired in compliment. some tears fell at this Instance of national Humility."[88]

The *George Washington* incident led to calls for war among the American consuls. O'Brien urged the immediate deployment of six frigates under the command of "such an active man as Commodore Truxton."[89] Eaton was particularly infuriated. In response to O'Brien's letter informing him of the episode, he copied it to the secretary of state and added an impassioned afterword referring to the incident as "our immortal shame" and claiming that "nothing but blood can blot the impression out." He closed with "will nothing rouse my country!"[90] The new Jefferson administration was none too pleased about the incident either. Incoming Secretary of State James Madison's instructions to the consuls explained that the impressment had "deeply affected the sensibility not only of the President, but of the people of the United States" and that, though it may have been temporarily favorable to American interests, the incident was not closed. He instructed them specifically that "the President wishes that nothing may be said or done by you, that may unnecessarily preclude the competent authority from animadverting on that transaction in any way that a vindication of the national honor may be thought to prescribe."[91]

For all these negative reactions, however, the *George Washington* incident offered America diplomatic advantages beyond placating Algiers. The first of these was getting American representation at the Sublime Porte for the first time. In 1799, with American trade in the Mediterranean expanding rapidly, the Adams administration had begun planning for a mission to Istanbul. That April, Secretary of State Pickering wrote to William Smith, the new minister to Portugal (Humphreys having been transferred to Spain), to appoint him to go to Istanbul and attempt to negotiate a commercial treaty. Smith concurred that this would be a good idea, thinking that positive Ottoman relations might help with Barbary issues and that the time was right for the United States to move into the Eastern Mediterranean trade. Unfortunately, the mission was suspended owing to chaos engendered by the French invasion of Italy. In August of 1799 President Adams was still hoping to send Smith to Istanbul (or Constantinople, as American records of the era consistently refer to it), but nothing came of the plans.[92]

The *George Washington* was the first opportunity for the United States to make formal contact with the Ottoman Porte. Captain Bainbridge received letters of recommendation from the consuls in Algiers and visited the English and Danish ambassadors upon arriving in Istanbul. He reported that the British ambassador "received me politely, but made no offers of public services," while the Danish ambassador "offered his services to the U.S. flag in the most friendly terms."[93] The ship spent six weeks in Istanbul, where Bainbridge made contact with Kapudan Pasha (commander of the navy) Küçük Hüseyin, who traditionally dealt with European maritime powers. Bainbridge reported that the flag of the United States "was treated with the greatest respect, in Constantinople & was taken under the immediate protection of the Captain Bashaw, who is a person of the greatest influence in the Turkish Empire."[94]

The Ottoman Sultan Selim III was furious that Algiers and Tripoli had continued friendly relations with the French after Napoleon's invasion of the Ottoman province of Egypt in July 1798 and the Ottoman Empire's subsequently joining the Second Coalition in war on France. The sultan detained the Algerian ambassador and his gifts and refused those of Tripoli outright. The Kapudan Pasha sent representatives to Tripoli and Algiers aboard the *George Washington* to insist that the regencies declare war on France. O'Brien believed that Ottoman outrage over the regencies' support for France would lead the empire to reestablish control over them, but the only concrete effect was that Algiers expelled its French expatriate community. Even this offered America an opportunity to improve its goodwill in Europe. When Bainbridge arrived in Algiers, O'Brien informed him of end of the Quasi-War with France via the Convention of 1800, news of which had reached O'Brien during the *George Washington*'s voyage. When the thirty-five to sixty (sources vary) French citizens in Algiers were expelled the following week, Bainbridge delivered them to Alicante. This act raised American status with both Algiers and France. Robert Montgomery, who had initiated negotiations with Morocco as a private citizen back in 1783, was still in Alicante. He was now an official representative of the United States, having been appointed as consul in 1793.[95] Montgomery reported that multiple French citizens and officials had visited him "to thank me in a formal manner for the civility & humanity received from Capt Bainbridge and the American officers at large."[96] Thus, Captain Bainbridge and his crew were the first serving naval officers among the ranks of American sailors engaging the Barbary Powers and with Europe regarding North African affairs. Many others would follow.[97]

This informal diplomacy with the Ottoman Empire and France raised America's profile in Europe, but exchanges of favors with other "second powers" paid more tangible dividends. The strongest examples of this were the long-standing relationship with Sweden in Algiers and the developing relationship with Denmark, which became more concrete via dealings with Tunis and Tripoli. In the summer of 1800, Tunis declared war on Denmark and expelled their consul. Eaton acted as temporary agent for Denmark during this conflict. Shortly, six Danish vessels were captured, and their masters came to Eaton with the plan that he purchase the ships, which they would then redeem via Danish credit from Livorno. After Eaton put a bid in for the ships, the captains came to him looking to cancel the plan, as they were uncertain of their ability to get credit, but it was too late to withdraw his bid. Eaton was stuck with the ships, which he planned to resell to recoup his expenses. Eaton also assisted the commodore of the Danish Mediterranean fleet with intelligence and assistance in negotiations. The commodore, in turn, offered to guarantee the Danish captains' credit, and Eaton sold them back their ships at cost. Upon the return of peace, Denmark also asked Eaton to provide "advice and directions" to their new consul.[98]

In gratitude, the King of Denmark, via the "Board for the affairs relating to the states on the coast of Barbary," sent Eaton a gold box ornamented with the royal initials. Eaton worried that the gift might be an issue under the emoluments clause of the United States Constitution, which, to minimize the risk of divided loyalty, forbids United States officeholders from accepting "any present, Emolument, Office, or Title, of any kind whatever, from any King, Prince, or foreign State" without congressional approval. Eaton wrote to the new secretary of state, James Madison, for guidance, expressing concern that refusing the gift would insult the Danes. Madison informed him that he would have to petition Congress directly if he wanted permission to keep it. Eaton responded that he would bring the matter up when he returned to America, and though the box is mentioned in his claim to Congress in 1806, there is no record of its ultimate fate.[99] In any case, though the box may have had significant cash value, the letter accompanying the gift made the true dividends very clear, citing the "friendship and intimacy which subsist, and, we trust, will continue still increasing between both governments."[100]

The Danish letter also mentioned that, in the spirit of reciprocity, Danish consuls would be ordered to "avail themselves of every opportunity that may occur for being of any service to the interests of the government of the United States and the individuals of the American nation."[101] Not only was the recognition as a partner nation gratifying, but the opportunity for reciprocity came quickly. Less than a year after the outbreak of the Tunis-Denmark conflict, Bey Yusuf of Tripoli ordered the flagstaff in front of the American consulate chopped down, expelled James Cathcart, and declared war. As he prepared to depart, Cathcart left instructions, funds, and the keys to the consul house with Denmark's Consul Nicholas Nissen, who stepped in as America's representative in the regency. Nissen was a natural choice and would soon serve as interlocuter for United States Navy commanders prosecuting the war and attempting to provide for peace, as well as providing relief for American prisoners. Nissen had previously served in a similar capacity for Sweden, and the three nations were very close in Barbary.[102]

Just how close had become obvious in the summer of 1800 when Eaton was acting as Denmark's agent in Tunis. America had become not only treaty-worthy but alliance-worthy. The United States, Denmark, and Sweden had very similar profiles in the Mediterranean. All three had extensive merchant marines trading and engaging in the carrying trade, were neutral powers, and had small navies with no bases in the Mediterranean. In addition to their shared experiences in the Mediterranean, the three countries had also shared the experience which had led to the Quasi-War, with the merchant shipping of all three falling prey to French predation. France had passed a law authorizing its armed vessels to seize (and its admiralty courts to condemn) any vessel carrying British goods or without a certified *rôle d'équipage* (muster roll). Since this was not a standard part of ship's papers outside of France and, with high crew turnover, very difficult to keep accurate and get repeatedly certified, the effect of this law was to annul the principle of "free ships, free goods" and to open almost all neutral shipping to French predation. In June 1798 *Claypool's American Advertiser* printed, "Danes and Swedes share the same fate as Americans." This shared victimization not only brought the countries closer but also reversed the lack of a navy that had mooted Thomas Jefferson's 1786–90 visions of an anti-Barbary alliance. The Quasi-War was winding down by 1800, but it had led to a significant naval build-up, with the inventory rising from its three-frigate beginnings in 1797 to a peak of forty-nine vessels. This was not a major navy by the standards of the era, but it was a credible one.[103]

While a war with any of the Barbary powers would be a burden for any one of the Danish, Swedish, or American navies so far from home, Sweden proposed a coalition of the three. Swedish diplomat Baron Lars von Engerstrom had apparently floated the idea as early as 1794, when America's navy was still nonexistent and Denmark's and Sweden's were, as Secretary of State Pickering put it, "mere *parade*."[104] After the expansions driven by the Quasi-War, Engstrom, now the Swedish minister to Berlin, made a more formal proposal in early 1800, which he communicated via the local American minister, John Quincy Adams.[105] John Marshall, best known for his next position as a Supreme Court justice, had taken the reins as secretary of state in June, after Pickering's dismissal for opposing President Adams's plans for peace with France. One of Marshall's first tasks was to write President Adams's son John Quincy in Berlin to ask him to inform von Engerstrom that the United States would have to decline the proposed anti-Barbary coalition for the time being. He was concerned that the ongoing Quasi-War made it hazardous to station American frigates in the Mediterranean. Moreover, he was convinced that in order to be treaty-worthy the United States had to live up to all its obligations, however "unreasonably burthensome." As much as President Adams liked the idea of an alliance, the United States had treaties of peace with the North African powers. Marshall also noted, however, that given their history, it was likely that one or more of the Barbary powers would break its treaty with the United States, in which case America would "be at perfect liberty, and will be well disposed, to make any reasonable arrangements with Sweden and Denmark for the purposes mentioned in the note of the Swedish Minister."[106] That perfect liberty came on 14 May 1801, when the American "Flagstaff was chopp'd down . . . and War was declared in form [formally] by the Bashaw of Tripoli against the United States of America."[107]

By the outbreak of the Tripolitan War (1801–5), the United States was able to operate in North Africa as both Americans and Europeans expected a sovereign nation would. The wave of funding and authority that Congress released in response to the 1793 captures enabled not only peace with the Barbary regencies but also the germination of the United States Navy. By 1796 American politicians and diplomats were able to demonstrate sovereignty and America's commitment to their view of the law-bound Vattelian regime via their interactions with the regencies. Additionally, American diplomats were now able to act in partnership with Europeans, rather than only as petitioners upon them. In this era, the strongest ties were formed with similar powers. The United States, Denmark, and Sweden had very similar profiles in the Mediterranean as neutral powers heavily involved in merchant shipping but with limited and distant navies. Especially after the three exchanged favors on Barbary issues, Sweden and Denmark saw America as not simply treaty-worthy but alliance-worthy. It was not long before a rupture with Tripoli would free the United States to act on the proposal.

4

A Coalition of the Willing

THE MULTINATIONAL TRIPOLITAN WAR, 1801–1805

WHEN CAPTAIN DANIEL MCNEILL and his thirty-two-gun frigate the USS *Boston* arrived in Tripoli harbor on 15 May 1802, they found friends—Swedish Rear Admiral Rudolf Cederström with one of the four frigates of his Mediterranean squadron. The *Boston* had previously fallen in with Cederström in January in Malaga, Spain, and had arranged coordination between him and America's squadron commander, Commodore Richard Dale, in Toulon, France, later that same month. The two commanders had agreed to several cooperative measures, including a combined blockade of Tripoli, and with the *Boston*'s arrival, that plan came to fruition. McNeill and Cederström had been in place for only one day when they had the opportunity to engage Tripolitan ships, the first American coalition combat operation since the Revolutionary War.[1]

On 16 May the *Boston* spotted a small Tripolitan vessel and gave chase. The enemy ship fled for shallow waters where the American frigate would be unable to continue, but misjudged and beached itself. Seeing the engagement, Tripolitan officials sortied six gunboats to come to the beached ship's assistance. The gunboats headed toward the *Boston* until they saw the Swedish frigate bearing down on them from the windward, at which point they retreated toward the port. As Cederström maneuvered to cut the gunboats off, the Swedes came in range of the Tripolitan forts, and they exchanged fire. The land-based guns managed to shoot away some rigging on the Swedish frigate but caused no casualties or major damage. The effects of the Swedish bombardment of the forts were minimal as well. The crew of the *Boston* could not join in that attack, because their orders only allowed engagement of armed ships. Instead, the *Boston* maneuvered to engage the gunboats until a new and much larger sail suddenly appeared to windward.

The Swedish frigate stood off from the harbor to get out from under the fort guns, and the *Boston* gave chase to the new sail. As they approached, the *Boston* discovered that this was not a fresh threat but actually another Swedish frigate coming to join the blockade. The Swedish and American vessels having moved off, the Tripolitan gunboats took the opportunity to make for their beached comrade. The combined force drove back toward the gunboats and fired four broadsides at them. As the keelless gunboats could operate in very shallow water, they were able to escape back to the port, though one lost a mast. The *Boston* was not hit in the engagement. Though the gunboats fired several rounds of heavy shot, they all went over, leaving the minor breakage in the rigging on Cederström's flagship as the only damage the allies suffered. As the *Boston*'s purser was writing his account of the engagement the following day, the Swedes began once again cannonading the forts, a show of force in which the United States Navy could not take part. Nonetheless, this minor engagement, sometimes grandiosely referenced as "The Battle of Tripoli Harbor," marked a new chapter for America as a partner nation.[2]

This chapter examines the Tripolitan War of 1801–5. It argues that, far from being an example of American exceptionalism, as popular histories and even some scholars would have us believe, this war was, in fact, multinational. Not only did the United States engage in combined naval operations with Sweden in the early portions of the conflict, but America also cooperated with various powers in the Mediterranean throughout. The United States Navy received basing and logistic support from Britain and the "Two Sicilies" (Sicily and Naples under the same ruler), the latter of which provided direct military support to the bombardment of Tripoli in 1804 as well. The United States also cooperated militarily with the deposed former bey of Tripoli and governor of Derne province, Hamet Karamanli. Further, Denmark represented American interests in Tripoli, and British and Ottoman officials in Egypt facilitated the Derne expedition of 1805.[3]

This chapter also examines the role of the United States Navy in the legal and diplomatic regimes of the early republic, as demonstrated in the Tripolitan War and as compared to the Quasi-War with France. It argues that the Adams and Jefferson administrations took remarkably similar positions on constitutional questions related to hostilities that fell short of war. Both administrations interpreted Congress's war powers under Article I, Section 8, of the Constitution as applying not only to declaring wars but also to regulating all hostilities. The Jefferson administration went slightly further in this interpretation than the Adams administration had, maintaining that congressional authorization was required before the executive branch could conduct military action even after an enemy had declared war upon the United States. Adams, of course, was not faced with the question, as neither side in the Quasi-War formally declared war. Both administrations also showed similar approaches to the conduct of distant operations, providing naval commanders with broad guidance on rules of engagement and aims but leaving questions of dealing with foreign diplomats and navies largely to the commanders' discretion. Given communication lags that measured in months, this is perhaps unsurprising, but the diplomatic role played by naval officers was striking, in terms of both ad hoc coordination with friendly forces and diplomacy. Not only did commanders negotiate directly with foreign governments, but the second United States representatives to Tunis and Tripoli were both naval officers released by their commanders to fill the role, adding to the tradition of American sailors as Barbary diplomats.

Shortly after taking office, Thomas Jefferson determined to send a naval squadron to the Mediterranean as a show of force and to protect American commerce in case of a rupture. The rules of engagement for this squadron were hotly debated within the administration. While everyone agreed that the force would not initiate hostilities, how to respond if one or more of the regencies did so was less clear. After debate, the squadron was sent to the Mediterranean with contingent orders that authorized defensive force and even sinking North African vessels under certain conditions. They could not, however, make captures, even of ships that had attacked them, as the Constitution specifically reserved the role of setting capture rules to Congress.

Commodore Dale's contingent orders also reflected the young republic's growing relationship with Sweden on North African affairs. While his instructions did not mention military cooperation, they specified that if the local American consul were to be expelled and American prisoners taken, Dale should work through the local Swedish consul "to afford them usual relief and comfort."[4] Though when that came to pass, it was actually the Danish consul through whom Dale worked, Dale also took the initiative to arrange an ad hoc military alliance with the Swedish navy.

Aside from their operations against Tripoli, the Swedish-American force also faced friction with Tunis and Morocco. Ironically, given that Sweden and the United States were both vocal supporters of neutral shipping rights, the tensions centered on the subject of the shipping rights of North African neutrals, which interpreted those rights much more broadly than did even the free-trade stalwarts fighting Tripoli. The controversy led to disputes about international law and, in the case of Morocco, came close to spilling into open hostilities. The Moroccan crisis was exacerbated by the fact that the coalition still did not understand that Morocco's approach to corsairing was motivated primarily by gaining diplomatic leverage, rather than widespread prize taking. Commanders envisioned a Moroccan rupture as entirely closing the Mediterranean to their nations' trade and tied up significant force to watch and overawe Morocco, reducing the force available to deal with Tripoli. The disagreements with Tunis and Morocco highlight several important points about international law. The disputes illustrate American leaders' views of the law of nations and how central they found upholding it to "being respected as a nation." The disputes also highlight how much less unified and codified "the" law of nations was than Americans, with their veneration of Vattel, often considered it. North Africans had agency in questions of international law, and many matters were open to multiple interpretations.

American cooperation in the Tripolitan War was not limited to Sweden. As Benjamin Armstrong has pointed out, the United States and British navies cooperated on logistics issues in the Mediterranean during this era, though they also competed for labor and accused each other of enlisting the other force's deserters. Indeed, this issue led American commanders to seek alternate bases to replace the British ports of Gibraltar and Malta. English-speaking sailors unhappy in one navy found harbor in another too easily in these ports. Officers clashed about this and other issues, contributing to a duel between a junior American officer and a British commissary clerk in Malta. The United States found cooperation with Sicily less fraught, and the squadron moved its main operating base to Syracuse in 1803. Not only did Sicily offer basing, but its sister kingdom of Naples supplied gun and mortar boats for Commodore Preble's bombardment of Tripoli in 1804.[5]

While scholars often report this loan of vessels, less noted is that the force also included almost a hundred Neapolitan sailors, gunners, and bombardiers. Additionally, a Sicilian pilot enabled perhaps the most famous exploit of the war. In October 1803 the frigate USS *Philadelphia* had run aground in Tripoli harbor, leading to the capture of her entire crew. The *Philadelphia* herself represented a major threat in Tripolitan hands, and Commodore Preble determined to destroy her before attacking the city. Although Lieutenant Stephen Decatur commanded the operation to burn the *Philadelphia* in Tripoli harbor, and the raid is memorialized as an American triumph, it would not have been possible if not for Sicilian assistance. It was Salvador Catalano, originally Preble's local pilot in Syracuse, who brought the ketch *Intrepid* into Tripoli and orchestrated the ruse that got the ship alongside the *Philadelphia*. After the war, Catalano accompanied the fleet back to America and became naturalized, making him perhaps the first example of a tradition of foreign auxiliaries to United States forces becoming American citizens.[6]

The best-known joint venture of the Tripolitan war, of course, is the 1805 overland expedition led by William Eaton and the former bey of Tripoli Hamet Karamanli, which took the city of Derne and gave the United States Marine Corps hymn the line "to the shores of Tripoli." While Hamet's contribution to this operation is widely acknowledged, the enterprise also depended on logistical and diplomatic assistance from British agents in Egypt and permission and facilitation from the Ottoman governor. The "American" expedition was truly multinational, with only about a dozen Americans, a few dozen each of Hamet's troops and mercenaries, and approximately 250 Arab auxiliaries. Though the expedition's success has often been overstated, not least by Eaton himself, it did put pressure on Bey Yusuf Karamanli to conclude a peace with the United States that saved face for both sides. American officials bragged of peace "without tribute," while Yusuf was able to claim that he had exacted payment, the ransom Tripoli received for American prisoners. Further, it brought to conclusion a multinational conflict during which the United States had, as Samuel Cooper had put it so long ago, successfully interacted on "the great theater of nations with advantage and glory," if not, perhaps, so much glory as some Americans in the Mediterranean hoped for.[7]

Projecting Power

With the end of the Quasi-War in late 1800, the United States Navy downsized considerably but did not entirely disband. Congress passed the "An act providing for a Naval Peace Establishment," authorizing the president to demobilize the fleet except for thirteen frigates. The act specified that six frigates be kept in constant service, even in times of peace, while the others could be laid up in storage. John Adams signed this act (among many others) on his last day in office, 3 March 1801, ensuring that Thomas Jefferson would be unable to demobilize the whole navy. Perhaps Adams had forgotten Jefferson's previous arguments of 1786 and 1790 that America needed a small navy, or perhaps he feared that the Republican-Federalist acrimony of the previous years had hardened Republican antimilitarism to the point that the Jefferson administration would not retain any military force not required by statute. In either case, Jefferson inherited a navy of at least the six active frigates he had previously envisioned, with seven more required to be kept at least seaworthy.[8]

Jefferson had not changed his mind. In fact, though many other Democratic-Republicans held antimilitarist views that included the United States Navy, Jefferson saw the navy as necessary to enable the United States to respond to international challenges and opportunities to cooperate with sister nations, and as much less dangerous domestically than a standing army. A navy could not be called up quickly in a crisis like a citizen militia, as building warships demanded considerable lead time and expense. Moreover, unlike an army that could occupy territory, a navy was much less likely to be used to oppress the rights of citizens. Although the popular image of Jefferson's view of America was the idealization of self-sufficient yeoman farmers, as James Sofka has demonstrated, Jefferson's consistent vision of America was also one of international trade—in agricultural products, if nothing else—with that trade protected by a navy. Jefferson presented this analysis in the abstract in a 1785 letter to John Jay.[9] In his July 1786 letter to John Adams arguing for a naval response to the Barbary States, Jefferson specified that a collateral benefit of such a policy would be that it would "arm the federal head with the safest of all the instruments of coercion."[10] Although the Jefferson administration would later seek to augment the navy with a militia-like gunboat force for port protection, it never sought to disband the navy's core force of frigates.

With a small navy in hand, President Jefferson wrote to his secretary of state, James Madison, advocating a show of force in the Mediterranean in words reminiscent of those he had written to Adams in 1786. As he wrote to Madison, "I know that nothing will stop the eternal increase of demand from these pirates but the presence of an armed force, and it will be more economical & more honorable to use the same means at once for suppressing their insolencies."[11] With the Quasi-War over, Jefferson determined to send a squadron of three frigates and a sloop of war to the Mediterranean. After all, as Madison wrote to the consuls, "the force employed would if at home be at nearly the same expense, with less advantage to our mariners," so there was little downside. Although the administration was aware that Tripoli had been threatening war, it would be months before the news arrived that it had actually been declared the week before Madison wrote those letters. Given the uncertain state of affairs, Madison informed the consuls that the squadron's primary goal was to overawe the Barbary regencies, but that should war have been declared, "this force will be immediately employed in the defence and protection of our commerce."[12]

The limits of this "defence and protection" were hotly debated within the Jefferson administration. After all, if the United States was to be seen as a treaty-worthy respecter of law, it was important that its actions be consistent with internal as well as international law. As the Constitution gave only Congress the right to declare war, could the president send a squadron with orders to participate in hostilities, even contingent ones? This was not a new debate, as the Adams administration had struggled with similar questions during the Quasi-War. Perhaps surprisingly, given the Federalists more expansive view of executive power than that of Democratic-Republicans, the two administrations came to very similar conclusions about this constitutional issue, and one that is very different from more recent interpretations of presidential authority to use force short of declared war. Both administrations interpreted Congress's constitutional power "To declare War, grant Letters of Marque and Reprisal, and make Rules concerning Captures on Land and Water" as broadly empowering Congress with control over the regulation of hostilities, whether in declared war or not.[13]

The Adams administration's response to French captures of American merchant shipping in 1797 demonstrated the centrality of Congress's role in hostilities short of war in the early republic. Immediately after Secretary of State Pickering's report to Congress that French naval vessels and privateers had captured over three hundred American merchant ships in the previous year, the Adams administration sought congressional authority to counter French hostility. Adams requested a variety of measures, from completing the partially built frigates that had been left unfinished after the Algerian peace treaty, to authorizing American ships to arm in self-defense. Congress did not authorize all of these, however. Particularly, they denied the authority to arm civilian ships. This decision clearly shows that congressional authority in this instance was not predicated on its "power of the purse," as the measure required no government funds. Instead, Congress's authority came from the war powers enumerated above. Adams eventually authorized arming merchant vessels almost a year later by executive authority, arguing that the prohibition had been an executive order by Washington and therefore that lifting the ban was within his authority and not specifically related to hostilities.[14] Even this limited application of executive authority was highly controversial, however, with constitutional framer and Federalist Paper author James Madison calling it "a Usurpation by the Ex[ecutive] of a legislative power."[15] Both the executive and legislative branches agreed that other authorizations, such as capturing French vessels, depended entirely on congressional authorization. Congress granted authority to make captures, though limited to armed ships, after the March 1798 revelation of French treatment of American representatives in the XYZ Affair. Congress also formally authorized arming merchant ships in order to resolve the constitutional ambiguity of Adams's previous declaration.

In 1801, with Madison now serving as secretary of state, the limits of executive power over the military were unsurprisingly a key component in the planning for the deployment of the Mediterranean squadron. As the Constitution specified the president's role as the commander-in-chief of the armed forces, his inherent authority to order a peaceful cruise was not in question. But what if one or more of the North African powers were already preying on American shipping? The new administration debated the issue on 15 May 1801. Though several members of the cabinet argued that executive authority extended to authorizing force if another nation had declared war, others felt that only defensive use of force could be authorized without congressional approval. Even among those who felt offensive operations would be legitimate, only Treasury Secretary Albert Gallatin believed that another country's declaration of war gave the executive full freedom to conduct hostilities. Gallatin argued that another nation declaring war automatically put the United States in a state of war, which the executive had full power to direct. Others disagreed, Attorney General Levi Lincoln vehemently. The rest of the cabinet took a middle view that maintained that an enemy's declaration of war would at least imply the administration's authority to take offensive action against the hostile nation's armed ships. Even in that case, however, they disagreed on the specific rules of pursuit that would be appropriate.[16]

The administration finally decided on sending the squadron with complex and contingent instructions. Orders related to hostile engagement only authorized offensive action against Barbary vessels if all three of the regencies should have declared war, or against the vessels of Algiers if they alone had. In either of those cases, the squadron was authorized to "sink, burn, or otherwise destroy their ships & Vessels wherever you shall find them." While the reasoning behind this authority applying only if Algiers was part of the hostilities is not recorded, it may have been based on congressional guidance during the previous conflict with Algiers that the Jefferson administration considered still valid. In the case of hostilities with Tunis, Tripoli, or both, the squadron was authorized to blockade their harbors and to intercept and release any vessels that the cruisers had taken as prizes, as well as to offer convoy protection to American vessels. The squadron was neither authorized to take prizes itself, nor to keep prisoners, who should be repatriated "on any part of the Barbary shore most convenient."[17]

Even this carefully parsed interpretation of executive authority drew critiques from Federalist commentators. Alexander Hamilton, writing as "Lucius Crassus" in the Federalist New York *Evening Post,* argued the point also made by Gallatin that another nation's declaration put the United States in a state of war. Hamilton also felt that failing to authorize captures of hostile forces without congressional approval represented a ludicrous self-limitation of executive power. He maintained that this was analogous to an enemy army invading the United States before Congress declared war and authorizing American troops to kill invaders who came within range, "but not to disable them from doing harm, by the milder process of making them prisoners."[18] This stance was a marked turn from Hamilton's 1798 opinion about the Quasi-War that presidential power was limited to "authority to *repel* force by *force,* (but not to capture)" unless Congress authorized reprisals.[19] The difference, for Hamilton, was apparently the declaration of war that Tripoli had made but that France had not. Thus, under international law, the United States was already at war with Tripoli, with or without a congressional declaration, and the president's full war powers applied. Other Federalists disagreed and argued that Jefferson's authorization of the use of force, even with its contingent and limited rules of engagement, represented a hypocritical example of executive overreach.[20]

For all the controversy about hypothetical use of force, the squadron's primary purpose was to deter a rupture, not to respond to one, and its instructions were predicated primarily on peace. This focus on peace affected the choice of squadron leadership. The senior officer in the United States Navy was Thomas Truxton, hero of the Quasi-War, and he was Jefferson's first choice to lead the squadron. During America's navy-less interlude between the Revolutionary War and 1797, Truxton had worked as a civilian merchant captain.[21] By 1801, however, he was less interested in returning to peaceful sailing, even in command of a naval squadron. After he was offered command, he wrote that he was uninterested in commanding a cruise that would not include decisive engagement. In response, Samuel Smith, acting secretary of the navy, gave him the blunt choice to accept that the mission was primarily preventive or to go off duty and onto half-pay status.[22] Truxton responded that "peace can afford no field for me on the ocean" and thus upon completing the fitting-out process for the flagship USS *President*, he handed command of the ship and the squadron to Captain Richard Dale, who, as squadron commander, took on the courtesy rank of commodore.[23] After fitting out and coordination, the squadron sailed for the Mediterranean on 1 June 1801.[24]

Commodore Dale's instructions primarily dealt with showing the flag at North African ports and the contingent rules of engagement if a rupture should have occurred, but they also touched on international cooperation. He was ordered to put in at Gibraltar upon arrival and request permission from the governor to establish a logistics depot there. Dale was also given a list of ports at which the administration expected that the squadron would be welcome, a list that included the future bases of the American Mediterranean squadron, Malta and Syracuse. Further, if any American prisoners had been taken, and assuming that in that case the American consul would have been expelled, Dale was directed to work through the local Swedish consul "to afford them usual relief and comfort." This final instruction serves as a reminder of the sustained relationship between America and the Scandinavian nations in Barbary. Dale's written instructions did not address the notion of direct military cooperation, however. This issue was either discussed only in verbal orders or left entirely to Dale's discretion.[25]

The United States' First Westphalian Coalition

Although the Continental Army had served alongside French allies from 1778 to 1783, and the United States Army often cooperated with cobelligerent Indians in their operations against other Native American groups, the fully independent United States' first experience in coalition warfare with a sister nation partner was its 1801–2 cooperation with Sweden against Tripoli. Upon hearing of Tripoli's rupture with the United States, the government of Sweden renewed its proposal from the previous year for joint action in North Africa. The news had come much more quickly to northern Europe than to America. On 25 June 1801, only six weeks after Tripoli chopped down the flagstaff at the American consulate, John Quincy Adams wrote to Secretary of State Madison from Berlin to pass on Sweden's revived request for an anti-Barbary coalition. A Swedish envoy had agreed to a peace with Tripoli at a cost of $250,000 and a $20,000 annuity, but the government of Sweden decided not to ratify the treaty. Ex-consul James Cathcart, expelled from Tripoli and now headquartered in Livorno, heard in late June that Sweden intended to send a naval squadron to Tripoli instead of payment. In July the American squadron arrived in the Mediterranean, discovered the state of hostilities with Tripoli, and began blockade and convoy operations. By September, Commodore Dale had received requests from Swedish merchant vessels to join American convoys and had heard reports through consular sources of Swedish offers of military cooperation between the forces.[26] James Cathcart sent Commodore Dale a letter arguing against forming such a coalition, as he believed it would be contrary to the administration's intent, and he was dead set against "dividing the honor of setting an example to all Europe. Our aim is to establish a National character, which we must do, without the assistance of any of the powers of Europe."[27]

Commodore Dale was unmoved by this argument and felt no need to refer to Washington City for further instructions. After all, army commanders regularly made ad hoc arrangements with Native American groups to join in expeditions against mutual adversaries in America without specific government directives. Perhaps he made the call simply on the basis of military efficiency, or perhaps he had verbal instructions or a personal feeling for the value of America's working on an equal basis with an established, if minor, power of Europe. By 14 October the Swedish chargé d'affaires to Tunis was happy to announce that Lieutenant Colonel Tonquist of the frigate *Thetis*, the lone Swedish warship in the Mediterranean, had received orders to act in concert with the American squadron, and that the Swedish squadron "dayly expected in the Mediterranean" had the same orders.[28] The forces would be well balanced, as the inbound escadrille was precisely the same size as the American squadron, three frigates and a cutter. Though Commodore Dale had not yet met Tonquist to confirm and coordinate, or even to exchange signals, he lost no time ordering his subordinate commanders to cooperate with their Swedish counterparts. Captains Barron of the USS *Philadelphia* and Bainbridge of the USS *Essex* and Lieutenant Sterret of the schooner *Enterprize* (as well as Lieutenant Shaw of the *George Washington*, which was not technically part of the squadron but was in the Mediterranean on a transport mission) soon had instructions to offer convoy protection to any Swedish merchant vessels bound in the same direction as American ships of war, along with assurances that Sweden would reciprocate.[29] As the cooperation began, Commodore Dale wrote to David Humphreys, now serving as minister to Spain, about the value of working with Sweden and his desire to coordinate more closely. By the first week of November, the first joint American-Swedish convoy was to sail in the company of the *Philadelphia*. Dale was proud to be able to "Empress on the minds of those people, also, the European Nations, what the Government of the United States can do," calling it an extremely favorable "opportunity for the U.S. to Establish a lasting reputation."[30]

For the remainder of 1801, American and Swedish vessels operated separately, protecting mixed convoys. On 27 November an American warship finally fell in with the *Thetis* and was able to confirm the cooperation that so far had only been arranged indirectly. The *Essex* was cruising near Gibraltar, interdicting two Tripolitan corsairs that the American squadron found in port when they arrived in July. Unable to lawfully engage the enemy in a neutral port, Commodore Dale detached a frigate to block the corsairs or to engage if they came into international waters. Almost five months later, the *Essex* was still performing this mission when it met the *Thetis* having just completed a convoy out of the Mediterranean. Captain Bainbridge dispatched Lieutenant Decatur to the Swedish ship for coordination. The two captains agreed to head to Malaga and coordinate in port, which they did three days later. The alliance was no longer simply de facto, if it was not yet so formal as to deserve the appellation de jure.[31]

Swedish Vice Admiral Cederström's squadron arrived in early January 1802 and fell in with another new arrival, the USS *Boston* under Captain McNeill, at Malaga. McNeill had previously met with the *Essex* on Christmas Day, when Bainbridge passed him orders to report to Commodore Dale at Toulon. This enabled McNeill to inform Cederström where to find his opposite number.[32] The two commanders finally met in person at Toulon on 24 January to coordinate strategy and signals. Commodore Dale was unable to agree to a proposed joint attack on Tripoli itself, though he hoped such authorization was forthcoming. He also warned Cederström against attacking Tripoli on his own unless sure of success, as failure "would not only give them confidence, but experience."[33] Dale and Cederström were able to organize rendezvous points for convoys and for a joint blockade of Tripoli harbor. Dale explained that weather wouldn't allow for close blockade until at least April, but that armed ships appearing in Tripoli harbor before then might deter corsairs from going out. In fact, in anticipation of the coordination with Admiral Cederström, Commodore Dale had already ordered the *Boston* to Tripoli after it completed a convoy down the Mediterranean (eastward) and to "act in concert with any Swedish Ships of War in Blockading Tripoli and giving protection to the commerce of both Nations."[34]

By May the joint blockade of Tripoli harbor was in place, and on 16 May the Swedish and American ships fought as a combined force in the so-called Battle of Tripoli Harbor. It was to be the only documented instance of the combined squadron firing shots in anger. After this experience, the Tripolitans generally kept their gunboats in port, and though the combined squadron cooperated frequently on chasing down blockade runners, there are no records of any of those ships engaging in combat with the Swedish and American warships. The closest they came to joint combat again was on 22 July, when Tripoli sortied some gunboats and ran them over a reef in an attempt to lead the much larger USS *Constellation* to chase them over it and ground itself. The Swedish frigate *Thetis* joined the chase from several miles behind. Although the Tripolitans and Americans exchanged fire, once the *Constellation*'s soundings revealed the reef, the pilot wore ship to avoid it, and the engagement ended before the *Thetis* arrived.[35]

The Swedish forces occasionally bombarded the city and forts of Tripoli, but the American forces did not join in these actions, owing to their rules of engagement. Dale had written recommending a bombardment in November 1801 but had not yet received any response to that recommendation. Thomas Jefferson had likely not yet received the request for authorization to take the offensive when he delivered his first annual message to Congress on 8 December 1801. He had received dispatches describing the *Enterprize*'s solo encounter with a Tripolitan cruiser, however. In this encounter, the *Enterprize* had captured and disarmed the Tripolitan. Then, in accordance with Commodore Dale's instructions, Lieutenant Sterret released the battered cruiser to carry its crew back to Tripoli, rather than taking prisoners. Jefferson used this story to introduce a request for legislation authorizing offensive action.[36] In February 1802 Congress responded, passing "An act for the protection of the commerce and seamen of the United States, against the Tripolitan cruisers," which authorized American ships to "to subdue, seize, and make prize, of all vessels, goods, and effects, belonging to the Bey of Tripoli, or to his subjects."[37]

Word of this new authorization took some time to reach the Mediterranean. American and Swedish ships continued joint blockade and coordinated convoy operations for several months and found themselves complaining of merchant ships ignoring convoys and taking their chances. With Europe temporarily at peace thanks to Treaty of Amiens (25 March 1802, with the peace lasting until 18 May 1803), the Barbary corsair threat seemed secondary to the great opportunity of the European powers no longer restricting trade to enemy ports. Naval captains were learning the frustration that Joel Barlow had expressed back in 1796—that merchant captains "would sail into the mouth of hell, if the Devil was to turn Catholic so as to make a good market for codfish."[38] While the merchants may have taken solace in the blockade of Tripoli, the blockade was unable to keep all Tripolitan cruisers in port. In June the Swedish consul in Algiers reported that two Tripolitan galliots had escaped the blockade and arrived in Algiers.[39]

Captain Murray, in the newly arrived *Constellation*, reported on 5 July that there was little the blockading force could do to keep smaller boats from escaping. The large frigates could not approach the shore safely, and the small cruisers would row out close to shore, often at night. Since the larger number of frigates did not seem to improve the blockade, Murray recommended sending more schooners, and in the meantime reducing the blockade force to two frigates, freeing up the others for convoy duty. Admiral Cederström agreed. Within a few weeks, the cruisers that had leaked past the blockade found unconvoyed merchant vessels. Two Tripolitan galliots took the American brigantine *Franklin* and brought it in to Algiers (also misreported as Tunis) as a prize, then brought the nine passengers and crew members to Tripoli as prisoners, along with seven captured Swedes. Still, this represented a far less successful cruise than the one of the year before, in which Tunisian corsairs had captured six Danish vessels. The captured Swedes' ship had reportedly not been made a prize, as the USS *Enterprize* had recaptured it, though the crew had unfortunately already been taken off. The coalition was having some success, if only defensively. Additionally, Danish Consul Nissen in Tripoli was good to his word and was sponsoring the imprisoned crews.[40]

By autumn, the American replacement squadron under Commodore Morris was aware of the new guidance allowing for offensive action and had formal instructions to "cordially co-operate with the Swedes."[41] In September, Captain Murray reported coordinating with the Swedish Admiral for a bombardment of Tripoli, which would require gunboats and bomb ketches (mortar boats). Admiral Cederström felt that he could secure them by the spring of 1803, when the weather would favor such an attack.[42] But it was not to be. In October 1802 French diplomats arranged a peace between Tripoli and Sweden. America's first coalition came to an end just over a year after it began. William Eaton in Tunis was very upset, writing in his usual bombastic style that "thus ended the *coalition of the north!* Thus ends the alliance between Sweden and the U States!" In his eyes, by accepting French intervention *"the national honor and independence of Sweden are thrown into the scale to balance the obligation!"*[43] Joseph Barnes, the United States consul to the Island of Sicily, was more philosophical about the event. He suggested that America either also look for French intercession to end the war or make common cause with the Kingdom of Naples, which was "dreadfully oppress'd by those pirates."[44]

Baron Silverhjelm, the Swedish envoy in London, was directed by his government to explain to the United States Sweden's motivation in making peace. He rather sheepishly informed Rufus King, United States minister to Britain, that although Sweden esteemed the cooperation, royal enthusiasm for the war had waned owing to the lack of offensive authority on the American side, which led to a long costly conflict that King Gustavus IV wished to see end. Baron Silverhjelm asked Minister King to pass this explanation on to President Jefferson, which he did, forwarding the Swedish envoy's letter through Secretary of State Madison.[45]

Despite the anticlimactic end to Swedish-American joint military operation, this incident nonetheless illustrates the rising status of the United States in the European system. From a supplicant to European powers for assistance on Barbary affairs in the 1780s, the United States had reached the point where an established, if minor, European power felt the need to explain its sovereign decision to make peace in North Africa and to attempt to repair any damage it may have done to bilateral relations with the United States. Cathcart hoped for more, noting that Bey Hammuda of Tunis considered America "on par with Sweden or Denmark," while Cathcart thought the United States should be considered a major power like Britian or France, but this hope was unrealistic.[46] Being considered the equal of these minor powers, both by North Africans and Europeans, was a major improvement in American status.

North African Neutrality

Ironically, given their positions on the rights of neutral shipping, the biggest challenge that the Swedish/American coalition faced outside of its direct conflict with Tripoli related to other North African powers' claims of rights to send ships to Tripoli in spite of the coalition's blockade. This friction would continue after Sweden's separate peace, leading to tensions with Tunis and a near rupture with Morocco that diverted forces and attention from the Tripolitan War, and also illuminating several points of international law and the United States' view of it. Although American politicians tended to see Vattel as the authoritative source for international law, many nations disagreed. Further, even within Vattel, many points of law remained unsettled, with Vattel giving examples of contrasting usage. The issues of the rights of neutral shipping were particularly contested, leading to both inter-European contestation, such as the Leagues of Armed Neutrality (1780–83 and 1800–1801), and American-European disputes, such as the Quasi-War with France (1798–1800). In a memoir on maritime law written for the French government during the Quasi-War, Joel Barlow argued that North African views on neutral shipping were superior, from a natural law standpoint, to those of Europe. Not only did Barbary powers respect the principle of "free ships, free goods" as the European neutral powers advocated, but they also "adopted principles of public law more rational . . . than those of Europe," as "they admit no such thing as *contraband of war;* but allow a neutral vessel to carry any article, at any time to any place."[47] This principle went beyond the claims of American and European proponents of neutral shipping rights, who recognized the right of warring powers to prevent neutrals from shipping contraband to their enemies, though neutrals often argued that contraband applied only to directly military cargos, such as arms and munitions, and not more broadly to "dual-use" goods, as the warring powers sometimes argued. In 1802, after Sweden and the United States had declared the port of Tripoli to be in a state of blockade, the coalition would learn that the right of blockading powers to deny entry to neutral ships and to capture blockade runners was another principle that North African powers refused to accept.[48]

The first objection came from Tunis on 2 May 1802, when Bey Hammuda summoned William Eaton to complain of three Tunisian ships seized by American blockade ships, as well as one by a Swede. Hammuda claimed the right of free commerce and that blockaders could turn away his vessels but could not make prizes of them. He and Eaton held a disputation on the law of nations' precedents, with Hammuda claiming Venetian usage and Eaton responding that the United States did not consider that authoritative and followed English and French legal examples. When Hammuda retorted that the United States accepted the "principle of *free bottoms free goods,*" Eaton replied that "this principle was never construed to extend to a blockaded port" and refused to press for the prizes' release or for restitution.[49] This dispute did not lead to hostilities but did lead to two visits from American naval squadrons and a Tunisian embassy to the United States. Additionally, it was a key factor in Eaton's expulsion from the regency the following year.

While the issue of the Tunisian prizes remained shelved for several months, a captured imperial polacca (also known as a polacre, a trading ship similar to a xebec) brought the issue to the forefront again in early 1803. The Tunisians recognized the American right to make a prize of the European blockade runner itself but not to seize the Tunisian-owned cargo on board. During the disputation, the Bey Hammuda renewed Tunis's claim that according to North African usage their vessels could ignore the blockade, and claimed the right of self-indemnification via seizing American merchants entering Genoa and Naples, with which Tunis was (in a desultory manner) at war. Eaton immediately notified Commodore Morris of the threat, and Morris diverted almost the entire squadron to visit Tunis. The squadron arrived on 22 February, and negotiations continued through 3 March.[50] According to one witness to the negotiations, when Bey Hammuda hyperbolically declaimed "I know no Laws of Nations," one of the American representatives responded tellingly, "But we do & observe them, & we mean to make ourselves respected as a Nation."[51] Commodore Morris eventually agreed to restitution for the Tunisian goods aboard the imperial ship but argued that he could not agree to any restitution for the Tunisian ships, as they were the prizes of the previous year's squadron. That issue was shelved again, but the dispute had apparently proved the end of Hammuda's patience with Eaton. Hammuda brought up debts Eaton owed and previous acts of brawling and expelled him from the regency. Commodore Morris appointed one of his officers, Doctor George Davis, as chargé d'affaires in Eaton's stead, the first of several navy officers to serve as United States diplomats in North Africa. Davis would deal with the claim of restitution for the seized ships fitfully for the next two years. In August 1805, after making peace with Tripoli, the American Mediterranean squadron would once again visit Tunis to negotiate this issue. The squadron left with Tunisian Ambassador Mellimelli, who represented the Tunisian claim in Washington, eventually winning in-kind restitution from the Jefferson administration in the form of a brigantine ship and about half a hold of cargo. The United States Navy also left behind a new diplomat in Tunis to replace Davis, the USS *Constitution*'s surgeon, Doctor James Dodge.[52]

Just eight days after Tunis's original protest of the blockade, Morocco also objected. This rupture was to be more serious, in part because feelings of religious obligation influenced Morocco to interpret its neutrality in Tripoli's favor, and in part because Commodore Morris did not understand the difference between Moroccan corsairing and that of the regencies. The disagreement started with a simple request on 10 May 1802 from the Moroccan secretary of state to the Swedish and American consuls at Tangiers for passports to allow Morocco to send a shipment of wheat promised to the Tripolitan ambassador, who had requested assistance because of the poor harvest in Tripoli.[53] The consuls demurred, as "all sort of intercourse by sea with blockaded ports was pointedly opposite to the law of nations and common usage at this day."[54] For Emperor Suleiman, however, this was not simply a dispute about legal usage but touched on his responsibilities as a Muslim ruler under the obligation of almsgiving (*zakāt*) to provide promised relief to the poor of Tripoli. He was particularly concerned with religious obligation to Tripoli, as it served as the traditional refuge for the "grand resting time" of Moroccan pilgrims on their way to and from Mecca. By 17 June Morocco was no longer requesting passports but demanding them. James Simpson, United States consul to Morocco, recommended to Commodore Morris that the passports be granted. He argued that since the cargo was for charity and did not include contraband of war, it would be acceptable to let it through and that even though Morocco had no active corsairs at the time, a rupture would cause insurance rates on all shipments through the Strait of Gibraltar to skyrocket. Commodore Morris considered the demand unreasonable and maintained that it would set a bad precedent, so he refused the passports.[55]

On 25 June the governor of Tangiers expelled Simpson, who departed for Gibraltar after sending a circular letter to over two dozen ports warning of the danger of Moroccan corsairs, particularly "small armed Boats" in the strait.[56] That same day, Commodore Morris diverted forces from the Tripolitan campaign to set up a revolving convoy system for the strait. Just eight days later, however, a letter arrived from the governor of Tangier stating that he had misunderstood Emperor Suleiman's instructions, and that the emperor actually wanted to give time for Simpson to consult with his superiors on the subject. Simpson was restored to his position, and after negotiation he and his Swedish counterpart, Peter Wyk, issued passports for the wheat to be shipped to the Tunisian port of Jerba, instead of Tripoli. Everyone seems to have understood that the wheat would be transshipped there onto small coast-hugging vessels that the blockade could not intercept, and thus on to Tripoli. Since no one had to give permission for ignoring the blockade, however, the likely final destination was ignored.[57] Commodore Morris still felt the need to use his ships for observing and making regular appearances in Moroccan ports, even with the incident smoothed over. As he did not understand that Moroccan corsairing was usually very limited and aimed at obtaining leverage for negotiations, he envisioned the affair as an attempt by Emperor Suleiman to manufacture a rupture that would allow him to take "advantage of our trade, when he finds less force at Gibraltar to oppose his corsairs."[58] The perceived Moroccan threat would serve as a central justification for Morris's lack of action against Tripoli when he was recalled and brought before a court of inquiry.[59]

Controversy between the United States and Morocco over the blockade would rise again the following May. Since the arrival of the American squadron in the Mediterranean, it had been blocking the Tripolitan flagship, the thirty-gun *Meshouda*, in the port of Gibraltar, ready to engage if it should come out of port. The crew had long since abandoned the ship and taken passage home on a neutral vessel. In September 1802 Morocco claimed the *Meshouda* and demanded passports from the Western consuls in Tangiers.[60] James Simpson issued a passport calling for American ships of war to "suffer the said ship *Meshouda* to pass freely . . . entrance to Blockaded Ports excepted."[61] Simpson speculated that Emperor Suleiman might be feeling particularly obliged to Tripoli at the time, as his son Musa had just left on the pilgrimage (*haj*) to Mecca. For several months, however, little was heard of the *Meshouda*. Then, on 13 May 1803, the USS *John Adams* captured the *Meshouda* attempting to enter Tripoli and carrying contraband of war in the form of arms and munitions.[62] Morris wrote that she would not be condemned if it "proved that this was not the order of the Emperor."[63] Immediately upon receiving word of the capture, the Moroccan government disavowed the captain, claiming that he went to Tripoli against orders.[64]

Morocco was apparently not confident of the promise to return the *Meshouda*, however, and turned to a favorite diplomatic gambit, attempting to capture a ship as a bargaining chip. On 7 August the governor of Tangier issued orders to Captain Ibrahim Lubarez of the newly refurbished twenty-two-gun corsair *Mirbokha* to capture American ships. This gambit failed spectacularly, as Captain William Bainbridge, recently returned to the Mediterranean and now in command of the frigate USS *Philadelphia*, stopped the *Mirbokha* for inspection and found the crew of the American merchant brig *Celia* aboard. He detained the *Mirbokha* and chased down and recaptured the *Celia*. Rather than leverage, what Morocco had achieved was further loss and embarrassment.[65] Emperor Suleiman lost no time disavowing Governor Ashash's orders to the *Mirbokha* and any intent at a general rupture. He explained to all the consuls in Tangiers that there was no plan for general conflict with America and that, though Ashash had probably simply ordered the corsairs to "take some Vessel of theirs to detain her untill the Tripoline should be restored," even that act was unordered and beyond Ashash's authority.[66] Suleiman called for negotiations and also ordered the *Hannah* of Salem, an American merchant ship in port at Mogadore (Essaouira), detained. This led the new American commodore in the Mediterranean, Edward Preble, to order United States ships to capture Moroccan ones and bring them in to Gibraltar for inspections. Before this could spiral out of control, however, Emperor Suleiman met with Consul Simpson and, in the traditional Moroccan style, ordered the release of the *Hannah* as a goodwill gesture at the start of negotiations. Simpson convinced Preble to accept the Moroccan disavowals and give up the *Meshouda* and the *Mirbokha* as reciprocal gestures, and peace was restored by 12 October. Five months later, Congress approved federal funds to replace the prize money that the capturing crews had given up in the interest of peace. While a misunderstanding with Morocco had once again diverted naval focus on the Tripolitan conflict, Commodore Preble was less distracted by the issue than Morris had been. Morris had been removed for his lack of offensive action against Tripoli, and Preble was determined that the missed opportunity for the once envisioned spring campaign against Tripoli in 1803 would not be repeated in 1804. Preble sent the *Philadelphia* to Tripoli to maintain the blockade and began planning for his spring offensive.[67]

Engaging Europe on Tripolitan Affairs

After dealing with the Moroccan challenge, Preble moved to prepare the squadron for offensive operations the following spring. The first project he took on, somewhat surprisingly, was shifting the main American naval base in the Mediterranean slightly farther from Tripoli, moving it from Malta to Syracuse. Further, he moved from the port of a nation at war, the Peace of Amiens between England and France having broken down, to one still enjoying a respite from the great wars of Europe. In this move, Preble also moved from working with a traditional, if sometimes controversial, European partner to a new one. Thus he reduced friction with the British navy and built ties with the Kingdom of the Two Sicilies. As Benjamin Armstrong has admirably detailed, from Commodore Dale's first arrival in Gibraltar in 1801 the United States and British navies cooperated extensively on logistics issues in the Mediterranean, especially via Britain providing basing to the United States squadron in Gibraltar and Malta. This level of collaboration with Britain's erstwhile colonies is not as surprising as it might seem. The basing offer was actually reciprocal. The British navy's Halifax-based North American squadron had been wintering in the Chesapeake Bay for years. Further, the navies had a tradition of cooperation. While they had not fought as formal allies, they had shared a common foe in the West Indies during America's Quasi-War with France. In July 1798 the two navies set up a system of mutual signals to share information such as French movements. That same year, Captain Thomas Truxton of the United States Navy had Christmas dinner with the commander of the British squadron, Rear Admiral George Vandeput, in Hampton Roads, Virginia, before departing on his cruise to the Caribbean. But though the relationship between the navies was cordial, it was also fraught, particularly over the issues of poaching each other's sailors via impressment and welcoming deserters. Tensions over these issues often boiled over into conflict, which, if much less violent than the ship-to-ship action of the *Chesapeake-Leopard* affair over similar issues in 1807, nonetheless damaged relations between the two forces. Thus, Preble decided to seek a base away from the British navy, removing a tempting English-speaking haven for would-be deserters and a tempting labor pool from would-be impressers. He found the sanctuary he was seeking in the Sicilian port of Syracuse. The governor of Syracuse was eager to host the American squadron. If not yet drawn into the Napoleonic Wars, Sicily, like the United States, was at war with Tripoli, and the strong naval presence would deter Tripoli from cruising in the area. The governor therefore offered the use of the port and warehouse space free of charge. By December 1803 the squadron was well ensconced at Syracuse, with the detachment watching the Strait of Gibraltar having moved to Algeciras, Spain, to avoid similar friction with the British navy at Gibraltar itself.[68]

The planned spring offensive had already run into a literal obstacle, however. Just a week after arriving on station at Tripoli in late October, the *Philadelphia* had hit a submerged reef. While Captain Bainbridge was an old hand in the Mediterranean, he was not very familiar with Tripoli harbor. He had visited briefly in the *George Washington* in early 1801, on his way back to Algiers from his forced trip to Constantinople, but his tour as commander of the *Essex* had almost entirely been spent near Gibraltar, guarding the strait and confining the *Meshouda* in port before its transfer to Morocco. Whether through Tripoli reusing the "reef trap" tactic tried against the *Constellation* the previous July, or simply through ill luck, Bainbridge ran the *Philadelphia* hard aground just after breaking off pursuit of a fleeing Tripolitan ship on 31 October. Unable to get the ship off the shoal and surrounded by Tripolitan gunboats, after a resistance of a few hours, Bainbridge ordered the ship scuttled and the guns thrown overboard and surrendered his command.[69]

Suddenly, Danish Consul Nissen had hundreds of American prisoners to sponsor. American prisoners found him "extremely attentive" and noted that he "kindly offers every service of assistance."[70] The officers and crew of the *Philadelphia* settled into a captivity highly reminiscent of that of previous American captives in Algiers, with officers spending most of it in housing arranged for them by Consul Nissen and often free to move about the city, while enlisted sailors were housed in a *bagnio* and required to labor for the regency. This captivity led to the publication of two popular narratives, the second of which was a class-based critique of the first. The *Philadelphia*'s assistant surgeon, Doctor Jonathan Cowdery, enjoyed even more freedom of movement than most of the officers, as he served as a physician to the ruling class of Tripoli. He published his memoir, *American Captives in Tripoli*, upon his return to America, relating the captivity in a gentlemanly style reminiscent of a travelogue. In response, one of the sailors, a former newspaperman named William Ray, published an expansion and criticism of Doctor Cowdery's account, giving the view from below. While the sailors' captivity was much harsher than that of the officers, it was perhaps overstated by Ray's title, *The Horrors of Slavery*. Ray used the opportunity of the prisoners' technical status as slaves to critique not only North African "barbarism" and the American class structure but also the Southern states' practice of chattel slavery against a people "whose only sin is, That his, alas! a sable skin is." But for all the points on which Ray disagreed with Cowdery, they both had nothing but praise for Danish Consul Nissen, whom Ray called "a most worthy character" and noted that, because of his efforts on the prisoners' behalf, he "deserves the gratitude, not of us only, but every American."[71]

Several American diplomats sought to mitigate or end the captivity of the *Philadelphia*'s crew, from Cathcart sending money and clothing from Livorno, to Minister to France Robert Livingston writing to Talleyrand to ask Napoleon to intervene for the prisoners' release, to Consul General to Russia Levet Harris requesting similar intervention (via the Ottoman Porte) from Emperor Alexander of Russia. These latter requests incensed President Jefferson, as they presented the United States once again as a supplicant to European powers on Barbary affairs, rather than a functional partner. His note on the subject to Madison was measured, perhaps given Madison's supervision of the diplomats as secretary of state, but still made Jefferson's displeasure clear.[72] The president's letter to Secretary of the Navy Robert Smith, however, was more outspoken. "I have never been so mortified as at the conduct of our foreign functionaries on the loss of the Philadelphia. they appear to have supposed that we were all lost now, & without resource: and they have hawked us in formâ pauperis [the style of paupers] begging alms at every court in Europe." Jefferson found himself in the odd position of hoping that his diplomats' efforts did not bear fruit, as "this self-degradation is the more unpardonable as, uninstructed & unauthorised, they have taken measures which commit us by moral obligations which cannot be disavowed."[73] Jefferson urged Smith to exhort the Mediterranean squadron to take action before such interventions could come to pass. Fortunately for Jefferson's foreign policy, if not for the prisoners, while both courts took some pro forma efforts on the United States' behalf, neither had any measurable effect. Further, the Mediterranean squadron had already taken action before the news of the loss of the *Philadelphia* had even reached the United States.[74]

Preble was less concerned with the diplomatic ramifications of the loss of the *Philadelphia* than with the operational ones. The capture represented not only a major reduction in his squadron's offensive capacity but also a formidable threat to the squadron itself. The Tripolitans had managed to refloat the ship and dredge up and remount most of its guns. The ship, which Tripoli renamed *God's Gift (haddiyat allah)*, was by far the most powerful vessel in Tripoli's fleet or, for that matter, in that of any North African power. Preble determined that he must recapture or destroy the frigate before attacking Tripoli. Receiving intelligence via letters from Captain Bainbridge and Consul Nissen that the ship was moored under the guns of the shore batteries, Preble determined that an attempt at recapture would be unlikely to succeed. He therefore determined to send an expedition to burn the ship in the harbor.[75] Commodore Preble had access to a local-style vessel, the ketch (a schooner-like large boat or small ship) *Mastico,* which the *Constitution* had captured in late December under Tripolitan colors, though the captain claimed that he and the ship were Turkish. As Preble had evidence that the ship had taken part in the attack on the *Philadelphia,* he was convinced that it was a good capture, as "if a Tripoline, he is a prize; if a Turk, a pirate."[76] Preble thus took the vessel into American service, renaming it the *Intrepid,* and decided to use it to infiltrate Tripoli harbor.[77]

Commodore Preble's plan depended on intimate knowledge of Tripoli harbor and local language and procedures. Fortunately, he had access to someone with just such expertise. Palermo native Salvadore Catalano was serving as the *Constitution*'s local pilot and had been in Tripoli as recently as October 1803, when he witnessed the capture of the *Philadelphia*. In fact, it was his testimony to the Vice Admiralty Court of Syracuse that he had witnessed the *Mastico* take part in the capture that led to its condemnation and availability for American use. Preble offered Catalano a bonus of one hundred dollars for taking part in the operation to infiltrate Tripoli harbor, which he accepted. The raid was under the command of Lieutenant Stephen Decatur and launched his reputation as an American naval hero, but its success depended on a Sicilian expert. At sunset on 16 February 1804, the newly named *Intrepid* stood into Tripoli harbor under British colors. By ten o'clock, the little ship was in hailing distance of the *Philadelphia* (or *God's Gift*), and Catalano called out in the local trade language, Lingua Franca, claiming that they were from Malta (thus the British flag) and had lost their anchors in a gale. He asked permission to tie up to the larger ship for the night, which enabled the sixty Americans on the *Intrepid* to board. They took the *Philadelphia* and fired it in place. The Americans retreated to the *Intrepid* and, as Tripolitan cannon fire began, sailed away under the guidance of their expert pilot, leaving the *Philadelphia* to burn into an unsalvageable wreck.[78] In Lieutenant Decatur's report of the action, he closed with a commendation of "the important services rendered by Mr. Salvador the Pilot, on whose good conduct the Success of the Enterprize in the greatest degree depended."[79]

After his adventure, Salvadore Catalano remained in the service of the American squadron for the remainder of the Tripolitan War at a salary of thirty dollars a month. At war's end, he returned to the United States with the newly promoted Captain Decatur on the USS *Congress* in November 1805. Catalano naturalized as a United States citizen, and in January 1806 he took a job in the Washington Navy Yard at the same rate of pay. As so many immigrants have done, he remitted much of his salary to help support his family back home, in Palermo. When next he appears in the historic record—as a witness in Decatur's widow's claim for prize money for the *Philadelphia* in 1825—Salvadore Catalano was still working at the Navy Yard. Catalano represents not only an international element in the triumphant American story of the burning of the *Philadelphia* but also the first known example of what was to become an American tradition of local partners in American foreign wars immigrating to the United States after their service and becoming new Americans. Few of these partners turned citizens have had as great an impact on enabling United States operations. Catalano was key not only to the famous raid itself but also, by helping remove the threat of the *Philadelphia* in Tripoli harbor, to enabling Preble's spring offensive.[80]

That offensive would also depend on assistance from the subjects of King Ferdinand of the Sicilies, this time in a more official capacity of governmental cooperation with his mainland Kingdom of Naples. The loss of the *Philadelphia* had not only reduced Commodore Preble's firepower but also drove home the fact that large frigates alone could not effectively deal with coast-hugging vessels. Preble had anticipated this problem before departing and had requested permission from the secretary of the navy to hire or purchase some small vessels to be manned by American sailors. Originally, Preble had envisioned small cruisers to intercept Tripolitan corsairs, but now he was planning an attack on Tripoli harbor and revisited the plan Captain Murray and Admiral Cederström had discussed of using gunboats and bomb ketches to bombard the city.[81] The need now seemed urgent, and Joseph Barnes's comments of the year before about Naples pointed to a potential source. Naples was often at war with one or more of the Barbary regencies. Its close location and weak navy made it a tempting target, to the point that, as Barnes put it, "along the whole south Coast of Sicily, the Turks venture on shore and carry away whole families!"[82]

While such coastal raids were not common, they had been known to happen, and Neapolitan shipping was a common target of corsairs. Barnes's prediction that Naples would be willing to pay some of the costs of expanding American naval presence were borne out. In spring 1804 Naples was at war with all the Barbary powers, and while not planning to bombard Tripoli themselves, they were very willing to facilitate an American attack. In May the Neapolitan government "leased" six gunboats and two bomb ketches to Preble at no cost "under the Title of a friendly Loan" and also included arms and ammunition, again gratis.[83] Though the London *Times* expressed surprise at this partnership, given that the United States was not, like Naples, at war with all regencies,[84] the Neapolitan prime minister noted that the king "embraces very willingly the Opportunity of favoring the Government of the United States of America, by seconding its Operations against the Common Enemies."[85] While the vessels were commanded by American officers, and two schooners were laid up in order to free up United States Navy crew to man the gunboats, they also included a complement of ninety-six Neapolitan sailors and gunners, volunteers who were compensated by the United States Navy at twice their regular pay.[86]

Though the delay in gathering these forces postponed the planned spring offensive, Commodore Preble used the men and material loaned by Naples in a series of attacks on the Tripoli harbor in August and early September. Surprisingly, only one of the thirty wounded and none of the twenty-four squadron members killed during these engagements were Neapolitans, whom Commodore Preble commended in his after-action reports as having "answered my highest expectations." Preble was particularly impressed with the service of bombardier Don Antonio Massi. The commodore formally commended him to the government of Naples in multiple letters and even employed him as a prize master for some of the captured boats after the campaign. If the Neapolitan crew members mostly escaped injury, the boats did not. Two of the gunboats sustained significant damage during the 7 August engagement. Another gunboat was sunk outright, though this was a Tripolitan prize seized during the action on 3 August, not one of the Neapolitan boats. During another attack on 3 September, one of the bomb ketches was hit so severely that it came near to sinking.[87]

As the weather turned too rough for continued campaigning, the American squadron towed the gun and mortar boats back across the Mediterranean and returned them to Messina, where they paid off their crews. Preble then continued to Naples to pass on his report and thanks and to lay the groundwork for a similar arrangement under the new commander of the American squadron, Commodore Barron, for the next campaign season. There is no record that Naples sought any recompense for the damaged vessels. Apparently, the limited damage that Preble had done to Tripoli's harbor and fleet was considered payment enough.[88]

Unfortunately for Barron's plans, however, the French Revolutionary Wars were transitioning into the Napoleonic Wars, and the Sicilies were being drawn into the Third Coalition (1805–6). Naples expected to need all its military power at home in the coming campaign season and could not spare any for another American-led Tripoli campaign. Back in the United States, Master Commandant John Shaw proposed that the American gunboats built for local harbor protection could sail across the Atlantic with false keels bolted on. This plan was enacted, but they could not arrive in time for the beginning of the 1805 campaign season. The first American gunboats arrived in the Mediterranean in early June, too late, as it turned out, to participate in the campaign at all. Commodore Barron's spring offensive would instead be supported by an unlikely alliance with a former bey of Tripoli facilitated by British and Ottoman officials.[89]

Out of Egypt

Hamet (Ahmed) Karamanli was an improbable candidate for a partnership with the republican United States of America. The second son of Bey Ali Karamanli (reigned 1754–93), Hamet had held the titular reins of power for five months in 1795 when the family retook power from Ali Burghul, an Ottoman adventurer who had held Tripoli for two years. The Karamanli family had been contesting among themselves for power internally when Burghul intervened, and though they came together to expel him, the contest resumed after Burghul was deposed in January 1795. Ali Karamanli sought to cement the succession of Hamet against the ambitions of his younger brother Yusuf by having Hamet take the beyship while Ali was still alive. This failed to forestall Yusuf, who expelled Hamet from the city in June of the same year and took power. Hamet would spend the following years as the sometime governor of Derne in the eastern portion of the regency, and sometimes in exile from the regency altogether. Meanwhile, Yusuf held Hamet's family in Tripoli as an attempted check on any ambitions to reclaim power. American diplomats first encountered Hamet in exile in Tunis. Shortly after the Tripolitan War began, the ex-consul to Tripoli James Cathcart suggested to the consul to Tunis, William Eaton, that the United States consider "effecting a revolution in favor of Hamet the Bashaws Brother who is at Tunis," in order to install a friendly ruler.

Should that prove impractical, Cathcart argued that having Hamet aboard when the navy arrived in Tripoli harbor would itself "strike such a panic in to his brother which could not fail to be subservient to our interest."[90] Eaton was intrigued and began to explore the notion with Hamet.[91]

In early 1802 Eaton convinced Hamet to go to Malta, where he hoped that the arriving squadron would pick him up on its way to Tripoli. Eaton spent considerable public money on this proposition on his own initiative, which opened him to censure but did not produce any results. Opinions on the value of the plan were mixed, but even those who supported it felt that it required government approval before acting on it. After his expulsion from Tunis in March 1803, Eaton returned to the United States and set out to get such approval. His efforts were boosted by the disastrous loss of the *Philadelphia* and the urge for decisive action that it engendered in Washington. At a 26 May 1804 cabinet meeting, the Jefferson administration decided that supporting the "ex-bashaw" was a legitimate stratagem against Tripoli and set aside $20,000 for the project. Four days later, Secretary Smith appointed Eaton as a special naval agent with orders to assist Commodore Barron, should he choose to participate in cooperation with Hamet, a decision that was left to the commodore's discretion.[92]

Few American officials in the Mediterranean expected much to come of the cooperation, as most saw Hamet as weak and even effeminate. In what way he was effeminate by their standards is never specified, but the implication is that it stemmed from his leaving his family in his brother's control, thus failing to maintain a proper masculine position as a head of household. Further, during Eaton's time in America, Hamet had temporarily reconciled with his brother and accepted a return to the governorate of Derne, only to abandon his position after another falling out and decamp to Egypt, again showing weakness and unmanly vacillation. Still, American officials considered the effort worthwhile.[93] As Commodore Barron put it, "If no other use can be made of him there will be no difficulty in placing him in possession of Derne & Bengaze. It may have a good effect, On his Brother."[94] Barron sent Eaton to Egypt in November 1804, with $20,000 in specie and the brig USS *Argus* to support the effort. Eaton accepted that the goal of this cooperation, from an American standpoint, was to influence Bey Yusuf toward making peace, at least when writing to his supervisor Commodore Barron before the operation, though he remained attached to the more quixotic idea of installing Hamet as the new bey. The first step in either version of this plan was to find Hamet and see what forces he might be able to raise.[95]

Eaton's party arrived in an unsettled Egypt on 25 November 1804, armed with letters of recommendation from Sir Alexander John Ball, the governor of Malta, to British officials in Egypt requesting that they assist Eaton's effort. It was assistance Eaton would rely on, as the rumor that Hamet was in Alexandria turned out to be incorrect. Instead, he was hundreds of miles up the Nile in a country that was still reeling from the French occupation (1798–1801). After the French withdrew, Ottoman forces vied with Egyptian Mamelukes for power, a struggle that became more complicated with the addition of Ottoman Albanian forces, which quickly split from the ethnic Turkish Ottomans. As of Eaton's arrival, Ottoman governor Khurshid Ahmed Pasha maintained a loose grip on power in Alexandria and Cairo with the vacillating support of Albanian leader Muhammed Ali, and Mamelukes held Upper Egypt. Hamet Karamanli had joined the Mameluke forces near Minya and was out of reach, and thus out of favor, with Khurshid Ahmed Pasha.[96]

British expertise and assistance were key to navigating the complex and volatile situation in Egypt. Immediately upon the party's arrival, British Consul to Alexandria Samuel Briggs facilitated a meeting with the local Ottoman governor and provided Eaton with transportation to Cairo to meet with Khurshid Ahmed. Briggs also set up a line of credit for the Americans, which was used by Eaton's party in Cairo and for maintaining and victualing the *Argus* during the long period of coordination. In Cairo, the Americans stayed in the British ministerial house and relied on British coordination with the Ottoman governor.[97] Eaton exalted, "His Britanic Majesty's Consul at Alexandra and resident at Cairo have the effect to give security and perhaps may add *success* to this expedition."[98]

Khurshid Ahmed was willing to facilitate Hamet's departure from Egypt with his few troops, which would reduce the factions at play, but he insisted on the expedition taking with it the "wild Arabs" of the *Awlad Ali* (Children of Ali), a nomadic tribe with a traditional range that straddled the Egyptian-Tripolitan border. Much of the tribe had come into central

Egypt to take part in the power struggle, with elements active near Alexandria and in Upper Egypt. By sending them to Hamet Karamanli, Ottoman Egypt rid itself of a destabilizing element, and the Eaton-Karamanli expedition gained a large, if undisciplined, force of irregulars. Khurshid Ahmed also gave Eaton permission to hire and remove mercenaries from Egypt, as that would represent one less source of insecurity in his fractious realm. The force that finally left Egypt in March 1805 consisted of Eaton and his six servants, one navy officer, eight United States Marines, sixty-three mercenaries hired by Eaton (most of whom were Ottoman Greeks), about ninety adherents of Hamet Karamanli, and approximately two hundred and fifty Arab auxiliaries. The decision to travel overland was not a strategic one for surprising the Tripolitan forces (who heard many rumors of the approaching force) but rather a tactic to keep the coalition together. Hamet feared that if he went by sea, "separating himself from the Arabs, they would lose patience, if not confidence also, and abandon his cause." Eaton had the same concerns about Hamet.[99]

Partially in an attempt to forestall the coalition splintering over arguments of leadership but seemingly mostly to gratify his ego, Eaton pressed Hamet to appoint him as the expedition's overall leader, thus obtaining what was likely Eaton's most prized possession—a commission as a general, if only over a tiny force and based on the authority of a long-deposed potentate. This commission was included as an article in a never-ratified convention signed by Eaton on behalf of the United States and Hamet, signing himself as the "Bashaw of Tripoli," so its validity is highly questionable. Nevertheless, the navy agent and former consul, who never served above the grade of captain in the United States forces, used the title "General" for the rest of his life. For all the guidance Eaton had been given about the assisting of Hamet being primarily aimed at pressuring his brother, the convention also committed the United States to "use their utmost exertions . . . to reestablish the said Hamet Bashaw in the possession of his Sovereignty of Tripoli," though the elided portion did offer some exceptions to this commitment, including the interests of the United States.[100]

When this combined force under "General" Eaton, with United States Navy fire support, succeeded in taking Derne on 27 April 1805, it accelerated peace talks and moderated Bey Yusuf Karamanli's demands. Eaton's notion that Yusuf made peace as quickly as possible before his brother could, with American aid, invade the city of Tripoli itself and depose him overstates the expedition's impact. In fact, Tripoli had requested, via Danish Consul Nissen, that the United States send a peace negotiator on March 18, when the combined force was still in Marsa, Matruh, Egypt, less than halfway through its march.[101] After taking Derne, Eaton claimed that with an investment of about $30,000 "I have no doubt, but he [Hamet] may proceed to the Walls of Tripoli."[102] Eaton admitted, however, that Hamet would need support from United States "regulars" to go any farther than standing outside the walls. Far from taking the capital, Eaton and Hamet's forces were having great difficulty even holding the city of Derne throughout May, and Commodore Barron argued that further support to Hamet would be very expensive and unlikely to succeed. Nonetheless, the joint expedition was a powerful factor in the negotiations. Prisoners reported that it alternately enraged and worried Bey Yusuf and made him eager to make peace.[103]

On 4 June 1805 the United States and Tripoli concluded a peace that saved face for both sides. American officials were able to tout the lack of a peace indemnity or annuity, while Yusuf was able to claim a payment due to the $60,000 ransom Tripoli received for the number of prisoners held above those exchanged one-for-one. American officials did not consider this payment "tribute," as such ransoms were a common part of prisoner exchanges.[104] For example, the Moroccan-American treaty that Barclay had negotiated in 1786 specified that, in case of war, prisoners would be exchanged on an even basis, and "if there shall prove a difficiency on either side it shall be made up by the Payment of one hundred Mexican Dollars for each Person wanting."[105] The Tripoli ransoms proved somewhat more expensive at about $200 per person but still reasonable. The peace was initially universally popular. Before Eaton returned to the United States and spread his dubious narrative of how only a little more effort could have deposed Yusuf, even Federalist newspapers were enthusiastic about the terms. When it heard the first vague reports of a treaty, for example, the New York *Evening Post* expressed concern over "whether peace has been *bought*" but reported satisfaction when they learned that there had been a ransom only for excess prisoners and that the agreement stipulated that *"a peace take place without any engagement on the part of the United States, for a future tribute."*[106]

Fittingly, given the partnerships that the United States had built around North African affairs and the diplomatic roles often played by American prisoners and navy officers, Danish Consul Nissen served as one of the peace negotiators. Nissen also offered his mentorship to the new American representative to the regency, former prisoner and surgeon of the USS *Philadelphia* Doctor John Ridgely. When the rest of the *Philadelphia*'s former officers were freed, before they even left Tripoli, they subscribed $700 to buy a thank-you present for Nicholas Nissen. They commissioned a silver urn in London, which reached him eighteen months later and renewed his correspondence with Captain Bainbridge. The thanks of the former prisoners was joined by that of a formal resolution from the United States Congress in 1806, echoing the gold box and formal certificate that Denmark had bestowed on Eaton for his support during their conflict with Tunis in 1801.[107]

After a shaky start, by the time peace was concluded with Tripoli in 1805, the United States had not only come through its first foreign war but was also operating militarily and diplomatically on a cooperative basis with established European powers. The United States had become treaty-worthy and, if not the major power that Cathcart envisioned, nonetheless a functional sovereign member of Vattel's previously exclusively European "republic of nations." This status was not due only to Barbary engagement, of course. It was influenced by many larger events, such as centralization under the Constitution, which built trust in the United States having the ability to agree to and enforce compliance with treaties. American prestige and engagement in Europe were also raised significantly by interactions with the great powers, such as the Jay Treaty with England, the ability to stand up to the subsequent Quasi-War with France and thereafter peace and agreement to neutral shipping rights via the 1800 Treaty of Mortefontaine, and, of course, the Louisiana Purchase. Still, cooperation in Barbary played an essential role in raising the United States fully into the "sisterhood of nations," and a much greater one than previous scholarship has appreciated. The problems of peace and war with the Barbary regencies were common problems of Europe. Other nations faced the same challenges and used the same methods to deal with them. America's engagements were a major opportunity to show viability as a sovereign nation and to build ties, especially with those European countries without New World interests.

Not only was the Tripolitan War an example of American engagement in Samuel Cooper's "great theater of nations," it was an enabler of America's ability to take that stage. The United States worked not merely like, but with, European nations in its engagement, both diplomatic and military, in North Africa. Yet the myth of American exceptionalism, which asserts that the United States did something new and different in this engagement, emerged even before the guns fell silent. On 29 March 1805, over two months before the conflict ended, Thomas Jefferson wrote from Monticello that "there is reason to believe that the example we have set, begins, already to work on the dispositions of the powers of Europe to emancipate themselves from that degrading yoke."[108] This vision of the Tripolitan War reached a wide audience in 1809, when Philadelphian political writer Tench Coxe (writing under the pseudonym Columbianus) published his series of essays on American uniqueness entitled "The New World: An Enquiry into the National Character of the People of the United States of America." In essay 10, while noting that other nations had also fought against Barbary powers, Coxe supported his exceptionalism thesis with the claim that American efforts exhibited "more of the coercive character, in proportion to our strength, and to our navy, than the treatment of those powers by any other nation." In the previous essay in the series, Coxe had asserted America's place "among civil societies" on the strength of the United States' respect for the law of nations, which he called "this half sacred law," and claimed that Americans "extended its benefits even to those Indians, who were not at that time within any of our municipal jurisdictions."[109] Once again, therefore, we see not only the tripartite division of Indian, Barbary, and European relations but also North African affairs supporting American striving for recognition in the Vattelian system.

By the end of the war against Tripoli, the United States was operating on a par with the smaller nations of Europe, particularly those with a shared interest in neutral shipping rights. Those rights were greatly threatened during the Napoleonic Wars, however, particularly by Britain. The United States Navy withdrew from the Mediterranean in 1807 in the run-up to the Embargo Act of 22 December 1807 and, thereafter, the War of 1812. During that conflict, Algiers refused a shipment of American naval stores sent as the annual peace annuity, expelled the consul, Tobias Lear, and began cruising for American prizes.[110] While the United States' response was in no way revolutionary, the end of the French Revolutionary and Napoleonic Wars (including the related War of 1812) would free European and American attention and forces to remove the Barbary System entirely.

5

Changing Tides

RISING AMERICA AND THE EBB OF CORSAIRING, 1807–1825

WHEN COMMODORE DECATUR'S SQUADRON arrived in Cadiz on 15 June 1815, they heard that Algerian corsairs were operating on the eastern side of the Strait of Gibraltar and immediately set sail for the Mediterranean. The next day, they spied the *Meshouda*, an Algerian frigate of forty-four guns, off the southern coast of Spain near Cabo de Gata. The squadron gave chase. Decatur's flagship, USS *Guerriere*, a new frigate less than a year off the ways, came into range first. Whether this was because it was the "fastest sailer," as one source claims, or because the older frigate *Constellation* cut off the *Meshouda* and forced it into range of the *Guerriere*, as other accounts offer, the flagship fired the first two broadsides. During this exchange, four Americans were wounded by enemy fire, and five were killed when one of the *Guerriere*'s cannons exploded, wounding thirty more.

Aboard the *Meshouda*, the first broadsides killed the captain, Rais Hamidou, who was also the admiral of the Algerian fleet. According to popular accounts in Algiers, Hamidou had recognized the squadron as Americans but had refused to "flee shamefully" and told his first lieutenant, "When I am dead you will have me thrown into the sea. I do not want the disbelievers to have my corpse." With Hamidou's death, most of the exposed crew fled below decks, although, with eight American warships surrounding it, the *Meshouda* would not have been able to fight free even given perfect handling. After a battle of about half an hour, the *Meshouda* was dismasted and surrendered. Decatur's squadron captured 406 Algerian corsairs aboard the *Meshouda*, about one-fourth of whom had been injured in the battle. The prisoners reported that they had lost around thirty dead, all of whom the Algerians had thrown overboard. Decatur sent the prize into Cartegena and set out in search of the rest of the Algerian squadron.

Three days later, the Americans fell in with a twenty-two-gun Algerian brig near the coast of Spain and gave chase. The brig fled and, after a chase of about three hours, reached shoal water. Having learned from the *Philadelphia* disaster, Decatur called off the frigates and let two of the squadron's schooners (the USS *Torch* and the USS *Spitfire*), the brig USS *Spark,* and the sloop USS *Epervier* continue the chase. These smaller ships were each outgunned by the Algerian brig, but collectively they carried over twice its weight of cannon, causing the brig to continue its flight until grounding itself near Cartegena. According to newspaper accounts, the Americans drew off "from respect to the neutral territory" but then reengaged when the Algerians fired on the schooner *Torch* (given as *Flambeau* in the papers), thus "violating the Spanish neutrality." The squadron captured the Algerian brig and eighty of its crew, killing about twenty in the engagement. An unknown number of the crew escaped in the ship's boats or, as given in a more colorful newspaper account, by jumping overboard and swimming to shore. Decatur's squadron also sent this prize into Cartegena, where its legal status became very murky, given the circumstances of the capture. The squadron then set sail for Algiers harbor, arriving on 28 June.[1]

This chapter argues that, unlike the Tripolitan War, the second Algerian conflict (1812–16) did little to enhance the United States' position in the European state system, though not because it failed to achieve American war aims. In fact, once the United States was able to turn its attention to the Mediterranean, its military and diplomatic efforts paid off remarkably well. Instead, this effort did little to build the country's reputation because at this point such success was largely expected. The War of 1812 vaulted the United States from an unseasoned minor power at the end of the Tripolitan War to an established, if still lesser, power by the time of the Treaty of Ghent. Although the war with Great Britain had gone relatively poorly on land, and the peace had gained the United States few of its war aims, ancillary conflicts and the Treaty of Ghent did settle two powerful challenges "internal" to America. By the end of the conflict the United States had suppressed the Red Stick Creeks in the Mississippi Territory and Tecumseh's pan-Indian confederacy in the Old Northwest and cut them off from the Westphalian system, and had gained control of disputed West Florida from Spain. Further, the simple act of successfully resisting a great power built both America's self-image and its reputation in Europe. American naval operations in that war had been strategically unimpressive, but tactical success in ship-to-ship actions against the world's foremost naval power impressed observers on both sides of the Atlantic. Finally, the United States Navy expanded greatly during the war, although much of the new construction came too late to see action. The Algerian conflict, then, was less about building repute, and more about displaying the United States' newly won national confidence in its place in the world.

This chapter further argues that the American-Algerian war did not bring about "the end of Barbary terror," as many popular historians have suggested, nor did the joint Anglo-Dutch expedition led by British Admiral Sir Edward Pellew, better known by the title Lord Exmouth, in August of 1816 "put a final end to the Barbary System," as others have argued.[2] The "Barbary System" was primarily a casualty of changing regional power dynamics. The end of endemic great power conflict in Europe freed forces and attention to concentrate on other matters. Further, the willingness of Europeans to accept corsairing as a necessary evil if it did more damage to rivals' trade than to one's own faded along with the lessening of great power conflict and mercantilist notions of trade as a zero-sum competition. Indeed, privateering of all types was losing its legitimacy throughout the Atlantic world, as irregular forces were often too independent and only loosely aligned with their sponsoring countries' goals. Many privateers were involved in illicit or semi-licit slave trading, an issue that connected them to North African corsairs and made both seem closer to pirates than to military auxiliaries. Both the American expedition to Algiers in 1815 and the Exmouth expedition a year later were enabled by this changing focus, but neither brought a sudden end to North African corsairing. Algerian corsairing continued in its regular pattern, if often suffering a paucity of legitimate targets, until the French invasion of 1830. Even after French pressure on Tunis and the Ottoman reassertion of direct control in Tripoli in the mid-1830s, occasional examples of North African privateering persisted for years.

Following the peace with Tripoli in 1805, the United States enjoyed two years of stable relations with the North African regencies, as the United States Navy continued to show presence in the Mediterranean and to supply diplomats to the regencies. In 1807 the Mediterranean squadron abruptly departed, called home after the British Navy ship HMS *Leopard* fired on the USS *Chesapeake* in a dispute about enlisting British deserters. Within months, discord broke out with Algiers over late American annuities. Though Tobias Lear was able to smooth over the breach, relations remained precarious. Additionally, American shipping patterns were disrupted by various American and European restrictions related to economic warfare. These issues also involved the regencies. American shippers used Tunis as a transfer location for goods headed to Europe in an attempt to work around the restrictions on direct trade. Additionally, both British and French navies and privateers captured American merchant ships and sent them in to North African ports for adjudication.

As war between Great Britain and the United States neared, Algiers refused a shipment of annuity goods and broke off relations. Algiers was suffering from a loss of legitimate targets, following a peace with Portugal and the expansion of British protection to some of Algiers's traditional prey, such as Sicily and Malta. Further, the dey of Algiers received a friendly letter from the Prince Regent that implied British support if Algiers experienced a rupture with any of Britain's enemies. Algiers thus expelled Tobias Lear and authorized its corsairs to capture American ships. The outbreak of the War of 1812, however, severely limited American shipping in the Mediterranean, as few merchants braved passing the British outpost at Gibraltar. In three years of "war," Algerian corsairs captured only one American ship and eleven captives. These captives, as had become traditional, came under the care of the Swedish consul, John Norderling. Although American papers railed once again about Britain unleashing savage allies against the United States in terms of both Tecumseh's Indigenous-American confederacy and Algerian corsairs, only the first of these was accessible to American offensive action. Algiers would have to wait.

Diplomatic relations with North Africa did not entirely cease during the War of 1812. Mordecai Noah was assigned as the new consul to Tunis, and he sent a mission to Algiers to attempt to ransom the eleven American prisoners, succeeding only for two of them. Interestingly, in a reverse of patterns from the 1780s, relations with Spain over Spanish American borderlands drove American engagement in North Africa. Apparently unbeknownst to Noah, he chose a problematic agent for the 1814 mission to Algiers. That agent, Richard R. Keene, was known for his involvement in land speculation and suspected also of supporting filibustering in Spanish Florida. President Madison and Secretary of State James Monroe feared repercussions on Spanish-American relations over the perceived endorsement of Keene implied by his employment on government business. They also lost confidence in Noah's judgment, recalling him from Tunis. Their use of reputed Muslim prejudice against Noah's Judaism as a face-saving reason for the recall stirred up a minor constitutional controversy at home, but the Keene issue seems not to have had the feared effect on relations with Spain. In Algiers, the remaining nine prisoners would next see an American diplomat when William Shaler arrived with a squadron of warships after the War of 1812 ended.

The signing of the Treaty of Ghent released a now large and experienced United States Navy for response to Algiers. The Madison administration sent two squadrons to the Mediterranean in 1815, one of three frigates and five smaller ships that could respond quickly, under the command of Commodore Decatur, and a follow-up under Commodore Bainbridge aboard one of America's new seventy-four-gun line-of-battle ships. This second squadron would not see action, as Decatur's squadron and the new United States consul to Algiers, William Shaler, brought an end to hostilities before Bainbridge arrived. Although the peace remained tentative for over a year, a new treaty was finally ratified in late December 1816. The final settlement benefited from the famed "Exmouth expedition" of August 1816, which destroyed the Algerian navy, thus increasing the American squadron's relative strength as it showed force to back up Shaler's diplomatic efforts.

Despite the fact that Exmouth had coerced all the regencies into declaring an end to European slavery in the aftermath of his 1816 engagement with Algiers, this did not bring an end to the corsairing system. Instead, captives were relabeled as prisoners of war rather than slaves, and the system went on much as before, though with an ever-decreasing list of safe and available targets. Algiers's 1827 rupture with France, though it brought in some prizes, would prove that the balance of power in the Mediterranean had shifted in ways that no longer allowed space for the Barbary System. Although there were a few echoes of North African privateering in the following years, France's colonization of Algiers in 1830 and the Ottoman invasion of Tripoli a few years later moved corsairing from a mainstay to a rarity.

A Precarious Peace

From the end of the Tripolitan War until departing the Mediterranean in 1807, the navy was an integral part of United States' peace with the North African regencies, both through shows of force and via detailing its officers to the regencies as diplomats. Indeed, many of those diplomats remained for years after their ships departed. This dynamic began immediately after hostilities with Tripoli ended. The Mediterranean squadron's August 1805 visit to Tunis was key to avoiding a rupture with that regency over the issue of Tunisian ships seized by the forces blockading Tripoli. With a large force in the harbor, Bey Hammuda agreed to send an ambassador to the United States to discuss the issue, rather than using the disagreement as a justification for hostilities. In November 1806 navy surgeon George Davis, who had previously served as the temporary chargé d'affaires to Tunis, was appointed as the new consul to Tripoli, replacing his fellow navy surgeon and temporary chargé d'affaires John Ridgeley. As he had done for Ridgely, Danish Consul Nicholas Nissen mentored Doctor Davis in his new position. Meanwhile, Doctor Dodge, the chargé d'affaires in Tunis, had died of natural causes. When the USS *Hornet* visited Tunis in December 1806 and discovered the situation, the captain detached his second lieutenant of marines, Charles Coxe, to handle American affairs in the regency. Consul General Tobias Lear confirmed Coxe in his position, and he served as consul to Tunis until 1813. The navy also contributed to the exchange of diplomatic favors among Western diplomats. For example, in early 1807 when Algiers went to war with Tunis, Danish Consul to Tunis Carl Holck found himself stranded. He was attempting to join his family in Livorno, but Algiers was seizing all merchant shipping leaving Tunis harbor, so Commodore Campbell took him as a passenger aboard the USS *Constitution*.[3]

In the summer of 1807 the American consuls found themselves suddenly without naval support when tensions with Britain led the United States Navy to withdraw precipitously from the Mediterranean. Secretary of the Navy Robert Smith had assigned James Barron to take the *Chesapeake* to the Mediterranean and serve as Commodore Campbell's replacement, with instructions to keep peace with the "Barbary Powers" via "a conciliatory comportment, and by displaying a force at all times prepared to protect our commerce."[4] Barron and the *Chesapeake* departed on 21 June but did not reach the Mediterranean. Instead, owing to a dispute with British naval forces in the Chesapeake Bay over the *Chesapeake* having enlisted British deserters, the HMS *Leopard* surprised Barron off the coast of Virginia on 22 June and opened fire when he refused to permit a search for the deserters. The encounter led the unprepared *Chesapeake* to haul down its colors after reportedly firing only a symbolic single cannon in reply. Less than three weeks later, Secretary of the Navy Robert Smith sent Commodore Campbell orders to bring the Mediterranean squadron back to America as quickly as possible. Campbell received these orders on 18 August, made arrangements for the *Hornet* to gather the contents of the squadron's store depots and ship them home, and departed the Mediterranean with the rest of the squadron on 8 September. The *Hornet*, after collecting the stores, followed on 18 October 1807. The United States Navy would not return to the Mediterranean until Decatur's squadron passed Gibraltar in June 1815.[5]

Keeping the peace with no naval presence and significant unprotected merchant shipping in the Mediterranean proved challenging for American diplomats. Not two months after the *Hornet*'s departure, Algiers seized three American merchant ships over the United States' delinquent annuities, which were due in naval stores and which were to have been sent with Barron's squadron. Tobias Lear was able to adjust the matter via a cash payment in lieu of the stores, and the ships were quickly released. Shortly thereafter, the news came that Algiers had actually captured four ships, but that the crew of the fourth had recaptured it, killing four Algerian corsairs in the process. Although Algiers first responded in December 1807 that the recapture would not affect the settlement, in March 1808 the issue suddenly arose again when Dey Mustapha summoned the Danish, Dutch, Swedish, and American consuls, demanding restitution for the slain corsairs from the United States and overdue consular presents or annuities from the rest. Lear paid $16,000 when offered the blunt choice between that and American merchant shipping being added to the list of targets for the next corsairing cruise.[6] American newspapers interpreted this demand as an act of extortion, undertaken either "for no other reason than he saw our property in the Mediterranean defenseless"[7] or because Algiers was acting at British instigation.[8]

The next near rupture happened not in a dispute over North African privateering but over a French seizure. American merchant shipping was frequently subject to capture for violating either British declarations of widespread embargo on shipping to France and its allies or French shipping restrictions put in place under Napoleon's "Continental System," or both. The Jefferson administration's Embargo Act of 1807's blanket prohibition on international merchant shipping departing from American ports had proved highly unpopular, leading to its reverse-spelled nickname in the Federalist press of "O-grab-me," and eventually its replacement. The Non-Intercourse Act of 1809 forbade only direct shipments to Britain, France, and their dependents. American merchants worked around this prohibition by departing for neutral ports, and there either transshipping their goods in other vessels or, having satisfied American regulations, taking their chances with British and French ones by continuing to a European port. One of the popular harbors for this mandated stop was Tunis, whose merchant marine flourished via both the expanded carrying trade opportunities and the flood of American ships sent into Tunis for sale by both British and French naval ships and privateers.[9]

A dispute over one such ship threatened the peace between the United States and Tunis in 1810. A French privateer sent in the ship *Liberty* of Philadelphia, which the French consul, authorized under French regulations to act as a sort of vice admiralty court, ordered sold at public auction. The Tunisian prime minister bought the *Liberty* and sent it, under Tunisian colors, on a voyage to Malta. There, the local American consul attempted to reclaim it for its original owners, claiming irregularity in the condemnation. This enraged Bey Hammuda, who ordered all American property in Tunis seized and held as surety against the return of his prime minister's ship. Before this dispute could spiral out of control, Charles Coxe sailed for Malta in August 1810 and was able to convince his counterpart to withdraw the claim. Coxe returned to Tunis and restored the *Liberty* to its new owner, resolving the dispute quickly enough to proceed with his planned wedding the next month to Fortuna Caravana, the daughter of an otherwise unknown expatriate colonel. The United States' precarious peace in the Mediterranean was maintained and lasted until the eve of the War of 1812.[10]

All Quiet on the Algerian Front

On 20 July 1812, with the United States and Britain "on the point of open hostilities" (actually, war had already been formally declared, though news of it had not yet reached the regency), Algiers refused a shipment of naval stores from America and expelled Consul Tobias Lear and all American citizens.[11] Thus began an oddly quiet period of warfare with almost no engagement between the contestants. Lear blamed the rupture primarily on the lack of legitimate targets for Algerian corsairing and on the United States' conflict with Britain. Algerian corsairs had lost two traditional targets in 1811 when the regency made peace with Portugal, and Britain brought Sicilian shipping under its protection. Lear warned at the time that Dey Ali "must make war upon some other nation, with or without cause, in order to employ his cruisers; and the extended and unprotected commerce of the U. States" offered the most tempting target. A year later, with the United States on the brink of war with Britain, the time seemed right. Lear assessed that Algiers considered (correctly) that conflict with Britain would keep the United States Navy too busy to deal with Algiers and that Dey Ali believed that Algiers had Britain's direct support. Although Britain and Algiers did not have an explicit alliance, a letter of friendship from the Prince Regent George (later George IV) of Britain to Dey Ali, which arrived in April 1812, included the prince's assurance that the British navy would protect the city of Algiers "so long as the present friendship shall subsist between the two nations." Lear interpreted this to mean that Britain and Algiers had "a treaty offensive and defensive" and that the United States was a target of it.[12]

Unlike with previous crises with Algiers, Lear was unable to prevent this rupture. Although the Federalist *Evening Post* published a poem celebrating Lear's expulsion as an occasion that would "save our purse" owning to his no longer being able to offer bribes of "thousands of pounds *without receipts*,"[13] he had actually been prevented from attempting such an accommodation by public law. On 1 May 1810 Congress had limited disbursements from consuls "to any one of the Barbary powers, or to the officers or subjects thereof" to $3,000 per year "without first obtaining a special approbation in writing, from the President of the United States, for that purpose."[14] As Lear had no time to seek permission to attempt to offer a cash payment, he instead sent a circular letter warning of potential Algerian predation on American merchant ships, asked Swedish Consul John Norderling to care for American affairs and any prisoners captured, and departed to Gibraltar. There, he discovered the state of war with Britain. The British seized and condemned the American store ship, and Lear was detained for seven months before British authorities allowed him to depart for Cadiz and thence to the United States, arriving in New York in April 1813.[15] Upon his arrival, Federalist papers seized on the event to attack the Madison administration, claiming that while "his masters have falsely insinuated" that Britain had instigated the Algerian war, Lear "knows how base the insinuation is."[16] Lear responded with a letter to the *National Advocate*, widely reprinted in other papers, stating, "So far am I from considering that insinuation *base*, that I have good grounds for believing it *true*."[17] Meanwhile, the Republican press revisited the rhetoric of Britain unleashing "savages" on the United States, which had been so prevalent in the 1780s, tying the War of 1812 to the conflict with Tecumseh's confederation in the Northwest and to the Algerian war. The *Aurora*, for example, called this the "triple alliance," noting that "whenever we are at issue with *Great Britain,* the *Indian* tribes and the *Algerine* rovers are let loose upon us in all their horrid modes of war."[18]

Yet on the Algerian side of this conflict, their mode of war was actually neither horrible nor particularly effective. The War of 1812 all but cleared the Mediterranean of American shipping, offering very few targets for Algerian corsairs. They captured only one unambiguously American merchant ship, and that near the very beginning of the conflict. On 25 August 1812 Algiers captured the brig *Edwin* of Salem, Massachusetts, and its crew of ten under Captain George Smith. Swedish Consul Norderling sponsored the crew, whose captivity paralleled that of previous North African captives, with the officers residing in housing arranged by the consul and the crew members living in the *bagnios* and having to labor for the regency. In April 1813 corsairs seized an American-owned and Spanish-flagged ship near Lagos, Portugal. Sources vary as to whether the ship was condemned but agree that the Spanish crew was released and only the American supercargo, James Pollard, was imprisoned. Soon, Pollard and Captain Smith went into business together as commission merchants in Algiers, paying a monthly sum for the privilege. Though an 1814 mission to attempt to ransom the prisoners failed to reach a general agreement, the agent was able to ransom two of Captain Smith's crew, leaving only nine American prisoners in Algiers. Here matters remained until the end of the War of 1812. Though the American privateer *Abellino* operated out of Tunis and Tripoli near the end of the war, it targeted British shipping and never engaged Algerian corsairs.[19] Algiers's 1813 cruise in the Atlantic that had led to Pollard's capture had also led to the only combat of the Algerian-American war before 1815. The *Globe* of Baltimore, an American privateer operating against British shipping out of Madeira, reportedly fought off a twenty-two-gun Algerian cruiser on 18 March 1813. This encounter was gleefully reported by the American consul to Madeira, the former Algerian prisoner and American consul to Tripoli James Cathcart, who expressed the hope that America would never again "pay tribute to such Miscreants."[20]

The rupture with Algiers, influenced by the outbreak of the War of 1812, was also sharply limited by America's involvement in that war. As the War of 1812 was itself a direct offshoot of the Napoleonic Wars, the Algerian war was, to a large extent, a second-order effect of the great conflict roiling Europe. Similar indirect consequences of the Napoleonic Wars were also roiling Spanish America, including its borderlands with the United States. Perhaps surprisingly, these issues too would become entangled with American interaction with the North African regencies.

Spanish Entanglements

As Rafe Blaufarb argues, "If any one individual bears responsibility for precipitating Latin American independence, that individual is Napolean Bonaparte," as his invasion of Spain and deposition of the Bourbon King Ferdinand VII "severed the links between Iberian and overseas Spain."[21] Not only did that separation lead to Latin American independence movements, but it also increased American covetousness of Spanish territory along the United States' borders. This covetousness was not new, of course. As early as the Louisiana Purchase (1803), Americans argued that West Florida (the coastal territory between the Mississippi and Perdido Rivers) constituted part of the purchase. This claim rested on the grounds that France had governed that territory as part of Louisiana up to its ceding of the territory to Spain in 1762, and that Spain had not defined the boundaries of the territory it ceded back to France shortly before the purchase, for all that West Florida had been governed separately for forty years. The United States also made a maximal westward claim, arguing for the entire (as yet unknown extent) of the Mississippi drainage. Yet except for the Lewis and Clark expedition (1804) to map and claim the portions "uninhabited" (by European-governed white settlements), and for the fact that Spanish territory was a potential target of the Burr Conspiracy's unsanctioned force (1806), Americans did little to threaten Spanish North America before 1808.

Napoleon's invasion of Spain turbocharged American complaints of Spanish territory as effectively ungoverned, serving as a refuge for Indian raiders and escaped slaves and an entrepôt for slave smugglers circumventing the 1807 "Act Prohibiting Importation of Slaves," which took effect on 1 January 1808.[22] Still, the federal government eschewed direct aggression until the War of 1812, when Spain's alliance with Britain legitimized American invasion. In the meantime, private citizens' schemes, plots, and outright violence targeted Spanish North America repeatedly, most notably the "West Florida Rebellion" of 1810 but also the many other filibuster expeditions and "corrupt speculations" that damaged America's reputation as a law-abiding nation. In a reversal of previous patterns from 1785, North American interactions between the United States and Spain would prove to affect American diplomacy in North Africa. When Mordecai Noah, consul-designate to Tunis, employed one of these agents of "grasping land Jobbers in New Orleans"[23] on a mission to Algiers, the potential fallout on relations with Spain led to Noah's recall, and the reasoning given led to a constitutional controversy.

Noah's representative on the Algiers mission, Richard R. Keene, had a long and contentious career on the edges of gentlemanly society. He first enters the historical record in 1798 when George Washington turned down his plea for funds and returned his papers; and as Washington "want[ed] no evidence of your request," he also sent back the original letter without copying it into his letter book, leaving the nature of the request a mystery.[24] Keene resurfaces next as a young attorney in Maryland in 1801, when he eloped with Eleanor Martin, the fifteen-year-old daughter of Luther Martin, a signatory of the Declaration of Independence in whose law office Keene had been reading. In response, Martin published a defamatory pamphlet denouncing Keene's ingratitude. While it is not clear how much effect the pamphlet had on Keene's prospects, he and Eleanor moved to New Orleans as part of the first wave of American settlers after the Louisiana Purchase. For a short time, he served as the Territory of Orleans's first attorney general, until Governor William C. C. Claiborne replaced him in 1804, whereupon he fought a duel with the lawyer who supplanted him. Thereafter, he was active in land speculation in West Florida. In 1807 things began to go rapidly downhill for Keene, as Eleanor died and he was arrested on suspicion of involvement in the Burr Conspiracy. He put up some of his property as bail and continued his involvement in land and filibuster schemes. Eventually he moved to Spain to petition the Cortes directly for a large land grant in either Texas or East Florida. In 1811 President Madison warned Joel Barlow, now serving as minister to France, about Keene's schemes in the "corrupt speculations" letter quoted above. By this time, France had apparently agreed that the United States should seek possession of both East and West Florida to keep Britain from taking it, and Madison was concerned that Keene's activities could further discredit America's intentions and disrupt negotiations toward acquiring those territories from the Joseph Bonaparte regime in Spain. Indeed, Barlow managed to negotiate such a draft agreement, but with Bonaparte's reverses in the Peninsular War and Joel Barlow's death in 1812, nothing came of it.[25]

For all that Keene's unsavory reputation did not have the feared effect on American diplomacy in Spain, it had a surprising effect in North Africa, further illustrating the entangled nature of diplomatic affairs throughout the Atlantic world. In April 1813 Mordecai M. Noah was appointed the new consul to Tunis. He was instructed to look for an opportunity on his way to Tunis to arrange the ransom of the American prisoners then held in Algiers, if it was possible to secure their release for $3,000 apiece or less, and to give the impression that the mission was private, rather than government sponsored. Noah found his opportunity at Cadiz, where he met Keene living in the house of the United States consul, Richard Hackley. Keene had by that time become a Spanish subject, in order, Noah presumed, "to cover some commercial views," which was accurate as far as it went. In addition to Hackley, United States Naval Agent Richard Meade, later to become an outspoken critic of Keene, also recommended him as an agent for the ransom attempt. Noah thus agreed to a contingency payment, under which Keene would receive the difference between any amount actually paid and the $3,000 maximum per man. Keene proceeded to solicit letters of credence from every source he could (the Cortes, the British commanding officer in the Mediterranean, etc.), which upset the Department of State when discovered, as Monroe felt it made the envoy seem far too official. Keene departed for Algiers in January 1814, where, despite the traditional assistance of Swedish Consul John Norderling and other European intermediaries, he was quickly stymied by Dey al-Hadj 'Ali's disinterest in ransoming his few American prisoners. In response to Keene's queries, the dey responded, "Tell the consul, and the agent of his government, and of the American merchants in Cadiz, my policy and my views are to increase, not to diminish the number of my American slaves," likely as he was aware how much more attention and funds had been forthcoming after the few prisoners of the 1780s became over a hundred in 1793.[26]

As Keene's renumeration for this mission was solely contingent, he then got creative. With the help of British Consul Hugh McDonnell, Keene convinced the dey to release two American prisoners as recompense for a British deserter under the dey's protection who had converted to Islam. Then the British frigate *Franchise* called in Algiers and proposed to discharge four recalcitrant French-speaking impressed sailors there. On the theory that they would be enslaved if stranded in Algiers and that they qualified as American citizens because they claimed to be from New Orleans and to have lived there at the time of the Louisiana Purchase, Keene claimed them from McDonnell as well. While Keene carefully avoided confirming their claim, he also argued that he needed to accept it based on their statements and the fact that McDonnell had turned them over to him, which he would be unlikely to do if they "belonged to France." For his part, Noah also had his suspicions, given that they spoke very little English, but he seems to have carefully avoided investigating too deeply. There is no record, for example, that he asked them anything about New Orleans, where he and they had theoretically lived at the same time. Instead, he simply accepted their sworn statement before Consul Hackley in Cadiz that they had lived in New Orleans until 1806 and were thus "native citizens of the United States." Noah paid Keene $15,852 for his "six prisoners" redeemed and expenses, which came to over $18,000 with the premium paid on the bill of exchange.[27]

When this bill reached Washington, James Madison and James Monroe alike were outraged. Considering Noah's actions "going beyond orders, employing a most obnoxious character, expending the public money unnecessarily," they determined to recall Noah from his position as consul to Tunis.[28] Their main concern seems to have been the selection of Keene in the first place, followed by Noah and Keene's indiscreetly intimating the government's involvement in the ransom attempt. The first they perceived would damage the United States' reputation with Spain, and the second its negotiating position with Algiers. Nonetheless, they felt that making these concerns public would only exacerbate the issue, so President Madison suggested that Monroe cite "the ascertained prejudices of the Turks agst. his Religion, and its having become public that he was a Jew" as the reason for the recall.[29] Monroe did so, but this sop that the recall was primarily because his religion would be a major obstacle to his ability to function in the consular role did not have the desired effect of providing a face-saving excuse. Instead, not only did the controversy over Noah's accounts and employment of Keene later become public knowledge, but the professed religious discrimination also added an additional layer of controversy. Nonetheless, avoiding discussion of their main concerns did keep Noah from commenting on them while still abroad. As the editors of Madison's papers noted, international relations "regarding the Spanish-American borderlands were too tense, and Keene's suspected involvement too deep, to risk giving Noah an opportunity to comment on this state of affairs."[30]

Yet comment Noah did. Upon his return home, Noah published a book that was half travelogue and half defense of his conduct and complaint about his recall and the reasoning behind it. While this book did not come out until 1819, by which time relations between the United States and Spain had stabilized, with the signing of the Adam-Onis Treaty making the immediate concerns moot, the religious issue continued to resonate. Noah cited not only the United States Constitution's prohibition of any religious test for public office but also the long history of Mediterranean leaders employing Jewish diplomats and their record of success. Finally, he invoked the famed Article 11 of the United States–Tripoli Treaty, quoting it in its entirety and emphasizing the fact that it was confirmed by the Senate and its statement that the United States *"is not, IN ANY SENSE, founded on the Christian religion,"* and that thus "no pretext *arising from religious opinions,* shall *ever* produce an interruption of the harmony existing between the two countries."[31] Noah sent copies of this book to many eminent Americans in an effort to bolster his reputation. In John Adams's letter of thanks, he expressed his admiration for "Israelites" and that he "wish[ed] the Jews again in Judea an independent nation," though his assessment that if "no longer persecuted they would soon wear away some of the asperities & peculiarities of their character possibly in time become liberal Unitarian Christians" probably did not delight Noah.[32] Noah's public relations blitz did not lead to his restoration to an office of equal rank, as he had hoped, but he does seem to have met his goal of having his "letter of recall to be struck from the files of the Department of State, as being a document, not only unconstitutional and discreditable, but calculated to impair, very materially, the rights of an increasing portion of the community."[33] The letter is not included in James Monroe's papers, and the only known source for it is Noah's book itself.

North Africa's Changing Place in Mediterranean Diplomacy

Noah's book is also illustrative of both the effects of the state of war, both in Europe and between the United States and Britain, on Mediterranean diplomacy and, more significantly, the changing status of the North African regencies within that regime. Even before Noah took up his office in Tunis, he faced significant obstacles in obtaining the traditional consular presents. While the goods he needed were available in Marseilles, in an issue reminiscent of Richard O'Brien's scramble to redeem letters of credit for cash to conclude the original treaty with Algiers in 1796, Noah was unable to secure specie to pay for them. Merchants were also reluctant to accept American government credit owing to the suspension of commercial shipping and "occasional reverses of our arms on land." Noah was advised that he would have to travel to Paris "where we had a Minister and a Banker," but even there, circumstances "rendered it impossible to obtain money." Eventually he was able to purchase gifts in Marseilles when a private merchant from Boston offered to stand surety.[34]

These gifts, of course, were de rigueur for a new consul to any of the regencies by long-standing tradition. But their meaning, and indeed European views of their propriety itself, were undergoing a profound change. As argued in chapter 1, in the seventeenth and eighteenth centuries

European powers treated the Barbary powers as sovereign, and their corsairing as legitimate acts of war. Yet in the nineteenth century that view was waning, led by a growing power imbalance favoring Europe and an increasing distaste for slavery, even the non-chattel "ransom slavery" of the corsairing states, and of privateering as a legitimate way to make war. As Christian Windler argues, Europeans' earlier view of the regencies was not due to deeply held Westphalian notions of the equality of sovereign states, but rather that it fit into "the context of early modern diplomatic cultures which were marked by highly ambiguous practices of competing claims to superiority."[35]

Consular gift giving fell squarely into this cultural competition. North African leaders interpreted these gifts as tribute and even the *jizyah* that permitted Christians to live peacefully under Muslim rule, whereas Europeans were divided on whether they were tribute or bribes and therefore shameful, or expressions of largesse toward pseudo-clients and therefore signs of European superiority. These issues, and indeed the "dramatic new imbalance of military and economic power in the Mediterranean," would only tilt further toward European views in the coming decades, leading to the end of diplomatic gift giving and, shortly thereafter, to European colonial domination of North Africa.[36]

Another manifestation of this competition over claims of superiority was the ceremony of consular audiences with North African leaders. As early as 1799, William Eaton had complained about the requirement to publicly kiss the dey of Algiers's hand, though his former prisoner colleagues found it unremarkable.[37] By the time Noah met Bey Mahmoud of Tunis in 1814, the consuls were more universally resistant to this "humiliating and most degrading custom."[38] In 1816 they won the concession of a separate audience chamber, so that the traditional hand kiss was at least not a public spectacle and thus considerably less objectionable. Nonetheless, Noah's replacement, Thomas Anderson, caused a minor rupture the following year when he initially refused to kiss the bey's hand, stating that he would not even kiss the president of the United States' hand.[39] This increasing power imbalance and the return of peace to Europe quickly led to movements to suppress Barbary corsairing. Noah calls out this changing dynamic in ways that could fairly be described as Orientalist in the "writing on the East in service of imperialism" way meant by Edward Said in his seminal work *Orientalism*. When reflecting on the Algiers-Tunis War of 1807, Noah opined that "the Mussulmen in the north of Africa, are wholly ignorant of the military art," and a hundred thousand European troops could take the whole of North Africa, or twenty thousand "any of the kingdoms in the Barbary States." Writing in 1819, he mused that "the tranquility which now prevails in Europe, affords a proper opportunity to agitate the question of the conquest of Barbary," suggesting that Russia might take this on. Barring conquest, he called for an international force to properly patrol the Mediterranean. Here he seems to be influenced by the discussions of the Congress of Aix-la-Chapelle the previous year.[40]

Tranquillity Disarrayed

Before such concerns could be prioritized, however, Europe would have to deal with a return to continental conflict, with the escape of Napoleon from Elba in February 1815 and the spasm of warfare it engendered. The so-called One Hundred Days captivated Europe but had much less impact on American efforts in North Africa than one might expect. To Noah, it was mostly notable only in that a pair of Bourbon loyalists took refuge in Tunis and that shortly thereafter a new French consul arrived to replace the Bourbon appointee. While the Bourbon loyalist chargé d'affaires protested, the bey recognized the new representative, Debois de Tainville. Noah followed suit, hosting a dinner for de Tainville at which all the other consuls were also present, though they refused to acknowledge the tricolored flag now flying on the French Consulate. A few months later, "when the powers of Europe combined once more to drive Bonaparte from France, and the white flag was again restored," Noah repeated the process.[41]

The One Hundred Days was more concerning to naval and political leaders in the United States planning the Algerian expedition commonly called the Second Barbary War. As soon as the Treaty of Ghent was ratified, President Madison requested on 23 February 1815 that Congress declare "the existence of a state of war between the United States and the Dey and Regency of Algiers and planning began."[42] President Madison reviewed Secretary of the Navy Benjamin Crowninshield's instructions to Commodore Decatur on 20 April and added that he should cooperate with "several nations, particularly the Dutch," who were "understood to be at war with Algiers."[43] The news of Napoleon's return to power reached Washington nine days later, leading Crowninshield to advise that plans might need to change. The cruise was officially delayed on 29 April, leading to two weeks of debate.[44] President Madison was concerned about convulsions in Europe and suggested a pause in both the expedition and in any post–War of 1812 disarmament, such that America would be "free to chuse the course, recommended by further information."[45] After a week of consideration and further news, he felt that Decatur's squadron should likely continue, as some merchant ships had probably already departed under the impression that the navy would be in the Mediterranean to protect them. Madison recommended, however, that the navy should avoid French ports and that Crowninshield should consider decreasing the size of the deployment to the minimum force required to "overmatch that of algiers, and suffice for a blockade; diminishing thus the stake exposed."[46] After consultation, President Madison was less concerned that the United States Navy might face danger from any of the European combatants. He felt that public sentiment in Europe was in favor of "an Expedition agst. the kidnapping & enslaving of Christians," and thus the nations of Europe would not interfere.[47] Decatur himself was eager to be about it, and Crowninshield worried that a delay after word of the expedition had gone out might give Algiers time to prepare. On 12 May, President Madison agreed and authorized the mission, which sailed eight days later.[48]

The Long-Delayed Response

The United States that responded to Algerian predation after the close of the War of 1812 was very different from that which had built its first three frigates in response to Algerian predation twenty years before. The War of 1812 had built national unity and willingness to spend on military might and removed some significant military and diplomatic challenges. For all that the invasion of Canada had failed miserably, American ground forces fared better against the Red Stick Creeks and Tecumseh's confederacy, each of which had received some support from Britain. The Creek (1813–14) and Tecumseh's (1810–13) Wars had led to defeat for both the traditionalist Creeks and the Northwest pan-Indian confederacy. The Treaty of Ghent cemented that defeat. While British Undersecretary of State Henry Goulburn renewed a long-proposed "Indian buffer state" plan during peace negotiations, the notion was quickly dropped. Britain made peace with the United States without any conditions regarding their erstwhile Indian allies, except a nebulous clause requiring Britain and America to return any Indian "possessions, rights, and privileges which they may have enjoyed . . . previous to such hostilities," provided that that the Indians "shall agree to desist from all hostilities."[49] As Leonard Sadowsky has argued, the end of the War of 1812 "essentially marked the removal of American Indian nations from contact with the Westphalian system" and brought an end to the "borderlands diplomatic regime that had existed for a century." In removing the potential for large-scale British-supported Native American threats on its frontiers, the peace not only victimized Indians but also released significant United States resources for other military endeavors, such as responding to the long-simmering Algerian conflict. The old tripartite division of international affairs, with Indians serving as a bridge between European and Barbary affairs, was thus stood on its head.[50]

But these tangible returns were not the ones that excited either American or European observers, who were much more impressed with the United States for having "successfully" stood up to British power. So different was the nation and so much more imagined as capable of sovereign action, that Americans widely referred to the War of 1812 as a "second war for independence," with the term common in newspaper accounts, patriotic toasts, and as the title of a history of the war rapidly written and published by subscription in 1815.[51] Observers in Europe agreed that the war had raised the United States both in actual capacity and in esteem. The naval successes, though most were limited to ship-to-ship actions with little strategic impact, nonetheless made great (or in Britain, doleful) press. Upon receiving news of the Treaty of Ghent, for example, the London *Times* argued against ratifying it until Britain "could close the war with some great naval triumph" in an attempt to reverse the rise of America's naval reputation and the fall of Britain's.[52] In America, anti-navalism, either on moral or on fiscal terms, was all but extinct. Secretary of the Navy Crowninshield wrote to the congressional Ways and Means Committee recommending against selling or breaking up the United States' expanded navy, arguing that "the destinies of the nation appear to be intimately connected with her maritime power and prosperity; and as the creation of a navy is not a work to be quickly performed, it seems necessary not only to cherish our existing resources, but to augment them."[53] His argument fell on receptive ears.

As soon as the Treaty of Ghent was ratified, President Madison requested on 23 February 1815 that Congress declare "the existence of a state of war between the United States and the Dey and Regency of Algiers."[54] Bypassing the legislative ambiguities of the Tripolitan conflict, the congressional committee that reported on the president's request expressed their opinion that the acts of Algiers since 1812 constituted waging war on the United States. Congress then passed "An Act for the protection of the commerce of the United States against the Algerine cruisers," which, rather than directly declaring war on the part of America, stated that "the Dey of Algiers, on the coast of Barbary, has commenced a predatory warfare against the United States" and authorized military action in response.[55] The Madison administration immediately organized two squadrons to put that response into action. The first would be led by the hero of the burning of the *Philadelphia* in Tripoli harbor, Stephen Decatur. His flagship, the USS *Guerriere*, was the first frigate laid down by the federal government since the Quasi-War (though several others had been built via subscription) and was pointedly named after a British frigate captured and destroyed by the USS *Constitution* under Captain Isaac Hull during the War of 1812. The second squadron was led by the captain who had grounded the *Philadelphia* and spent the rest of the Tripolitan War in captivity, William Bainbridge. Bainbridge had refurbished his reputation from that incident by capturing and destroying the British frigate HMS *Java* during the War of 1812, coincidentally also while commanding the *Constitution*. Bainbridge's flagship, the USS *Independence*, was one of the United States Navy's first seventy-four-gun line-of-battle ships.[56]

President Madison appointed Decatur, Bainbridge, and the new consul to Algiers and former junior member of the American diplomatic delegation at Ghent, William Shaler, as peace commissioners, with authorization to pay a "reasonable" ransom for American prisoners, if required, and the "expediency of disguising it if not to be avoided."[57] Writing from England to his mother, Abigail, John Quincy Adams predicted how this mission would further elevate America's reputation in Europe. He first noted how drastically the reputation of the United States, "in the general scale of civilized Nations," had risen in response to the War of 1812, asserting that "no American visiting in Europe in 1815 can avoid perceiving how much more individual Consideration he derives from the reputation of the Nation to which he belongs, than he could have derived in 1811," and crediting that largely to American naval victories. The war with Algiers, he asserted, "opened a new field of honour" and added, "May the glory of rescuing ourselves and all Christendom from the piratical Barbarians of Africa, be reserved for the American Navy!"[58] The expedition went almost as well as Adams could have desired, though Europe's response to it disappointed him.

In fact, by the time Adams wrote, the active campaign was already over. After the two quick victories off the Spanish coast, Decatur's squadron arrived in Algiers harbor on 29 June 1815, standing between the remainder of the Algerian fleet and its home port. Dey Omar had ruled Algiers for less than four months, having inherited the American war from his predecessor and, far from having profited by it, had already lost two of his strongest ships and his admiral. Further, he was likely aware that his theoretical British allies had not only lost interest in Algiers with the end of the Napoleonic Wars but had agreed at the Congress of Vienna to future talks about European cooperation in suppressing the slave trade, including Barbary captivity. Omar's first priority was to end the conflict quickly. He sent Swedish Consul Norderling out to the fleet to negotiate on his behalf, and his demands were remarkably light and primarily aimed at securing the release of the nearly five hundred Algerian prisoners in American hands and of his two captured warships. Decatur and Shaler were unwilling to make the return of the warships part of the treaty but offered it as a friendly gesture after the peace was signed. Dey Omar accepted, and within twenty-four hours of the squadron's arrival, a new peace was signed. While it offered no cash payments, annuities, or ransom to Algiers, it did involve the free repatriation of almost five hundred more Algerian prisoners than the nine Americans released, which would have cost Algiers over $48,000 under the prisoner exchange terms of the American treaty with Morocco, or twice that at the rate America had paid Tripoli a decade previously. Thus, the agreement was much less severe to Algiers than often depicted. Decatur then dispatched the *Epervier* to the United States with his dispatches and the original treaty, the released American prisoners, and captured Algerian flags. Sadly, the *Epervier* was last seen by a passing ship on the 9 August, a few days' sail from the United States and preparing for an approaching storm. The storm turned into a two-day gale, and the *Epervier* went down with all hands, including those just released from almost three years in captivity.[59]

Decatur's squadron continued to Tunis and then Tripoli to show the flag. At each of these stops, he received a complaint from the American consul there that the locals had allowed the British to recapture prizes sent in by the American privateer *Abellino*. The United States considered these recaptures to be violations of the North African ports' neutrality but claimed the value from Tunis and Tripoli, rather than England, as the regencies had signed treaties that specified protecting American property in their waters. Both regencies paid the demanded reparations, though Tripoli offered ransom of prisoners in lieu of part of the payment. Commodore Decatur accepted the release of eight Neapolitan prisoners, and returned them to the Kingdom of the Two Sicilies in token of "the grateful sense entertained by my Government of the aid formerly rendered to us by His Majesty during our war with Tripoli."[60] Decatur's squadron then swept back up the Mediterranean, meeting Bainbridge's squadron coming in but leaving them no mission but to show off America's increased naval power.[61] The expedition seemed a triumph, but John Quincy Adams was surprised to note that though "our Naval campaign in the Mediteranian has been perhaps as splendid as any thing that has occurred in our annals since our existence as a Nation. It has excited little attention in Europe." He attributed this issue to grander affairs holding Europe's attention and possibly even to jealousy.[62] The "grander affairs" issue was almost certainly true, as the expedition took place during the One Hundred Days of Napoleon's return to power and warfare. Jealousy seems very unlikely, however. More likely, Europeans had simply come to consider American military and diplomatic success normal. The War of 1812 had cemented the new republic's place as an established power within the Vattelian system, and the Decatur expedition was just such an action as would be expected of a fully sovereign and vigorous nation. It earned some approbation but little wonder.

Barbary Corsairing's Legitimacy Crisis

Europe's appreciation for American success was partially grounded in a growing distaste for Barbary corsairing. A significant driver in the anti-corsairing movement was the overlap between privateering and slave trading, both in the chattel sense and in ransom slavery, which was increasingly seen as just as illegitimate. With Napoleon's invasion of Malta and dissolution of the Hospitaller corsairing system (1798), the practice was no longer mutual but only practiced by "barbarians." Further, even "civilized" privateers were often part of illicit or semi-licit slave trafficking. The treaties at the end of the Napoleonic Wars began calling for an end to the slave trade with the 1814 Treaty of Paris committing France and England to attempt "at the approaching congress, to induce all the powers of Christendom to decree the abolition of the slave-trade." This movement grew stronger through the Congress of Vienna and the Second Treaty of Paris, and by the time of the Congress of Aix-la-Chapelle (1818), this issue was specifically tied to Barbary corsairs. British Secretary of State for Foreign Affairs Robert Stewart, better known as Viscount Castlereagh, submitted a proposal for the Quintuple Alliance to suppress both, though it foundered on British concerns about a Russian fleet in the Mediterranean and other countries' disinclination to allow foreign powers the right to search ships under their flag. Nonetheless, Britain and France agreed to less formal cooperation, due to "the necessity of their discontinuing the depredations and acts of violence committed by armed vessels of these regencies."[63]

Perhaps surprisingly, the American government agreed not only with the sovereignty arguments but also with the need to suppress the slave trade and the privateers' problematic connection with it. For all that the United States had a growing appetite for enslaved labor to work in the expanding network of cotton plantations, the prohibition on importation of slaves continued to tighten. Americans complained bitterly of privateers bearing letters of marque from Latin American revolutionary governments smuggling slaves into the United States, especially at the close of the War of 1812. Jean Lafitte in Galveston, Spanish Texas, and Louis-Michel Aury, who moved from there to Amelia Island in Spanish Florida, made the majority of their profits from the human cargos they seized from slave ships and sold primarily in the United States.[64] The privateer problem became so bad that President Madison suggested diverting the second squadron under Commodore Bainbridge from the Mediterranean as "a naval force of some sort is much wanted to repress depredations & enforce our laws in the Gulph of Mexico, and in the neighborhood of New Orleans." But the Barbary threat remained a higher priority and the squadron had already sailed.[65] It frustrated James Madison that Britain did not prioritize the same way, complaining that Castlereagh "makes a limping retreat from the British obligation to force the Barbarians out of the practice of enslaving [Christia]ns. . . . Why more delicate towards the Dey of Algiers, than the Kings of Spain & Portugal? True, G[reat] B[ritain] does not mak[e] war in form agst. them, but she disregards their sovereignty, in seizing & adjudging their slave ships. Let her do the same with the slave ships of the Barbarians."[66] Madison's desire to see British action against North African corsairing would come a year later with the famed Exmouth expedition, but even thereafter, Barbary predation would continue, if in an increasingly desultory manner.

The Barbary System Dwindles

For all of its success, the 1815 Decatur expedition did not bring an end to the Barbary System, nor even to American issues with the North African regencies. In April 1816 the United States and Algiers came near to renewed conflict. The primary issue was that of the warships captured by Decatur. Following the peace agreement of June 1815, the American squadron had relinquished its claim to the ships, and Algiers had reclaimed the *Meshouda*, but Spain had refused to release the brig, claiming it had been illegally captured in Spanish waters. The issue was exacerbated by the loss of the original treaty in the *Epervier*, which left the United States without a signed copy. When the USS *Java* (another American frigate named after a British ship destroyed in the War of 1812) arrived with a ratified copy of the treaty, Dey Omar argued that it was not the original and that the United States had broken the treaty by failing to restore the captured brig. William Shaler insisted that the brig had been a separate issue not part of the treaty and that Spain's refusal to release it was not the United States' responsibility. Issues became heated enough that Shaler withdrew to the fleet during four days of negotiation. Rather than calling for an immediate rupture, the parties agreed that Dey Omar would communicate his claims to President Madison directly and that the two nations would maintain a truce during the exchange of letters. Dey Omar's letter claimed that the failure to restore the brig annulled the 1815 treaty and offered to instead restore the 1795 treaty, which included a requirement for the United States to pay an annuity in naval stores. On Secretary of State Monroe's urging, Madison rejected both that offer and Dey Omar's interpretation of American responsibility for Spain's retention of the brig, though he did offer America's good offices in attempting to convince Spain to return it.[67] He pointedly sent the reply, which included the phrase "as peace is better than War, War is better than tribute," with Commodore Isaac Chauncey in the USS *Washington*, one of the new seventy-fours.[68]

In the interim between Dey Omar's letter and President Madison's reply, Algiers came under a joint British-Dutch attack that many scholars mark as the event that ended the Barbary System. It did not, but the damage that it caused left Algiers in a poor position to resist American demands when they arrived. The British Mediterranean fleet under Lord Exmouth had visited Algiers harbor in April 1816 to emphasize that Sardinia and Naples were now under British protection and had ransomed all prisoners from those nations as part of the visit. In late May rumor apparently reached the Algerian town of Bona that the dey had declared war against the English because Exmouth had demanded the burning of the Algerian fleet. Local forces responded by attacking all European coral fishers in the town operating under the British flag, most of them Neapolitans. While Exmouth had not made such a demand in April, when the British fleet returned in August in company with a Dutch squadron, they did, eventually, destroy the Algerian fleet by fire. First came several days of negotiations, however, during which Dey Omar imprisoned British Consul McDonnell and several members of the British Navy. American Consul Shaler sponsored them during their brief imprisonment, which was recognized by a letter of thanks from Lord Exmouth. After negotiations failed, the fleet of twenty-four British ships, joined by the six-ship Dutch Mediterranean squadron, bombarded Algiers on 31 August 1816. According to after-action reports, the battle was relatively inconclusive until an Algerian frigate caught fire (in some reports, a small British vessel maneuvered alongside and set it alight). The wind reportedly caught the frigate's flames and spread them to the entire Algerian fleet.[69] As part of his terms after the battle, Exmouth insisted on the "abolition of slavery of Europeans" and the immediate release of all currently held. Algiers agreed and freed all 1,606 Europeans in captivity.[70] Exmouth then proceeded to Tunis and to Tripoli and "requested" that they also abolish holding Europeans in slavery, with which they complied. As dramatic as this sounds, however, the Barbary System went on.[71]

By the time the American squadron arrived in Algiers with President Madison's response, Algiers was already seeking to reestablish its fleet, but it was clearly in no position for a fresh rupture with the United States. In November 1816 Algiers purchased a European ship and converted it into a corsair. This ship (either a frigate or a sloop, depending on the source) represented the entirety of the Algerian fleet, compared to the ship of the line, three frigates, and five smaller ships of the American squadron that arrived in December. As such, Shaler and Commodore Chauncey were able to negotiate a peace based on the 1815 treaty, with only the removal of one article that had stipulated that Algiers would not allow enemies of the United States to send captured American ships into Algerian ports.[72] American observers noted, however, that Algiers was preparing for a return to offensive warfare and resented the American terms. By February 1817 an unnamed European expatriate in Algiers noted that the regency had "wholly remedied the consequences of one of the blooddiest battles which the shores of Africa have witnessed." He predicted a quick return to corsairing, noting that the abolition of slavery meant little, as European captives would be treated the same "either as slaves or as prisoners of war."[73] This proved prophetic. Algerian corsairs were reported cruising as early as April, and by August the Algerian fleet was up to eleven corsairs and had captured ships belonging to Spain and Hamburg, with Algiers holding their crews as prisoners of war in the *bagnios* in exactly the same manner as when such captives had technically been considered slaves.[74]

In 1825, while still serving in Algiers, William Shaler completed a book entitled *Sketches of Algiers, Political, Historical, and Civil*, which, though it purported to show corsairing as a thing of the past, instead showed that it continued, but that American power had risen enough for it no longer to be a serious threat to the United States. If Noah's book has some elements of Orientalism, Shaler's is Orientalist throughout. That is to say that his book "others" Middle Easterners by focusing on stereotypical depictions of Eastern eroticism, violence, and Islam in ways that seem designed to support imperialism. In Shaler's case, he advocates for another power's imperialism, rather than his own country's, calling for Britain to colonize Algiers. Still, the fact that an American official has joined the discourse of colonialism as a positive civilizing force says interesting things about America's relative power in this era. Shaler does not give in to stereotypical accounts of "Christian slavery" in the regency, however. Instead of lurid accounts of cruelty and sexual exploitation, he states that, when it had existed, European slaves' "condition here was not generally worse than that of prisoners of war in many civilized, Christian countries," and that "female captives were always treated with the respect due their sex."[75]

Shaler oddly treats corsairing as though it were an outdated system of maritime predation, while often noting details that contradict that notion. Though he states that "since 1815, they have derived no benefit from pillage" in his description of what he considers a former practice, Shaler documents continuing annuity payments from Naples, Sweden,

Denmark, and Portugal just two pages later. He also reports that although the European powers agreed at the Conference of Aix-la-Chapelle to seek an end to the Barbary System and that a combined British and French squadron visited Algiers in 1819 proclaiming that "the states of Barbary are prohibited in future from cruising or making war upon any Christian European power," Algiers "refused to agree to this arrangement," citing international law and treaty rights.[76] Shaler seems to be basing his claim that Algiers no longer derived "benefit from pillage" on the fact that the Register of Prizes had been blank for three years while he was writing. However, as he himself notes, from 1821 to 1823 the Algerian fleet had been engaged as auxiliaries to the Ottoman fleet, fighting against Greek rebels, and that upon their return Algiers had begun a war with Spain. That war was to be particularly lucrative for Algiers. Although the corsairs registered only two prizes from other countries (one each from Tunis and the Papal States) from 1824 to 1826, they captured at least a dozen prizes from Spain. Corsairing seemed so well established in 1826 that Dey Hussein promulgated a new law clarifying the disbursement of proceeds among the corsairs, the state, and religious institutions.[77]

In 1827 Algiers began its ill-fated war with France, and the final captures in the Register of Prizes are French ships captured between August and October of that year, when the French blockade that would end in invasion was already in place. Indeed, though it was not recorded in the register and may thus have never been condemned, newspapers reported that an Algerian corsair captured a French merchant in January 1830, just months before France would invade and colonize Algiers. In the following decades, with Tripoli taken under direct Ottoman control, and Tunis under French pressure to reign in corsairing, the practice dwindled but still did not entirely disappear. Two "Barbary privateers" were reported off the coast of Menorca as late as February 1840. In 1847 an Algerian felucca (a small ship or large boat with lateen sails) based in Oran was one of four ships that reportedly took advantage of the Mexican-American War (1846–48) to obtain Mexican letters of marque to cruise against American shipping. By the time of the Paris Declaration Respecting Maritime Law of 1856, in which powers including Britain, France, and the Ottoman Empire agreed, among other measures, no longer to issue letters of marque to private vessels, the Barbary System of state-sponsored corsairing had already stumbled to a slow end, a victim of changing power dynamics and changing norms of warfare.[78]

The Tripolitan War had helped raise the United States to the level of a minor power in the Vattelian system, but minor powers were often subject to North African maritime predation, especially those without a robust naval presence in the Mediterranean. Though the consuls in the North African regencies were able to keep the peace for a few years, the rapidly dwindling number of legitimate targets for corsairing and America's widespread and unprotected merchant shipping in the Mediterranean made an eventual rupture highly likely even without implicit British support. The timing of Algiers's decision to go to war worked out poorly, however, as the War of 1812 had begun first, leading to an exodus of potential American targets.

Unlike the Tripolitan War, the second Algerian conflict (and the first in which the United States engaged militarily) did little to change the United States' place in the Vattelian system. That had been accomplished by the War of 1812, which boosted America's reputation, nationalism, naval establishment, and taste for military spending. Instead, this conflict highlighted a change that had already occurred and reaffirmed America's position on the world stage. The United States was a power now and would keep a respectable naval presence in the Mediterranean (except for occasional recalls for the ships to participate in other conflicts, such as the American Civil War and the Spanish-American War) from 1815 through the present day.

The conflict also did little to change the "Barbary System." That system was a casualty of changing patterns of competition and power, in which the American expedition was only a small part. The Exmouth expedition was a larger part but still far from "the end of the Barbary System" of North African state-regulated corsairing. Instead, the system ended gradually. Corsairs found fewer legitimate targets, and those they did find grew in relative power. Further, the end of military and mercantile great power competition between England and France removed an umbrella of acceptance that "the enemy of my enemy is my friend." The Conference of Aix-la-Chapelle's joint decision to seek an end to the Barbary System, and British and French cooperation to attempt to enforce it, failed at the time. However, it showed new norms and power dynamics in Europe—ones that had no room for corsairs, who now seemed much more akin to pirates than to privateers, who were themselves also beginning to look illegitimate.

Perhaps ironically, the North African regencies, who in the seventeenth century had served as drivers of Vattelian international universalism, were increasingly excluded from a more Eurocentric culturally driven "universal order" led by the Concert of Europe. As Christian Windler put it, "Reciprocity as understood by members of the European state system in the early nineteenth century applied only to those whom the European governments considered civilized."[79] The putative ties between the rulers of the regencies and the Ottoman Empire served as an excuse to deny the sovereignty of the regencies, and their continued participation in a corsairing system that Europeans now defined as piracy legitimized the military domination that Noah had called for in 1819.

Conclusion

WORKS OF HISTORY OFTEN tell us as much, or even more, about the era in which they were written as they do about the period they purport to illuminate. As well as attempting to consider the Barbary encounters from a new perspective—that of the law of nations—this study directly combats the presentism all too common in Barbary historiography. Despite my best efforts, I am certain that some of my own and my era's subconscious and implicit biases have made it into my interpretation as well, and I can only apologize for any that remain. The Barbary Wars have seen a large resurgence in interest in the early twenty-first century, unsurprisingly often via conscious analogy to the "War on Terror" that began after the attacks of 11 September 2001. This is not a unique phenomenon. The memory of North African contestation has been reexamined and reimagined multiple times since the contests ended, brought back by issues such as the North African campaign of World War II and by the United States–led intervention in the Libyan civil war in 2011. Interestingly, however, the first American mobilization of the memory of United States–Barbary contention involved neither North Africa nor Muslims. Instead, Americans used the purported lessons of the Algiers and Tripoli conflicts to justify the United States' actions related to the Mexican-American War (1846–48).[1]

In late 1845, during the negotiations for the annexation of Texas, President James K. Polk sent United States Army forces into the strip of land disputed between the Republic of Texas and Mexico in an act that historians contend amounted to a deliberate provocation, a verdict with which participant Ulysses S. Grant agreed later in life.[2] The pro-expansion *Philadelphia Public Ledger* defended this move as preventive and invoked the Barbary powers in its claim that America had "never waged war against any nation ... till after it had suffered numerous outrages, and all peaceful means of justice had failed."[3] In April 1846, after the annexation but with the border still disputed, Mexico supplied the United States with its seemingly desired outrage when a Mexican cavalry detachment attacked an American patrol within the disputed territory. In defense of the American response in the battles of Palo Alto and Resaca de la Palma, and of General Taylor's crossing into Mexico, all before the United States' declaration of war, the *Detroit Advertiser* invoked a highly imaginary Barbary precedent. In this version, the Tripolitan conflict took place under President Washington, who sent a naval expedition to Africa in response to "acts of depredation similar to those of Mexico against the United States" without a declaration of war. Washington then theoretically communicated those acts to Congress, which "provided means of attack to be used until peace should take place." Therefore, according to the *Detroit Advertiser*'s narrative, President Polk had simply followed "the Course of Washington" and deserved no censure.[4]

This justification for aggression against Mexico was widely promoted, appearing in at least twenty separate newspapers, sometimes in slightly different prose but all with the same basic narrative and moral conclusion. The version in the *Detroit Free Press* even included the specific claim that Mexico, "in practice like the Barbary States, captured and confiscated American vessels in time of peace."[5] Reports that Mexico had given letters of marque to four feluccas operating in the Mediterranean that were taking in prizes "to the south of Mogadore, on the Barbary coast" reinforced the connection between the new enemy and the old.[6] These connections likely resonated well, as a fictional tale of felucca-sailing, uncivilized, "lawless pirates" of Barbary had recently reached a widespread American audience. In November 1846 popular author Charles J. Peterson published "Beatrice Vernon" in his *Ladies National Magazine*. This short romance and adventure story featuring a United States Navy officer who had "won his wife" by rescuing her from the clutches of "brutal barbarian" corsairs was immediately picked up by the papers, being republished almost as often as the "Course of Washington" story justifying the Mexican-American War.[7] Via these reminders of "Barbary depredations" and the imaged history of Washington intrepidly deploying the navy in response and only seeking congressional approval post facto, the memory of the Barbary Wars was mobilized to support American imperialism and executive overreach. Even had the correct administration been cited, the authors of the Jefferson administration's carefully parsed instructions to the actual first cruise of the Mediterranean squadron would likely have been taken aback by the mid-nineteenth-century interpretation of the early republic's place in the world and of the executive's power over war making.

This study began with my frustration with the endemic use, even in scholarly works, of the term "Barbary pirates" when I was aware that the eighteenth-century definition of piracy did not include those acting under sovereign authority. To be sure, many legitimate privateers "turned pirate" when they thought they could get away with it. Captain William Kidd, for example, was a respected privateer before he was tried for piracy after capturing a British-captained and Indian-owned ship under the pretext that a pass signed by the French East India Company among the ship's papers made it a French vessel and thus a lawful prize. Even that act was theoretically law-bound, however, for all that it was a spurious argument. Had Captain Kidd taken the ship into a legitimate admiralty court, he would likely have had to release it but would not have been considered a pirate.[8] Pirates were those who acted outside the law, the "enemies of all mankind." Since North African corsairs were authorized by their governments, I considered the term pirate inappropriate. As I began to research the issue further, I discovered that corsairs were considered legitimate not only by the laws of their homelands but also by the law of nations. In the eighteenth century, European countries, even if they deplored the dubious casus belli under which Barbary powers would make war in order to create legitimate targets, nonetheless considered North African corsairs legitimate privateers.

From that kernel, it became clear not only that the new government of the independent United States accepted this interpretation of the law of nations, but also that American interactions with the North African states were intricately bound up with issues of international law and sovereignty. American diplomats (and, later, naval personnel) were not simply attempting to solve direct issues with North African predation. They also aimed to show the United States' respect for law and treaties and its ability to act as a sovereign nation to the established members of the Vattelian "republic of nations," a group among which the United States wished to be numbered and considered, as Eliga Gould put it, "treaty-worthy." This is, of course, not the only legitimate perspective from which to view United States–Barbary contestation,[9] but it is one that offers valuable insights into the foreign policy and aspirations of the early American republic. As Gould argues convincingly, the American prioritization of treaty-worthiness was "amply clear from the tripartite division with which Americans imagined the Republic's international relations, starting with 'sister nations' in Europe, as Thomas Jefferson wrote in his first address to Congress in 1801, followed by the North Africa's Barbary States, and ending with what Jefferson called 'our Indian neighbors.'"[10] This study focuses on the intersection between the first two of these tiers.

American diplomats' early attempts at engaging Europe on North African affairs after the Moroccan capture of an American merchant ship in 1784 and two Algerian captures in 1785 revealed that the United States was unable to act as a sovereign nation. The new republic was utterly dependent on pro bono help from European powers. Friendly assistance bore some fruit in the case of Spain, both in terms of direct dealings with Morocco and in terms of building diplomatic relationships that would lead to the negotiation of the ill-fated Jay–Gardoqui Treaty. For the most part, however, European nations' self-interest trumped their desire to aid the fledgling United States. Though Spain was willing to negotiate a general treaty, it was unwilling to budge on the issue of navigation rights on the Mississippi. France, though offering good offices in negotiations with Algiers, did not follow through. French officials furtively ordered their representative in Algiers not to advance American interests in the Mediterranean, as it might threaten French trade. Britain was of no help either. In fact, many Americans believed that the British were actively encouraging North African powers to prey on American shipping. The

United States was clearly incapable of dealing with Algiers and securing the release of prisoners. This inadequacy helped convince some to favor a stronger central government. Even after the ratification of the Constitution, the Washington administration's efforts to deal with Barbary challenges, especially after over a hundred more Americans were captured in 1793, exposed the republic's continuing weakness. It also made clear that America's natural partners on these issues were not the great maritime powers of Europe but the small neutral ones that shared the United States' interests and limitations in the Mediterranean.

After the funding and naval construction unleashed by the 1793 captures and, especially, the Quasi-War with France, the United States was much more capable of acting as a conventional sovereign nation. Further, American diplomats in North Africa had built ties, especially with Denmark and Sweden, on Barbary issues, culminating in Sweden's proposed anti-Barbary alliance. Thus, the Tripolitan War (1801–5) was, in many ways, the United States' debut on the European stage. Through their interactions with the North African regencies and with European nations on Barbary affairs, American politicians, diplomats, and naval personnel were able to demonstrate America's capability as a sovereign nation and their commitment to the American understanding of the Vattelian regime of international relations. The most powerful expressions of this "sisterhood of nations" were direct military cooperation with Sweden and the jointly ruled Kingdoms of Sicily and Naples. By the war's close, the United States had taken on issues common to the previously exclusively European "republic of nations" and handled them in ways the other members deemed appropriate. This was not because, as Americans are so fond of imagining now, the United States did something new, different, and even exceptional in Tripoli, but because it had done something normal. It had successfully faced a standard problem of European nations and used traditional means to deal with it, including partnering with other powers. These engagements showed American viability and trustworthiness and built ties, especially with several small European nations. As the Tripolitan War ended, the United States was well ensconced as one of the minor neutral powers—a place earned largely through interaction with its sister nations on North African issues.

As a minor neutral power, the United States was much buffeted by the great power contestation of the French Revolutionary and Napoleonic Wars. On two occasions, the United States was drawn into the periphery of these wars, both times primarily in response to great power pressure on American shipping. In the first instance, the United States fought against France in the Quasi-War of 1798–1800. In the second, America began with an attempt at economic warfare against both sides via the Embargo Act of 1807 but eventually fought against Britain in the War of 1812. The United States Navy's 1807 departure from the Mediterranean made peacekeeping with the regencies difficult. With implicit British support, Algiers went to war with the United States in 1812, though the conflict remained largely unfought until 1815. The United States was preoccupied with its contest with Britain, which also removed almost all potential American targets from Algerian cruising ranges. When America did engage Algiers after the end of the War of 1812, however, it did so with much improved relative power and the ability to act unilaterally. The United States was no longer an upstart power struggling for a place in the Vattelian system. Instead, it demonstrated itself as an established, if moderate, power on the European stage.

Although both have been depicted as crushing blows to North African corsairing, neither the American expedition of 1815 nor the Anglo-Dutch Exmouth expedition of the following year were catastrophic shocks to the Barbary System. Although it is true that Exmouth exacted promises to "end European slavery," state-controlled North African corsairing continued, and captives were simply rebranded as prisoners of war rather than slaves. The end of the endemic great power competition between Britain and France and the demise of mercantilist theories of the value of damaging others' trade, however, led to a decline of all privateering, and especially the unabashedly predatory version practiced by the North African regencies. Rather than encouraging predation against enemy shipping, Britain and France began cooperating to suppress corsairing. In 1819 a joint Anglo-French fleet attempted to bring the Barbary System to an end. Though that effort failed, it indicated an increasingly powerful Europe now cooperating against the practice. The Barbary System could not endure, though it ended gradually rather than suddenly. Soon thereafter, Europe would come together against all forms of privateering via the Paris Declaration Respecting Maritime Law of 1856. The United States would never become a party to that treaty, though it has not issued letters of marque since the declaration. In the best Vattelian tradition, the United States government now considers privateering unlawful owing to the customary international legal force of the Paris Declaration, despite never having signed it.[11]

For Americans of the twenty-first century, the history of Barbary contestation is an important reminder that functioning within the international system depends not only on power relations but also on working within international regimes and norms.

APPENDIX 1

The Al Koraschi Ebnallad Letter

On 3 May 1785 the *Pennsylvania Packet* published the satirical letter below, using a purported Algerian threat to critique Philadelphian society. Though some scholars have approached this as a genuine threat, or at least an expression of a genuine fear felt by Americans of the era, this "threat" is clearly a literary device. As mentioned in chapter 2, not only is the style obvious satire, but also the name of the purported dey is not that of any ruler of Algiers, or even an Anglicization of a valid name construction, and the *hijri* date given, while a valid date, would require the letter to have been written well before the American Revolution, corresponding to 9 July 1750. I hypothesize that this letter and its introduction from the "translator" may have been the work of noted Philadelphia wag Francis Hopkinson, a signer of the Declaration of Independence and then serving as judge of the Philadelphia Admiralty Court.

To the PRINTERS

The general concern of the following intelligence, which is just arrived by the packet, induces me to request you will publish it without loss of time—It may afford a hint to the legislature upon the defenceless situation of our river and the neglect of a station, which were it in proper order might protect us from the first approaches of a foreign invasion; at present, any paltry pirate, with a sloop of 20 guns, might lay Philadelphia under contribution, and in such a case the grossness of the insult, would not be palliated by the following gallant requisitions of the Algerines, a demand of either sort would throw us into great confusion, and whatever volunteers there might be among the ladies, I fancy most of our rich men would bear away their wealth as precipitately as possible. I am, &c. Y.Z.

P.S. The Translation is very faithful.

By Al Koraschi Ebnallad, Sovereign and Supreme Dey of Algiers, Lord of the Algerine Territories and the Atlantic Ocean.

WHEREAS the strength of our arms, the ferocity of our character, and the nature of our religion, have long continued a general hostility on our part against all those Christian powers who do not bow down to the dust before our throne, and alleviate our wrath by rich and judicious presents; and whereas certain inhabitants of a country, lately the abode of much more respectable animals than themselves, to wit, North-America, having withdrawn themselves from a subjection to their masters, nearly as mild as that which we inflict on our slaves, have not yet submitted to our prerogative or acknowledged our clemency, wherefore we have proposed to let loose our corsairs upon them; and whereas we have received certain information of the riches and abilities of the said country, particularly of the city called Philadelphia, and of the number of serviceable virgins therein, with which we might recruit our seraglio and revive our satiated appetite; we do, therefore in consideration of the before-written, hereby promulgate to the inhabitants of the said territory, that we shall shortly dispatch two of our own vessels to the river called Delaware, with directions to anchor before the said city, and reduce it instantly to ashes, unless it be redeemed by the humiliation of the inhabitants, and the following presents, to wit.

One hundred thousand pounds of their money.

Thirty thousand pounds of their most costly manufactures, and 40 of their most beautiful and virtuous damsels, not under 12 or above 18, descended from honest parents, free from mole, blemish, or latent imperfections.

And, as we are informed, these Christians affecting to secede from the true, holy and single faith of the Mussulmans, have divided their own wretched doctrines into many sects and tribes; therefore, in order to enable ourselves to decide between them, we require, that each of those sects to supply us with one fair and unblemished virgin of the above description, and one of their most zealous priests, so that we may discover the difference in each mode of belief, by its effects, as well on the bodies as the souls of its sectaries.

And for the sake of their future happiness and tranquility, we shall communicate to them our decision, in order, that laying aside all controversies and disputes, which are fit for women only, they may live as peaceable and serene as our own slaves: and we further declare, that their entire and immediate compliance with those our demands, will alone ensure our future compassion.

Done at Algiers, on the eighth of the Moon of Chaban, from the Hegira of our blessed Prophet, 1163.[1]

I base my hypothesis that Francis Hopkinson wrote this piece of satire largely on the research of Mary Shepherd. Shepherd argues for Hopkinson as the author of the controversial 1767 farce *The Disappointment,* and many of her findings also fit this letter. Part of her case for Hopkinson's authorship of *The Disappointment* revolves around her uncovering (from printing equipment signatures) that John Dunlap published the play and that Hopkinson was known for his political satire pieces published in Dunlap's newspaper, the *Pennsylvania Packet.* Further, not that it was an unusual pseudonym, Hopkinson had been known to publish under the name Y.Z. and to make risqué social critiques.[2] A short follow up to the Ebnallad letter printed only in the *Pennsylvania Packet* the following February particularly smacks of Hopkinson's style. The story claims that the Dey of Algiers had renewed his demand for American virgins and then notes "a correspondent observes, that Congress would have no difficulty in providing the quota could the article of *virginity* be dispensed with."[3]

APPENDIX 2

Article 11 of the 1796 Treaty Between the United States of America and Tripoli

On 4 November 1796 the bey of Tripoli, Yusuf Karamanli, signed the "Treaty of Peace and Friendship between the United States of America and the Bey and Subjects of Tripoli of Barbary" negotiated by Richard O'Brien, with the assistance of Spanish Consul General de Souza and under the authority of American Peace Commissioner Joel Barlow. Famously, Article 11 denied any religious justification for war between the parties and also any Christian foundation to the government of the United States. The entirety of that article's English text reads:

> As the government of the United States of America is not in any sense founded on the Christian Religion,—as it has in itself no character of enmity against the laws, religion or tranquility of Musselmen,—and as the said States never have entered into any war or act of hostility against any Mehomitan nation, it is declared by the parties that no pretext arising from religious opinions shall ever produce an interruption of the harmony existing between the two countries.[1]

The Arabic text on the facing folio, however, does not match this text and, in fact, does not appear to be an article in the treaty at all but rather a letter from Dey Hassan of Algiers to Bey Yusuf of Tripoli exhorting him to make peace with the United States. This fact remained undiscovered until Hunter Miller had the text translated in 1930 as part of the preparations for publishing the first volumes of the United States Government Printing Office's *Treaties and Other International Acts of the United States of America*. The translator he engaged, Dr. C. Snouck Hurgronje of Leiden, commented that the letter replacing the eleventh article was "drawn up by a stupid secretary who knew just a certain number of bombastic words and expressions occurring in solemn documents, but entirely failed to catch their real meaning." He concluded, therefore, that the passage was untranslatable, particularly the first three-fourths, which simply made up a formal, but unintelligible, introduction, and instead offered an attempt to "give the reader an impression of the nonsensical original."[2]

When I first encountered this assessment, I felt it overly harsh, but after doing my best to decipher the obtuse original, I understand Dr. Hurgronje's frustration. With the help of a colleague, I was able to puzzle out most of the lettering but still could not make large portions of the introduction make sense. I was, however, able to confirm that Dr. Hurgronje's assessment that Article 11 does not appear in Arabic and a letter from Dey Hassan of Algiers to Bey Yusuf of Tripoli is in its place. The letter seems less to be a notice of Algiers's peace treaty with the Americans and a recommendation that Tripoli observe it, as Dr. Hurgronje interpreted it, and more a letter of introduction for American peace negotiators and a recommendation that Tripoli assent to peace with America. Like Dr. Hurgronje, I offer my work more as an impression than a translation:

> God grant them the determination of kings, worthy counsel, goodness, and intellect, and may matters run to the good of the country and its servants. All of the goodness of heaven has been put in its place and the shelter of security is [spread?] at the hand of the landmarks of Mount Ayr [reference unknown].
>
> The matter for them [presumably the Americans] is passed via a meeting with well-protected Algiers, may God grant it blessings and victory and assist him [presumably Hassan Pasha] in doing good deeds. May all attempts to destroy it be brought down in all ways, and may it perform God's work in the age of its [tomb?] before victory makes it blessed.
>
> Peace has been spoken of lightly as a good thing, preferable and fine [illegible] through His protection, our brother and our protector, our friend the emissary, may God make them [illegible], residing in the well-protected Tripoli, may God bless it and grant it victory, [illegible], and everlasting generosity. [Illegible] make haste toward ridding ourselves of all our neglectfulness, lest the works be lost. The [illegible] attended [illegible] a praiseworthy

hand, glorified as active, beloved with [illegible], and ordered provision with the spirit of countless blessings and a pure and sincere relationship.

[This next portion is particularly muddled and resists literal translation. It seems to include some sort of aphorism about children growing well when suckled on good milk and a reference to everyone receiving salt.] May it endure for us and for you until resurrection and the day of religion's solution.

May Americans in well-protected Tripoli remain untouched and be protected under care from all hatefulness, as is the case with all [nationalities?], and that no one inflicts injury upon them, and they suffer no hurt. Similarly, Tripolitan people in the country of the Americans will be [illegible], with thriving upon their heads, all traveling freely and without one being treated differently than another until they travel well and in good health. Thus and [illegible].³

Dr. Hurgronje's "impression" may be less literal than mine (though some differences may be due to my difficulty with the Maghrebi script of the original), but it is an easier read:

Praise be to God who inspires the minds of rulers with causes of well being and righteousness! The present matter may be in the interest of the land and the servants [of God] in order that things may be put in their place. This whole affair has been opened [by omission of one letter, the Arabic reads "victories" instead of "opened"] by the intermediary of the exalted honored Prince the Lord Hassan Pasha in the protected [by God] Algiers, may God strengthen him and give him victory and help him in accomplishing good things. Thus in the beginning and in the end and may the acquiescence in his order take place by considering all his affairs, and may his endeavor repose on the fitness of his reflection. So may God make it the beginning of this peace a good and graceful measure and an introduction having for result exaltation and glorification out of love for our brother and friend and our most beloved the exalted Lord Yussuf Pasha [here follows the same word as in Article 10: *al munshi*? "residing" or "governing"] in the well protected [by God] Tripoli, may God strengthen him by His grace and His favor amen! Because our interests are one and united because our aim is that acts may succeed by overflowing justice and the observance [of duty?; of treaties?; of the Sacred Law?] becomes praiseworthy by facts entirely amen by making successful safety and security by permanence of innumerable benefits and pure and unmixed issue. Prosperity accompanies highness and facilitation of good by length of the different kinds of joy makes permanent, Praise be to God for the comprehensive benefit and your perfect gifts. May God make them permanent for us and for you thus till the day of resurrection and judgment as long as times last, amen!

Further if there are American people coming to the well protected Tripoli they wish to be by your carefulness honored [and free] from all disagreements as are indeed all the [Christian] nations so that nobody molests them and no injury befalls them, and likewise people from Tripoli if they proceed to the country of the Americans they shall be honored elevated upon the heads nobody molesting or hindering them until they travel [homeward] in good state and prosperity. Thus. And greetings![4]

NOTES

Introduction

1. "Diary of George Washington, March 1790," Entries for 22 and 23 March 1790, *Founders Online;* Richard O'Brien to Thomas Jefferson, 12 July 1790, *Founders Online*. Richard O'Brien also spelled his last name "O'Bryen" in some of his early letters, including this one. To avoid confusion, I use the spelling O'Brien throughout.
2. Richard O'Brien to Thomas Jefferson, 13 June 1789, *Founders Online*.
3. "Instructions to the American Commissioners, May–June 1784," *Founders Online*.
4. "Diary of George Washington, March 1790," entry for 23 March 1790, *Founders Online*.
5. Thomas Jefferson, "III. Report on American Trade in the Mediterranean," 28 December 1790, *Founders Online*.
6. Recent examples include Davis, *Christian Slaves, Muslim Masters;* and Oren, *Power, Faith, and Fantasy*.
7. Kilmeade and Yaeger, *Thomas Jefferson and the Tripoli Pirates,* xvii.
8. Gould, *Among the Powers of the Earth,* 12.
9. Thomas Jefferson, "First Annual Message to Congress, 8 December 1801," *Founders Online;* For additional examples of Jefferson's use of this tripartite division, see, for example, his annual messages of 1802 and 1804, as well as letters to Congress on 27 October 1807 and 8 November 1808, *Founders Online*. On the limitations of diplomacy in China, see Samuel Snow to James Madison, 22 September 1805, *Founders Online*. On the controversy over whether Indian polities were sovereign foreign nations, diplomacy with whom was a federal responsibility, or subject to state-level negotiation and compulsion, see Sadosky, *Revolutionary Negotiations,*148–75.
10. John Adams to William Knox, 15 December 1784, *Founders Online*.
11. Rufus King to James Madison, 14 May 1803, *Founders Online*.
12. Vattel, *The Law of Nations,* 15–17.
13. Thomas Jefferson to James Madison, 3 August 1793, *Founders Online*.
14. For examples of Jefferson's use of Vattel in treaty discussions, see Thomas Jefferson, "Report on Negotiations with Spain, 18 March 1792"; Jefferson, "Notes on a Cabinet Meeting," 6 May 1793; and Jefferson to Edmond Charles Genet, 17 June 1793, all on

Founders Online, among many others. For his use of "republic of nations," see Jefferson to James Monroe, 16 October 1816, *Founders Online*.

15. Edmund Randolph to James Madison, enclosure to 27 January 1784 letter; Benjamin Franklin to Richard Oswald 14 January 1783; III. The American Commissioners' Memorandum in Support of Article 23 of the Draft Prussian-American Treaty of Amity and Commerce, 10 November 1784, all on *Founders Online*.
16. Onuf and Onuf, *Federal Union, Modern World*, 107.
17. Samuel Cooper, "A Sermon Preached before His Excellency John Hancock."
18. Sadosky, *Revolutionary Negotiations*, 204.
19. See, e.g., the *AHR* forum discussion Tyrrell, "American Exceptionalism in an Age of International History"; McGerr, "The Price of the 'New Transnational History"; and Tyrell, "Ian Tyrell Responds." Quotations from Bender, *A Nation Among Nations*, 61, 93.
20. Examples of studies examining international law as a model for federal union include Bender, *A Nation Among Nations*; and Onuf and Onuf, *Federal Union, Modern World*.
21. Gould, *Among the Powers of the Earth*, 4–18, 65–67.
22. For a general discussion of practical usage of prize law, see Petrie, *The Prize Game*. For more specific examination, see Benton, "Legal Spaces of Empire"; Benton, *A Search for Sovereignty*; Tucker, "Piracy of the Eighteenth-Century Mediterranean: Navigating Laws and Legal Practices," in his *The Making of the Modern Mediterranean*; Talbot, "Ottoman Seas and British Privateers"; and White, *Piracy and Law in the Ottoman Mediterranean*.
23. Diplomatic histories include Parker, *Uncle Sam in Barbary*; and Irwin, *The Diplomatic Relations of the United States with the Barbary Powers*. Primarily military histories include Toll, *Six Frigates*; and London, *Victory in Tripoli*. Lambert, *The Barbary Wars*, combines the diplomatic and military approaches.
24. For domestic impacts of Barbary contestation, see Allison, *The Crescent Obscured*; Peskin, "The Lessons of Independence" and *Captives and Countrymen*.
25. Sheffield, *Observations on the Commerce of the American States*, 205.
26. Lambert, *The Barbary Wars*. Other publications in the tradition include Hannah Farber, "Millions for Credit," which examines the efforts to gather specie to pay Algiers's peace indemnity from the standpoint of establishing American credit and credibility in Europe as well as North Africa. Armstrong's "A Ketch Named Mastico" and "Against the Common Enemies" examine issues of United States naval cooperation with European powers on Barbary issues to counter the popular American exceptionalism narrative of the Barbary Wars. Abigail Mullen has expanded on that theme in her recently published *To Fix a National Character*.
27. Sadosky, *Revolutionary Negotiations*, centers on the intersection of Native and European diplomacy from the colonial era through Cherokee removal in the late 1830s.
28. On Thomas Jefferson's foreign policy and Barbary affairs as representing continuity, rather than a departure, see Sofka, "The Jeffersonian Idea of National Security; Revisited," in Marzagalli et al., *Rough Waters*.
29. For locations of early consulates and their roles, see Emory Johnson, "The Early History of the United States Consular Service. 1776–1792," *Political Science Quarterly* 13, no. 1 (March 1898): 19–40; and James Madison to Tobias Lear, 1 June 1801, *Founders Online*. Consuls to North Africa were somewhat of an exception to the consular role described above, as no American merchant companies were headquartered there, and

consuls were expected to protect trade as much as to facilitate it. Thus, the appointees were salaried and occupied a middle ground between the concerns of other consuls and those of more traditional ambassadors.

30. On privateering, see n. 22 above. On the legality of requiring ransom for prisoners and the state's responsibility to redeem its captive citizens, see Vattel, *The Law of Nations*, 556–57. For an account of Indian captors expecting ransom for American prisoners during the time of the early republic, see Helen Hornbeck Tanner, "The Glaize in 1792: A Composite Indian Community," *Ethnohistory* 25, no. 1 (Winter 1978): 15–39. On present and annuity-based diplomacy between Americans and Indians, see, e.g., John F. Hamtramck to Secretary of War Henry Knox, 31 March 1792, *Founders Online*. This practice was common in borderlands diplomacy of North America for over a century, as discussed in Richard White, *The Middle Ground: Indians, Empires, and Republics in the Great Lakes Region, 1650–1815* (New York: Cambridge University Press, 1991).
31. On Barbary interactions influencing American national identity formation, see Peskin, *Captives and Countrymen*; Allison, *The Crescent Obscured*; and Dzurec, *Our Suffering Brethren*.
32. E.g., Richard O'Brien's copy of the United States–Tripoli Treaty of 1797, United States Department of State, *State Department Consular Despatches*, Algiers, vol. 2, National Archives; and Zahhar, *Mudhakkirāt Al-Ḥājj Aḥmad Al-Sharīf Al-Zahhār*, 71.
33. John Adams to Thomas Jefferson, 31 July 1786, *Founders Online*.
34. Secretary of State John Marshal to John Quincy Adams, 24 July 1800, in Knox, *Naval Documents Related to the United States Wars with the Barbary Powers* (hereafter *Naval Documents*), 1:364–65.
35. Richard Dale to David Humphreys, 28 October 1801, *Naval Documents*, 1:610–11.
36. Thomas Jefferson to Robert Smith, 27 April 1804, *Founders Online*.
37. Alexander Hamilton to George Washington, 14 April 1794, *Founders Online*

1. The Barbary System

1. Cathcart, *The Captives*, 5, claims that he served as a midshipman aboard the CNS *Confederacy*. Goodin, *From Captives to Consuls*, 20–25, casts doubt on his claim, noting he may instead (or also) have served with his uncle on the privateer *Tyrannicide*.
2. Jones, "The Dreadful Effects of British Cruelty"; Goodin, *From Captives to Consuls*, 16, 22.
3. Parker, *Uncle Sam in Barbary*, 88.
4. Cathcart, *The Captives*, 5.
5. Jones, "The Dreadful Effects of British Cruelty," 438.
6. Cathcart, *The Captives*, 273.
7. This interpretation is most prevalent in jingoistic popular histories of America, with the best-known recent example being Kilmeade and Yaeger, *Thomas Jefferson and the Tripoli Pirates*. Other examples include London, *Victory in Tripoli*; and Richard Zacks, *The Pirate Coast: Thomas Jefferson, the First Marines, and the Secret Mission of 1805* (New York: Hyperion, 2005).

8. This interpretation can be found in the scholarly literature, e.g., Davis, *Christian Slaves, Muslim Masters;* and Oren, *Power, Faith, and Fantasy.* It can also be found in some popular works, including, interestingly enough, some Arabic language defenses against the pirate interpretation above, such as Ben Ahmadi, "An-Nashat al-Bahria Aljiza'iria."
9. For O'Brien's use of the term Barbary System, see Richard O'Brien to James Madison, 25 November 1801, *Founders Online.* For its use by fellow consuls, see, e.g., William Eaton to James Madison, 22 October 1802, and Tobias Lear to James Madison, 11 January 1804, *Founders Online.* Quotation about money as the god of Algiers from Richard O'Brien to Thomas Jefferson, 8 June 1786, *Founders Online.* Examples of the "capitalist enterprise" approach to corsairing among scholars include Lambert, *The Barbary Wars,* and Dávid and Fodor, *Ransom Slavery Along the Ottoman Borders.*
10. Anooshahr, *The Ghazi Sultans and the Frontiers of Islam,* 58–61, 65.
11. The Sublime Porte was a common period term for the Ottoman central administration, derived from the name of the gate that gave access to the central administrative buildings. Often shortened to simply "the Porte."
12. For shared maritime laws of predation, see Tucker, "Piracy of the Eighteenth-Century Mediterranean," in his *The Making of the Modern Mediterranean,* 123–38; and White, *Piracy and Law in the Ottoman Mediterranean.* For actors combining licit and illicit predation, see Benton, *A Search for Sovereignty;* and White, *Piracy and Law.*
13. See Dávid and Fodor, *Ransom Slavery Along the Ottoman Borders,* for discussion of ransom slavery in various incarnations. For a recent example of "slave market" rhetoric, see Oren, *Power, Faith, and Fantasy,* 22. For public ownership and public works employment of captives, see, e.g., the captivity narratives of James Cathcart and John Foss in Algiers, and Jonathan Cowdery and William Ray in Tripoli. Cathcart, *The Captives;* Foss, *A Journal of the Captivity and Sufferings;* Cowdery, *American Captives in Tripoli;* and Ray, *The Horrors of Slavery.* For discussion of agency among chattel slaves, see Berlin, *Many Thousands Gone;* and Morgan, *Slave Counterpoint.*
14. Oren, *Power, Faith, and Fantasy,* 18, offers essentialized visions of corsairs as "Arabic-speaking pirates" who styled themselves "as mujahideen—warriors in an Islamic holy war," though he does not make it clear whether he accepts that self-styling. Davis, *Christian Slaves, Muslim Masters,* argues that North African corsairing, particularly the enslavement of Christians, had deep roots but was especially a response to Spain's expulsion of the Moors. In his conception, Muslim corsairing represented a response to "the wrongs of 1492, for the centuries of crusading violence that had preceded them, and for the ongoing religious struggle that has continued to roil the Mediterranean well into modern times." Davis argues that this set off a continual and almost unchanging conflict, though he does find some room for political and economic motives. "In the three-centuries long Christian-Muslim *jihad* that began around 1500, piracy and slaving became policy instruments of state for both sides: enslaving ordinary civilians not only deprived the enemy of thousands of useful, productive citizens but also provided serviceable labor and a significant source of income through ransoming." Ibid., xxv, 141.
15. Moalla, *The Regency of Tunis and the Ottoman Porte,* 12, 64, 127.
16. Baepler, *White Slaves, African Masters,* 3.

17. Lambert, *The Barbary Wars*, 31, 37, 118.
18. On the "Northern Invasion" as the impetus for corsairing, Fodor claims this interpretation as generally agreed upon, stating that "a general consensus seems to exist concerning the underlying causes of the phenomenon: the Mediterranean piracy (*corso*) was the attempt of impoverished societies excluded from the mainstream of development to compensate themselves—at least in part—for the losses caused by the commercial ascendancy of the northerners." In his case, he is speaking of Maltese corsairing, an activity that he, like Lambert, refers to as capitalist. Tucker concurs in her discussion of Tunisian corsairing, quoting Fodor's statement above. By the seventeenth century, as Tucker notes, "protection payments" began to replace much of the direct income from corsairing. See Pál Fodor, "Maltese Pirates, Ottoman Captives" in Dávid and Fodor, *Ransom Slavery Along the Ottoman Borders*, 223; Tucker, "Piracy of the Eighteenth-Century Mediterranean," in his *The Making of the Modern Mediterranean*, 126.
19. Panzac, *Barbary Corsairs*, 21, 101 (spelling of *mudjahid* per original).
20. Anooshahr, *The Ghazi Sultans and the Frontiers of Islam*, 65.
21. All references to the Algerian Register of Prizes come from the version translated into French by a colonial archivist in Algiers: Albert Devoulx, *Le registre des prises maritimes* (hereafter *Register of Prizes*). Other Algerian documents translated into French by Devoulx are found in his *Tachrifat*, 47–48.
22. Richard O'Brien's copy of the United States–Tripoli Treaty of 1797, *Consular Despatches*, Algiers, vol. 2.
23. Zahhar, *Mudhakkirāt Al-Ḥājj Aḥmad Al-Sharīf Al-Zahhār*, 66, 71 (author's translation from Arabic). A sultana was a gold coin weighing about 3.45 grams, worth about 2.2 dollars at the time. Thus, the share was about 17.5 dollars each.
24. Quran, 9:30 (author's translation from the Arabic, which in terms of the Quran is therefore considered commentary). Other common translations exist, specifically for the second-to-last word, which comes from the root "to make small" and is thus sometimes translated as "belittle," "humble themselves," or "feel themselves subdued."
25. White, *Piracy and Law in the Ottoman Mediterranean*, 222–64.
26. Grotius, *The Law of War and Peace*, 188, 713.
27. Vattel, *The Law of Nations*, 595.
28. Grotius, *Law of War and Peace*, 715.
29. Vattel, *The Law of Nations*, 255; Michael Talbot, "Ottoman Seas and British Privateers."
30. Baron Paget to Alexander Mavrokordatos, February 19, 1697/March 1, 1698, and Baron Paget to William Raye, May 2/12, 1697, as quoted in Talbot, "Ottoman Seas and British Privateers," 62.
31. Greene, "The Ottomans in the Mediterranean," 113–14.
32. Richard O'Brien to Thomas Jefferson, 12 July 1786, *Founders Online*. The Holy Roman Empire is alternately referred to as the German or Austrian Empire, or more commonly simply "the Empire," in American documents of the late eighteenth and early nineteenth century.
33. Gøbel, "The Danish 'Algerian Sea Passes.'"
34. "A Proclamation; Requiring passes, formerly granted to ships and vessels trading in the way of the cruizers belonging to the governments on the Coast of Barbary to be

returned into the Office of the Admiralty of Great Britain; and other passes, of different forms, to be issued," 22 February 1765, as published in the *Caledonian Mercury* (Edinburgh, Scotland), 4 March 1765.
35. *The Pennsylvania Packet*, 2 August 1787, 2.
36. The term "good prize" indicated a legitimate capture subject to confiscation, often referred to by the French term *bon prise*, even in languages other than French.
37. *Register of Prizes*, 18–19; James Taylor to House of Gibbs, 17 January 1794 (misdated as 1793), *Consular Despatches*, vol. 1.
38. Joel Barlow to U.S. Minister at Paris, 14 March 1797, *Consular Despatches*, vol. 1.
39. Braudel, *The Mediterranean and the Mediterranean World*, 606–42; Fusaro et al., *Trade and Cultural Exchange in the Early Modern Mediterranean*.
40. White, *Piracy and Law in the Ottoman Mediterranean*, 145, 156–57.
41. Molloy, *De Jure Maritimo Et Navali*, 55.
42. White, *Piracy and Law in the Ottoman Mediterranean*, 267. Asma Moalla represents a dissenting voice to this interpretation. She argues in particular that Tunis was a functional governorate of the Ottoman Empire during the period of this study, basing her arguments largely on parallels in the administrative and military structures of the empire and the regency. While these parallels are accurate, I would argue they do not imply any sort of dependence. She further argues that the reason that the regencies did not pay regular taxes as other governorates did was that they were exempt in return for supplying ships to the Ottoman fleet and "waging the corso against the Christian enemies of the Porte." Here she elides the fact that the most common disputes between the regencies and the Porte were failures to send ships when summoned and corsairing against powers that were at peace with the Ottoman Empire. Moalla, *The Regency of Tunis and the Ottoman Porte*, 12.
43. Moalla, *The Regency of Tunis and the Ottoman Porte*, 50–53.
44. When Thomas Barclay visited Morocco in 1786, he reported a fleet of ten ships, but five of them were being used as transports. He also noted that there were "no Prisoners or Christian Slaves" held by the Empire. Tomas Barclay to the American Commissioners, 10 September 1786, *Founders Online*; Colley, *The Ordeal of Elizabeth Marsh*, 51, 58–59, 66, 82–83.
45. Joel Barlow to Thomas Jefferson, 18 March 1796, *Naval Documents*, 1:140–42; Richard O'Brien to David Humphreys, 1 March 1798, *Naval Documents*, 1:239–40; *Register of Prizes*, 10–12.
46. "Concerning Defenses of Algiers and Tunis," copied from *The Register in the US Chancery at Tunis*, April 1799, *Naval Documents*, 1:315–17; Panzac, *Barbary Corsairs*, 48; Richard Dale to Admiral Cederström (given as "Soderstrom"), 2 February 1802, *MS 45 Letterbook of Commodore Richard Dale*, NAV.
47. *Register of Prizes*, 10–12, 59–62.
48. Vattel, *The Law of Nations*, 532; Lieutenant Maley to Secretary of the Navy, 27 August 1800, in Knox, *Naval Documents Related to the Quasi-War*, 6:293–99 (hereafter *Quasi-War Documents*). The term "to take in" or "to send in" a ship was the act of compelling it (usually by occupying it with a prize crew) to go to a certain port for legal adjudication.
49. *Register of Prizes*, 59–62.

50. For an outstanding comparative study of American chattel slavery with the experience of Americans enslaved in North Africa, see Sears, *American Slaves and African Masters*.
51. Panzac, *Barbary Corsairs*, 114.
52. Hershenzon, *The Captive Sea*, 168.
53. Vattel, *Law of Nations*, 566.
54. Cathcart, *The Captives*, 6, 47–48.
55. White, *Piracy and Law in the Ottoman Mediterranean*, 96–97.
56. Richard O'Brien to [?] Chamic, 28 April 1787, *Consular Despatches*, vol. 1; Panzac, *Barbary Corsairs*, 116–17; Cathcart, "Diplomatic Journal and Letter Book," 357 (though Cathcart cites a different price that seems off by an order of magnitude, he does confirm the existence of a set price for captives in private hands in Algiers); Cowdery, *American Captives in Tripoli*; Ray, *The Horrors of Slavery*.
57. Oren, *Power, Faith, and Fantasy*, 22.
58. Cathcart, *The Captives*, 54, 60.
59. Cathcart, *The Captives*, 50–53, 107–8, 157, 177; Joel Barlow to Secretary of State, 18 October 1796, *Consular Despatches*, vol. 1. A prisoner who was working as secretary to the French consul to earn money for his own ransom sent Benjamin Franklin a warning that Americans might be targeted by Algerian corsairs two years before the first American captures. [Jean-Antoine?] Salva to Benjamin Franklin, 1 April 1783, *Founders Online*.
60. Oliver Spencer, *The Indian Captivity of O. M. Spencer*, ed. Milo Quaife (Chicago: Lakeside Press, 1917), 95–96.
61. Vattel, *The Law of Nations*, 566.

2. American Sovereignty Checked

1. *Pennsylvania Packet*, 24 February 1785, 2; *The Freeman's Journal, or The North-American Intelligencer*, 22 June 1785, 2.
2. Richard Parker, *Uncle Sam in Barbary*, has particularly good discussions of European mercantile concerns and American suspicions of European duplicity.
3. Sheffield, *Observations on the Commerce of the American States*, 2.
4. Sheffield, *Observations on the Commerce of the American States*, 204–5.
5. Benjamin Franklin to Robert R. Livingston, 22[–26] July 1783, *Founders Online*.
6. "I. A Plan of Treaties, 18 June 1776," *Founders Online*; "The Continental Congress: Instructions to Franklin, Silas Deane, and Arthur Lee as Commissioners to France, [24 September–22 October 1776]," *Founders Online*; "Treaty of Amity and Commerce Between The United States and France; February 6, 1778," The Avalon Project: Documents in Law, History, and Diplomacy, YLS.
7. Roberts and Tull, "Moroccan Sultan Sidi Muhammad Ibn Abdallah's Diplomatic Initiatives toward the United States, 1777–1786," 239. For an example of using this letter to claim Morocco as the first country to recognize Unites States independence, see "Morocco: The Bilateral Relations between Morocco and the USA." *MENA Report*, 20 November 2013.

8. Etienne D'Audibert Caille to the American Commissioners, 14 April 1788, *Founders Online*.
9. John Jay to President of Congress, 30 November 1780, and enclosures in Wharton and Moore, *The Revolutionary Diplomatic Correspondence of the United States*, 4:169–74; Harris, *Journals of the Continental Congress, 1774–1789*, 28:146–47 (hereafter *JCC*).
10. *JCC*, 28:146–47. In fact, it is not clear if Congress's letter was ever sent, as the only archived version of it is as an enclosure in a later letter, with a blank for the specific day it was sent.
11. Robert Montgomery to the Emperor of Morocco, 4 January 1783, Mss.B.F85, *Papers of Benjamin Franklin*, APS.
12. *JCC*, 26:144.
13. John Adams to Robert Montgomery, 18 June 1783, *Founders Online*.
14. Robert Montgomery to John Adams, 2 August 1783, *Founders Online*.
15. Eliaho Leve to Robert Montgomery, 23 April 1783, *Papers of Benjamin Franklin*; John Adams to Robert Livingston, 12 July 1783, *Founders Online*; Giacomo Francisco Crocco to Benjamin Franklin, 15 July 1783, *Founders Online*.
16. Giacomo Francisco Crocco to Benjamin Franklin, 25 November 1783, *Founders Online*.
17. Benjamin Franklin to Giacomo Francisco Crocco, 15 December 1783, *Founders Online*.
18. Thomas Jefferson, "III. Report on American Trade in the Mediterranean," 28 December 1790, *Founders Online*; *JCC*, 26:154. The disposal instructions derive from Jefferson's report and were omitted from the resolution itself, likely to add flexibility as to when the commissioners could offer presents.
19. Etienne d'Audibert Caille to Benjamin Franklin, 6 July 1784, *Founders Online*; Franklin's Journal, 26 June–27 July 1784, *Founders Online*; *Pennsylvania Packet*, 10 August 1784, 2.
20. *Pennsylvania Packet*, 24 February 1785, 2.
21. Oren, *Power, Faith, and Fantasy*, 22.
22. *The Freeman's Journal, or The North-American Intelligencer*, 22 June 1785, 2.
23. William Carmichael to Thomas Jefferson, 25 November 1784, *Founders Online*.
24. William Carmichael to Thomas Jefferson, 2 September 1785, *Founders Online*.
25. Roberts and Tull, "Moroccan Sultan Sidi Muhammad Ibn Abdallah's Diplomatic Initiatives," 248; "Extract of a letter from Madrid, August 15," *Pennsylvania Packet*, 12 November 1785, 2.
26. Rumor had the *London Packet* captured by Algiers with Benjamin Franklin aboard, and newspapers even printed letters supposedly from the ship's captain, Thomas Truxton, reporting their capture. These letters were fictitious, however, and Franklin and Truxton had already arrived safely in Philadelphia by the time some of them were printed. Truxton, who was a veteran of the Continental Navy, would go on to fame as the senior officer of the United States Navy during the Quasi-War with France.
27. Thomas Jefferson to John Adams, 4 September 1785, *Founders Online*.
28. "I. Commission," 11 October 1785, *Founders Online*.
29. Thomas Barclay to John Adams, 24 November 1785, *Founders Online*; Thomas Jefferson to John Adams, 27 March 1786, *Founders Online*.
30. Thomas Barclay to the American Commissioners, 10 June 1786; Thomas Barclay to the American Commissioners, 26 June 1786; The Moroccan-American Treaty of Peace

and Friendship, [28 June 1786]; Thomas Barclay to the American Commissioners, 10 September 1786, all in *Founders Online*.
31. Thomas Barclay to the American Commissioners, 10 September 1786, *Founders Online*; American Commissioners to John Jay, 27 January 1787, *Founders Online*.
32. Richard O'Brien to Thomas Jefferson, 25 September 1787, *Founders Online*.
33. Richard O'Brien to Thomas Jefferson, 25 September 1787, *Founders Online*; Richard O'Brien to William Armistead Burwell, 12 July 1805, *Founders Online*; Richard O'Brien to Andrew Monroe, February 1822, as printed in Randall, *The Life of Thomas Jefferson*, 2:324–25; Virginia Navy Board, "Payrolls and account of clothing of the Brig Jefferson, 1780–1781," Accession 44215, Virginia Navy Board record group (RG#2), Library of Virginia; Mathew Irwin to George Washington, 9 July 1789, *Founders Online*.
34. For examples of articles teasing about O'Brien's nautical phrasing, see "How Does It Look?," *Aurora General Advertiser*, 23 August 1808, 2; "Authentic News from Hayti," *Aurora General Advertiser*, 7 April 1809, 2.
35. Richard O'Brien, Isaac Stephens, and Zaccheus Coffin to John Adams, 27 August 1785, *Founders Online*; Cathcart, *The Captives*, 23–24.
36. Richard O'Brien to Thomas Jefferson, 24 August 1785, *Founders Online*.
37. "III. Supplementary Instructions to John Lamb," 11 October 1785, *Founders Online*.
38. Thomas Jefferson to Richard O'Brien, 4 November 1785, *Founders Online*.
39. William Carmichael to the American Commissioners, 3 February 1786, *Founders Online*; Pennsylvania Gazette, 31 May 1786, 2; *Vermont Gazette*, 26 June 1786, 3; *Pennsylvania Packet*, 28 May 1787, 3; "Intelligence from Algiers," *Independent Gazetteer*, 28 May 1787, 2.
40. "IX. The American Commissioners to the Comte de Vergennes, 1–11 October 1785," *Founders Online*; Parker, *Uncle Sam in Barbary*, 217–19.
41. John Lamb to the American Commissioners, 20 May 1786, *Founders Online*.
42. Richard O'Brien to John Adams, 12 May 1792, *Founders Online*; Richard O'Brien et al., to Thomas Jefferson, 8 June 1786, *Founders Online*. The letter does not detail what attributes Lamb showed that were ungentlemanly, though Cathcart's captivity narrative referred to him as much given to swearing, and a later letter from O'Brien implied that matters above simple trade were beyond him. The prisoners may have been particularly surprised by Lamb's unpolished manner given that he had been an officer during the Revolution. For more on norms of gentility, see Cox, *A Proper Sense of Honor*; and Foster, *New Men*. For notions of appropriate masculine behavior among Americans in a North African context, see Goodin, *From Captives to Consuls*, 34–52.
43. Thomas Jefferson to John Adams, 11 July 1786, *Founders Online*.
44. William Carmichael to Thomas Jefferson, 31 July 1786, *Founders Online*.
45. Paul R. Randall to the American Commissioners, 14 May 1786, *Founders Online*; William Carmichael to Thomas Jefferson, 17 December 1786, *Founders Online*.
46. John Adams to Thomas Jefferson, 31 July 1786, *Founders Online*.
47. Thomas Jefferson to John Jay, 23 May 1786; John Lamb to the American Commissioners, 20 May 1786; American Commissioners to John Jay, 28 March 1786; Thomas Jefferson to John Jay, 1 February 1787, all on *Founders Online*.
48. *JCC*, 34:393–96.
49. *JCC*, 34:419–20.

50. *JCC*, 34:451–53, 29:843–44.
51. Thomas Jefferson to John Jay, 4 May 1788, *Founders Online*.
52. *Pennsylvania Packet*, 26 February 1788, 3; Richard O'Brien to Thomas Jefferson, 28 April 1787, *Founders Online*.
53. Richard O'Brien to Thomas Jefferson, 25 September 1787, *Founders Online*; Enclosure: Richard O'Brien to Mathew and Thomas Irwin, 20 December 1788, *Founders Online*.
54. The most complete treatment of this issue is Peskin, *Captives and Countrymen*. For more focus on the issues surrounding the earliest captures, see Peskin, "The Lessons of Independence." The most recent treatment is Dzurec, *Our Suffering Brethren*, though I found this work added little to Peskin's. For discussion of the American interpretation of North African corsairs as British proxies in ongoing economic warfare, see Lambert, *The Barbary Wars*.
55. Americanus, "A Sketch of the Political State of America Number II," *Gazette of the United States*, 29 April 1789, 2–3.
56. E.g., O'Brien's letter complaining of Consul Logie's treatment of the prisoners was printed in at least four different states. My research found it in *Boston Independent Chronicle*, 25 May 1786; *Independent Gazetteer*, 27 May 1786; *Maryland Gazette*, 8 June 1786; and *Vermont Gazette*, 26 June 1786. Doubtless many other papers that I did not search printed it as well.
57. *Pennsylvania Packet*, 17 August 1786, 3.
58. The most developed accounts of this dynamic and its use as critiquing not only slavery but also other aspects of American culture are found in Allison, *The Crescent Obscured*; and Marr, *The Cultural Roots of American Islamicism*.
59. *Pennsylvania Packet*, 31 August 1786, 3.
60. Allison, *The Crescent Obscured*, 104–6. For a discussion of honor culture, including print wars, see Freeman, *Affairs of Honor*.
61. For a critiques of gender roles, see Allison's analysis of Susanna Rowson's 1794 play *Slaves in Algiers* in Allison, *The Crescent Obscured*, 74–77. For "pursuit of wealth and pleasure," see Anonymous, *The Algerine Spy in Pennsylvania* (Philadelphia: Prichard & Hall, 1787), reprinted as Markoe and Marr, *The Algerine Spy in Pennsylvania*, 62.
62. Recent examples include Dzurec, *Our Suffering Brethren*; and Jacob Crane, "Barbary(an) Invasions: The North African Figure in Republican Print Culture," *Early American Literature* 50, no. 2 (2015): 331–58. As an example of a source often quoted to support notions of American fear, see John Banister to Thomas Jefferson, 2 December 1785, *Founders Online*. While Banister does state that Americans "are greatly alarmed at the hostility of the Algerines," he continues "which puts a stop to our eastern Trade to Spain, and all Countries in the Mediterranean," making it clear that the alarm is not about a potential for attacks on the American coast.
63. Crane, "Barbary(an) Invasions," 340; Dzurec, *Our Suffering Brethren*, 39, 206.
64. As an example of comment-free reprinting, even of news the publishers knew to be incorrect, on 22 November 1785, the *Pennsylvania Packet*, among many other papers, republished without comment a letter putatively from Thomas Truxton reporting the capture of his ship by Algerian corsairs and his and Benjamin Franklin's imprisonment. This letter was published in spite of the fact that the *Pennsylvania Packet* had covered Franklin's safe arrival in Philadelphia on 15 September and toasts given in honor of

the event as recently as 10 November. It was only in December, with some readers having apparently expressed confusion, that the *Pennsylvania Packet* noted that the letter purported to be from Truxton was "generally discredited." *Pennsylvania Packet*, 22 November 1785, 2; 15 September 1785, 3; 10 November 1785, 2; 2 December 1785, 2.
65. *Pennsylvania Packet*, 3 May 1785, 2.
66. *Pennsylvania Packet*, 17 February 1786, 2.
67. *Pennsylvania Packet*, 21 March 1786, 2–3.
68. *Pennsylvania Gazette*, 19 April 1786, 3.
69. "From the *Boston Independent*" as reprinted in *Pennsylvania Packet*, 10 July 1786, 3.
70. Markoe and Marr, *The Algerine Spy in Pennsylvania*, 101–2.
71. *Pennsylvania Packet*, 3 April 1788, 2.
72. *Pennsylvania Packet*, 5 June 1788, 2.
73. III. Report on American Trade in the Mediterranean, 28 December 1790, *Founders Online*; VII. Senate Resolutions on the Algerine Captives, 1 February 1791, *Founders Online*.
74. VIII. The President to the Senate, 22 February 1791, *Founders Online*.
75. Richard O'Brien to Congress, 28 April 1791, *Naval Documents*, 1:28–30; *The Times* (London), 22 August 1791, 2.
76. George Washington, "Conversation with a Committee of the United States Senate," 12 March 1792, *Founders Online*; George Washington to Thomas Jefferson, 10 March 1792, *Founders Online*; Thomas Jefferson, "Memorandum of Conference with the President on Treaty with Algiers," 11 March 1792, *Founders Online*; United States Congress, "An Act making certain appropriations therein specified," *United States Statutes at Large*, volume 1: *Public Acts of the Second Congress, 1st Session, Chapter 41*, 8 May 1792.
77. Thomas Jefferson to John Paul Jones, 1 June 1792, *Founders Online*.
78. George Washington to Thomas Barclay, 11 June 1792, *Founders Online*.
79. For the dynastic struggle following Mohammed II's death and the barriers it created to American diplomacy, see Thomas Barclay–Thomas Jefferson correspondence of 1791–92; Thomas Barclay to George Washington, 27 December 1792; Thomas Barclay to Thomas Jefferson, 27 December 1792; David Humphreys to Thomas Jefferson, 23 January 1793, all on *Founders Online*.
80. David Humphreys–Thomas Jefferson correspondence, 23 January 1793 to 8 October 1793, *Founders Online*; James Simpson to Secretary of State, 25 November 1793, *Naval Documents*, 1:55–56; David Humphreys to Robert Montgomery, 1 December 1793, *Naval Documents*, 1:56–57.
81. Thomas Jefferson to John Paul Jones, 1 June 1792, *Founders Online*.

3. A Minor Power

1. David Humphreys to Secretary of State, 6 October 1796, in Knox, *Naval Documents Related to Wars with Barbary Powers*, 1:175–76 (hereafter *Naval Documents*); Miller, *Treaties and Other International Acts of the United States of America*, 2:312, 378; Richard O'Brien to Secretary of State, 16 February 1796, *Naval Documents*, 1:131–32; David Humphreys to Secretary of State, 5 August 1796, *Naval Documents*, 1:170–72.

2. "Treaty of Peace and Friendship between the United States of America and the Bey and Subjects of Tripoli of Barbary," signed 4 November 1796, ratified by United States Senate 10 June 1797, Article 11, YLS; Miller, *Treaties*, 2:377–79.
3. On inability to enforce treaties, see, e.g., *Pennsylvania Gazette*, 19 April 1786, 3. On Constitutional supremacy, see United States Constitution, Article VI.
4. David Humphreys, "Instructions to Robert Montgomery, U.S. Consul, Alicante, 1 December 1793," *Naval Documents*, 1:56–57.
5. Farber, "Millions for Credit."
6. William Eaton to Secretary of State, 21 July 1800, *Naval Documents*, 1:363; William Eaton to Elizabeth Eaton, 6 November 1800, in Prentiss, *Life of Eaton*, 180; William Eaton to Don Antonio Porcile, 25 April 1801, in Franklin and Lowrie, *American State Papers*, volume entitled *Claims*, 328.
7. Secretary of State John Marshal to John Quincy Adams, 24 July 1800, *Naval Documents*, 1:364–65.
8. III. Report on American Trade in the Mediterranean, 28 December 1790, *Founders Online*,
9. For anti-navalism, see, e.g., the sarcastic letter purportedly in support of establishing a navy in Benjamin Franklin Bache's *Aurora General Advertiser*, 12 February 1794, 2, which equates a navy with aristocratic leanings and a desire to subdue the population. This letter is possibly by Bache himself, who was famously anti-navy. It ends with a statement that it will be continued, and thus does not include an attribution. A search of the remainder of the month's issues does not reveal any continuation of the letter. For the cancellation clause, see United States Statutes at Large, "An Act to provide a Naval Armament," 27 March 1794, as printed in *Naval Documents*, 1:69–70.
10. "An Act making further provision for the expenses attending the intercourse of the United States with foreign nations; and further to continue in force the act intituled 'An act providing the means of intercourse between the United States and foreign nations,'" 20 March 1794, in Peters, *Public Statutes at Large*, 1:345.
11. For unspecified reasons, the budget was given to Humphreys as $800,000, rather than the $1 million appropriated by Congress. Edmund Randolph to George Washington, 19 July 1794, *Founders Online*; Secretary of State to David Humphreys, 19 July 1794, *Naval Documents*, 1:77–78; Richard O'Brien to David Humphreys, October 1794, *Naval Documents*, 1:82–86; "Presents exacted from the United States by the Dey of Algiers," 22 December 1794, *Naval Documents*, 1:89–90; Secretary of State to David Humphreys, 28 March 1795, *Naval Documents*, 1:94–96; David Humphreys to Joseph Donaldson, 18 May 1795, *Naval Documents*, 1:98–99.
12. David Humphreys to Thomas Jefferson, 29 April 1793, *Founders Online*; Cathcart, *The Captives*, 157; Secretary of State to David Humphreys, 19 July 1794, *Naval Documents*, 1:77–78; Secretary of State to David Humphreys, 28 March 1795, *Naval Documents*, 1:94–96; Cathcart, *The Captives*, 158–61.
13. Joseph Donaldson to Secretary of State, 3 May 1796, National Archives, Record Group 59, Consular Despatches, Algiers, vol. 1.
14. Cathcart, *The Captives*, 176; Joseph Donaldson to Secretary of State, 7 September 1795, Consular Despatches, Algiers, vol. 1; Parker, *Uncle Sam in Barbary*, 104.

15. Richard O'Brien to Secretary of State, 16 February 1796, *Naval Documents*, 1:131–32; David Humphreys to Dey Hassan Bashaw of Algiers, 16 February 1796, *Naval Documents*, 1:170–72; Cathcart, "Diplomatic Journal and Letter Book," 426.
16. David Humphreys to Secretary of State, 26 April 1796, *Naval Documents*, 1:151–53; David Humphreys to Secretary of State, 5 August 1796, *Naval Documents*, 1:170–72.
17. Cantor, "A Connecticut Yankee in a Barbary Court," 89–90.
18. For a detailed narrative of the efforts to gather payment and their implications for American credit, see Farber, "Millions for Credit."
19. Miller, *Treaties*, 2:377–79.
20. Joel Barlow to Secretary of State, 18 October 1796, Consular Despatches, Algiers, vol. 1.
21. Barlow, *Political Writings*, 35, 49.
22. Noah Webster to Joel Barlow, 13 October 1808, as printed in Todd, *Life and Letters of Joel Barlow*, 220–21.
23. For the Tripoli treaty and negotiations, see Miller, *Treaties*, 249–385. Miller gives the impression that Barlow made, or had made, a translation and added it to the left-hand folios, which would have been otherwise blank, but this is extremely unlikely. For an example of assuming that Barlow translated the Arabic text personally, see Sherman D. Wakefield, "The Treaty with Tripoli," *Freedom from Religion Foundation Legal Archives*, June/July 1997, https://ffrf.org/legal/item/16944-the-treaty-with-tripoli.
24. For ratification, see Lowrie, *Journal of the Executive Proceedings of the Senate*, 1:244. For McHenry's objection, see James McHenry to Oliver Wolcott, 26 September 1800, in Gibbs, *Memoirs of the Administrations of Washington and John Adams*, 2:420–21.
25. For the use of the Tripoli treaty to support Jefferson's secularism, see "To the People of the United States," *Aurora General Advertiser*, 22 September 1800, 2. For McHenry's response, see James McHenry to Oliver Wolcott, 26 September 1800, in Gibbs, *Memoirs of the Administrations of Washington and John Adams*, 2:420–21.
26. Joseph Donaldson to David Humphreys to Secretary of State, 24 October and 2 November 1795, *Naval Documents*, 1:120–21; "Copy of a Truce Concluded between the United States of America and the Regency of Tunis," 8 November 1795, *Naval Documents*, 1:121–22.
27. Cantor, "A Connecticut Yankee in a Barbary Court," 102–3.
28. Edward Rand to Joel Barlow, 23 June 1796, *Naval Documents*, 1:157–58.
29. Joel Barlow to Edward Rand, 2 August 1796, Consular Despatches, Algiers, vol. 2.
30. Gorham Parsons and Edward Rand, Petition to Congress for restoration of Schooner Eliza to former owners, 9 December 1797, *Naval Documents*, 1:225–27.
31. Secretary of State to Richard O'Brien, 21 December 1798, *Naval Documents*, 1:280–83.
32. Jessup and Deak, "The Early Development of the Law of Neutral Rights"; Nathaniel Skinner to George Washington, 15 October 1793, Consular Despatches, Algiers, vol. 1.
33. Thomas Jefferson to Robert R. Livingston, 9 September 1801, *Founders Online*.
34. Joel Barlow to U.S. Minister at Paris, 14 March 1797, Consular Despatches, Algiers, vol. 1.
35. Samuel Snow to James Madison, 22 September 1805, *Founders Online*; Edward Carrington to James Madison, 9 April 1807, *Founders Online*; Joel Barlow to U.S. Minister at Paris, 14 March 1797, Consular Despatches, Algiers, vol. 1.

36. Joel Barlow to U.S. Minister at Paris, 14 March 1797, Consular Despatches, Algiers, vol. 1.
37. Richard O'Brien, "Remarks and Observations Relative to the Affairs of the United States of America with the Bashaw of Algiers," undated but filed with late 1796 documents, Consular Despatches, Algiers, vol. 2.
38. Foss, *A Journal of the Captivity and Sufferings*, 144; Joel Barlow to Secretary of State, 18 August 1797, *Naval Documents*, 1:206–10; Joseph Donaldson to Secretary of State, 5 and 12 January 1797, Consular Despatches, Algiers, vol. 1; Joel Barlow to Secretary of State, 18 August 1797, *Naval Documents*, 1:206–10.
39. James Madison to William Eaton and Richard O'Brien, 20 May 1801, *Naval Documents*, 1:460–62.
40. John Adams to United States Congress, 23 June 1797, *Founders Online*.
41. Joel Barlow, "Certificate concerning the Commission of the Dey of Algiers to Richard O'Brien to purchase Two Cruisers in America," 12 January 1797, *Naval Documents*, 1:192; Richard O'Brien, "Remarks and Observations Relative to the Affairs of the United States of America with the Bashaw of Algiers," n.d., Consular Despatches, Algiers, vol. 2; "List of Candidates for Offices," June 1797, *Founders Online*.
42. Joel Barlow to Secretary of State, 4 May 1796, *Naval Documents*, 1:154–55.
43. Secretary of State to Joel Barlow, 4 May 1796, *Naval Documents*, 1:182–83; "List of Candidates for Offices," June 1797, *Founders Online*.
44. Prentiss, *Life of Eaton*, 19–54; "List of Candidates for Offices," June 1797, *Founders Online*. On the controversy over Eaton's court martial and Gaither's activities and cashiering, see their respective testimony at the trial of Aaron Burr in *The National Intelligencer and Washington Advertiser*, 12 October 1807, 2. The Blount Conspiracy was an abortive attempt, led by Senator William Blount, to prop up land prices in the Southwest by helping Britain seize Spanish Florida and Louisiana in exchange for guaranteeing American navigation rights on the Mississippi. Eaton arrested co-conspirator Nicholas Romayne in July 1797. *Philadelphia Inquirer*, 5 December 1797, 3.
45. Mullen, *To Fix a National Character*, 13; Richard O'Brien to David Humphreys, 1 March 1798, *Naval Documents*, 1:239–40; Secretary of State to Richard O'Brien, 29 December 1797, *Naval Documents*, 1:231–34; Secretary of State, "Special Instructions to Richard O'Brien, Esquire," 29 December 1797, *Naval Documents*, 1:234–36.
46. Secretary of State to James Leander Cathcart, 20 December 1798, *Naval Documents*, 1:275–76.
47. Prentiss, *Life of Eaton*, 20, 54; Allison, *The Crescent Obscured*, 164–65.
48. Wright and MacLeod, *The First Americans in North Africa*, 30. For more on American middle- and upper-class women's engagement in the public sphere through activities related to their "appropriate domestic roles," see Norton, *Liberty's Daughters*.
49. Wright and MacLeod, *The First Americans in North Africa*, 30.
50. William Eaton to Elizabeth O'Brien, 22 July 1799, Letter and commonplace book EA 200 1799 April 8 to 1802 February 13, William Eaton Papers, Huntington Library (hereafter Eaton Papers); Wright and MacLeod, *The First Americans in North Africa*, 30.
51. Sadosky, *Revolutionary Negotiations*, 94, 154.

52. For discussion of blurred class lines and competing cultural systems of republicanism and gentility, see Bushman, *The Refinement of America*.
53. Richard O'Brien to Secretary of State, 6 April 1798, *Naval Documents*, 1:320–21.
54. Richard O'Brien to Secretary of State, 6 April 1798, *Naval Documents*, 1:320–21.
55. Joel Barlow to Secretary of State, 18 October 1796, Consular Despatches, Algiers, vol. 2; Richard O'Brien, "Remarks and Observations Relative to the Affairs of the United States of America with the Bashaw of Algiers," n.d., Consular Despatches, Algiers, vol. 2.
56. O'Brien, "Remarks and Observations Relative to the Affairs of the United States of America with the Bashaw of Algiers."
57. O'Brien, "Remarks and Observations Relative to the Affairs of the United States of America with the Bashaw of Algiers."
58. Richard O'Brien to Secretary of State, 12 October 1798, in Knox, *Quasi-War Documents*, 1:523. Richard O'Brien to Secretary of State, 25 November 1801, *Naval Documents*, 1:625.
59. Tobias Lear to James Madison, 14 July 1803, *Founders Online*. For more on symbols of nationhood and their importance in the early republic, particularly during the Revolutionary War, see Irvin, *Clothed in the Robes of Sovereignty*. The discussion of passports here is in reference to a ship's documents, rather than an individual's, but a concurrent issue regarding protection for citizens was ongoing. The modern individual passport's forerunner was likely the sailor's "protection" document that certified United States citizenship and thus theoretically shielded one from impressment, most commonly, but not exclusively, by the British navy. For more on this issue and on national identity among sailors, see Perl-Rosenthal, *Citizen Sailors*.
60. James Cathcart to Secretary of State, 09 July 1799, *Naval Documents*, 1:331.
61. Richard O'Brien to Secretary of State, 12 October 1798, *Naval Documents*, 1:258–62.
62. James Cathcart to Secretary of State Pro tempore Charles Lee, 18 October 1800, *Naval Documents*, 1:382.
63. Joel Barlow to Secretary of State, 18 October 1796, Consular Despatches, Algiers, vol. 1.
64. James Cathcart to Secretary of State Pro tempore Charles Lee, 18 October 1800, *Naval Documents*, 1:382.
65. James Cathcart to James Madison, 4 June 1801, *Founders Online*.
66. William Eaton to James Madison, 8 June 1802, *Founders Online*.
67. William Eaton to James Madison, 6 March 1801, *Founders Online*; Richard O'Brien to John Gavino, U.S. Consul to Gibraltar, 10 January 1799, *Naval Documents*, 1:289. For discussion of the interpersonal relationship among O'Brien, Cathcart, and Eaton, see Allison, *The Crescent Obscured*, 153–86; and Goodin, *From Captives to Consuls*, 80–110. Peskin offers a different interpretation that sees Eaton's views of O'Brien and Catchart as an artifact of their time in captivity, leading to an unmasculine servility: Peskin, *Captives and Countrymen*, 137–62. For an argument that the interpersonal disfunction did not affect the consuls' ability to function as diplomats, see Parker, *Uncle Sam in Barbary*.
68. E.g., William Eaton to Secretary of State, 15 June 1799, *Naval Documents*, 1:326–28. James Cathcart to James Madison, 16 May 1801, *Founders Online*.

69. Richard O'Brien to James Madison, 24 June 1801, *Founders Online*.
70. William Eaton to Stephen Pynchon, 8 April 1799, in Prentiss, *Life of Eaton*, 156–61; William Eaton to James Madison, 1 February 1803, *Founders Online*; Allison, *The Crescent Obscured*, 163.
71. William Eaton to James Madison, November 1802, *Founders Online*.
72. Richard O'Brien to James Madison, 16 September 1802, *Founders Online*.
73. William Eaton to James Madison, 12 December 1801, *Founders Online*.
74. James Cathcart to James Madison, 21 March 1801, *Founders Online*.
75. All quotations from William Eaton to James Madison, 28 June 1801, *Founders Online*. For examples of cost-benefit analyses, see Barlow and O'Brien's calculations of the costs of a peace versus the benefits of Mediterranean trade: Barlow to Secretary of State, 17 April 1796, *Naval Documents*, 1:146–50; Richard O'Brien, "Remarks and Observations Relative to the Affairs of the United States of America with the Bashaw of Algiers," n.d., Consular Despatches, Algiers, vol. 2.
76. Journal of James L. Cathcart, 28 February to 13 April 1799, *Naval Documents*, 1:306–13.
77. William Eaton to James Madison, 12 September 1802, *Founders Online*. Eaton does not specify which minister he was conversing with in this incident, but such demands usually came from the prime minister.
78. James Cathcart to Secretary of State, 27 May 1800, *Naval Documents*, 1:356–57; James Cathcart to Secretary of State, 27 May 1800, *Naval Documents*, 1:382–84; Protest of James L. Cathcart, U.S. Consul, Tripoli, 29 October 1800, *Naval Documents*, 1:391–94; James Cathcart to Supreme Commandant, Tripoli, 19 February 1801, *Naval Documents*, 1:420–21; James Cathcart to the Bashaw of Tripoli, 14 May 1801, *Naval Documents*, 1:453.
79. Samuel Shaw to John Jay, 31 December 1786, *Founders Online*; Samuel Shaw to John Jay, 21 December 1787, *Founders Online*.
80. James Cathcart to James Madison, 29 November 1802, *Founders Online*; Richard O'Brien to William Eaton, 13 January 1800, Simon Gratz Autograph Collection, *Historical Society of Pennsylvania*. (The Historical Society of Pennsylvania holds portions of O'Brien's papers in several different collections. All can be found at https://discover.hsp.org/search/Results?lookfor="richard o'brien" and will be referenced collectively hereafter as O'Brien Papers.)
81. William Eaton, account dated 31 October 1802, Eaton Papers, box 3, 119.
82. Richard O'Brien to Secretary of State, 13 March 1800, *Naval Documents*, 1:350–51.
83. Rousseau, *Annales Tunisiennes*, 237, 239; William Eaton to Don Antonio Porcile, 25 April 1801, Franklin and Lowrie, *American State Papers, Claims*, 328; Prentiss, *Life of Eaton*, 120, 406–8; James Madison from William Eaton, 12 November 1802, *Founders Online*; Antoine Porcile to Thomas Jefferson, 22 July 1804, *Founders Online*. Eaton's claim for the Porcile ransom was part of his disputed accounts that the Department of State referred to Congress. Eaton made claims to Congress in 1804 and 1806 that were eventually settled, though the fate of the specific line items is not recorded. See Franklin and Lowrie, *American State Papers, Claims*, 323–32.
84. Memo of the Secretary of War, 10 May 1797, *Quasi-War Documents*, 1:5; Toll, *Six Frigates*, 76–86; Secretary of State to David Humphreys, 7 May 1800, *Quasi-War Documents*, 5:483–84; Richard O'Brien to William Eaton, 19 October 1800, *Naval Documents*, 1:384–85.

85. "Account of William Brown, commanding the ship *Brutus*, concerning the voyage to Constantinople, of the U.S.S. *George Washington*," 11 December 1800, *Naval Documents*, 1:385–88.
86. Richard O'Brien to Secretary of State, 27 January 1801, *Naval Documents*, 1:413–16.
87. Richard O'Brien to Captain William Bainbridge, 10 October 1800, *Naval Documents*, 1:380.
88. Extract from the log of USS *George Washington* Captain William Bainbridge, U.S. Navy commanding, 9 October 1800, *Naval Documents*, 1:378.
89. Richard O'Brien to Secretary of State, 22 October 1800, *Naval Documents*, 1:388.
90. William Eaton to Secretary of State, 1–11 November 1800, *Naval Documents*, 1:397–98.
91. James Madison to William Eaton and Richard O'Brien, 20 May 1801, *Naval Documents*, 1:460–62.
92. Secretary of State to William Smith, 2 April 1799, *Quasi-War Documents*, 3:9; William Smith to Secretary of State, 19 June 1799, *Quasi-War Documents*, 3:363–64; President Adams to Secretary of State, 24 August 1799, *Quasi-War Documents*, 4:121.
93. Captain William Bainbridge to Secretary of the Navy, 17 November 1800, *Naval Documents*, 1:401.
94. Captain William Bainbridge to James Leander Cathcart, 10 January 1801, *Naval Documents*, 1:410.
95. Captain William Bainbridge to James Leander Cathcart, 10 January 1801, *Naval Documents*, 1:410; Richard O'Brien to William Eaton, 27 January 1801, O'Brien Papers; Richard O'Brien to Secretary of State, 27 January 1801, *Naval Documents*, 1:413–16; Extract from the log of USS *George Washington* Captain William Bainbridge, U.S. Navy commanding, 31 January 1801, *Naval Documents*, 1:417; Thomas Jefferson to Robert Montgomery, 20 February 1793, *Founders Online*.
96. Robert Montgomery to Secretary of State, 19 February 1801, *Founders Online*.
97. Extract from the log of USS *George Washington* Captain William Bainbridge, U.S. Navy commanding, 9 October 1800, *Naval Documents*, 1:419. On the varying estimates of French citizens, it seems the major discrepancy is whether children were counted. O'Brien makes it "60 men women and children," Bainbridge logged "5 ladies and Thirty gentlemen," and Robert Montgomery reported "the Commissary and whole Commercial Relation of the French Republic at Algiers, in number about forty."
98. William Eaton to Richard O'Brien, 23 June 1800, *Naval Documents*, 1:362; William Eaton to Secretary of State, 21 July 1800, *Naval Documents*, 1:363–64; William Eaton to Elizabeth Eaton, 15 August 1800, Prentiss, *Life of Eaton*, 178–79; William Eaton to Elizabeth Eaton, 6 November 1800, Prentiss, *Life of Eaton*, 180–81.
99. William Eaton to James Madison, 17 November 1801, *Founders Online*; James Madison to William Eaton, 10 May 1802, *Founders Online*; William Eaton to James Madison, 9 November 1802, *Founders Online*; William Eaton to James Madison, 17 November 1801, *Founders Online*; Franklin and Lowrie, *American State Papers, Claims*, 328.
100. Prentiss, *Life of Eaton*, 209–10.
101. Prentiss, *Life of Eaton*, 210.
102. James L. Cathcart to Nicholas Nissen, 15 May 1801, *Naval Documents*, 1:453–54.
103. DeConde, *The Quasi-War*, 17; Toll, *Six Frigates*, 183.
104. Timothy Pickering to John Adams, 24 September 1798, *Founders Online*.

105. John Quincy Adams to James Madison, 25 June 1801, *Founders Online*.
106. John Marshall to John Quincy Adams, 24 July 1800, *Naval Documents*, 1:364–65.
107. Circular issued by James L. Cathcart, U.S. Consul, Tripoli, 15 May 1801, *Naval Documents*, 1:454–55.

4. A Coalition of the Willing

1. Daniel McNeill to William Eaton, 28 January 1802, Knox, *Naval Documents Related to the United States Wars with the Barbary Powers*, 2:41 (hereafter *Naval Documents*); Captain Richard Dale to Secretary of the Navy, 10 January 1802, *Naval Documents*, 2:16–17; Captain Richard Dale to Rufus King, 7 February 1802, *Naval Documents*, 2:52–53; Charles Wadsworth to William Eaton, 17 May 1802, *Naval Documents*, 2:154. Admiral Cederström's name is spelled Soderstrom by most American correspondents, though Coderstrum and Cederstrun also appear. I will use the spelling Cederström throughout to avoid confusion. The Swedish squadron consisted of the frigates *Thetis*, *Fröja*, *Camilla*, and *Sprengporten*. Which of the Swedish frigates was already in Tripoli harbor is unclear, but it seems likely to have been the *Fröja*, as it was serving as Cederström's flagship less than four months later and I have found no record of him shifting his flag.
2. Charles Wadsworth to William Eaton, 17 May 1802, *Naval Documents*, 2:154.
3. Technically, the name Kingdom of the Two Sicilies is anachronistic until 1816, though terms such as "the Sicilies" were in widespread use earlier. Sicily and Naples (also known as "the mainland Kingdom of Sicily") were in personal, but not yet constitutional, union under the Bourbon King Ferdinand from 1759. Ferdinand lost control of Naples when France invaded in 1806 in response to Ferdinand joining the Third Coalition. He regained control in 1815 and formally joined the two kingdoms into one the following year. For examples of the American exceptionalism presentation of the Tripolitan War, see Kilmeade and Yaeger, *Thomas Jefferson and the Tripoli Pirates*; and Oren, *Power, Faith, and Fantasy*.
4. Secretary of the Navy, "Instructions to Commodore R Dale," 20 May 1801, *Naval Documents*, 1:465–69.
5. This 14 February 1803 duel between Midshipman Joseph Bainbridge and commissary clerk (not secretary to Governor Ball, as often related) John Corcoran (also given as Cochran) was not directly related to the issue of sailor poaching, but the quarrel apparently began over insulting remarks about the United States Navy made in a theater, which then expanded into a physical confrontation, and finally a deadly duel. For an account of the duel and the myths that have grown up around it, see Sultana, "Coleridge, Stephen Decatur, and the Mysterious Duellist in Malta."
6. For commendations for Catalano's role in the Tripoli harbor raid, see Lt Stephen Decatur to Captain Edward Preble, 17 February 1804, *Naval Documents*, 3:414–15; and Midshipman Ralph Izard, Jr to Mrs. Ralph Izard, Sr, 20 February 1804, *Naval Documents*, 3:416–17. For Catalano's immigration and naturalization, see Secretary of the Navy to Hon. John C. Smith, 21 December 1805, *Naval Documents*, 5:386; and Salvadore Catalano to Secretary of the Navy, 26 November 1805, *Naval Documents*, 6:311.

7. On conditions in Egypt and Ottoman expectations, see William Eaton to Secretary of the Navy, 13 December 1804, *Naval Documents*, 5:186–89; Khurshid Ahmed Pasha to Hamet Caramanli, 9 February 1805, *Naval Documents*, 5:186–89. For expedition force numbers, see "Extract from the journal of William Eaton," 8 March 1805, *Naval Documents*, 5:398–99. On the conditions of the peace and the claims about it, see "Treaty of Peace and Amity between the United States and Tripoli," 4 June 1805, *Naval Documents*, 6:81–82; Tobias Lear to John Ridgley, 6 June 1805, *Naval Documents*, 6:93–94. Quotation is from Cooper, "A Sermon Preached before His Excellency John Hancock."
8. Peters, *Public Statutes at Large*, 2:110–11.
9. James Sofka, "The Jeffersonian Idea of National Security Revisited," in Marzagalli et al., *Rough Waters*, 172–73.
10. Thomas Jefferson to John Adams, 11 July 1786, *Founders Online*.
11. Thomas Jefferson to James Madison, 28 August 1801, *Founders Online*.
12. James Madison to William Eaton, 20 May 1801, *Founders Online*. Identical wording with one different capitalization in James Madison to Richard O'Brien, 21 May 1801, *Founders Online*.
13. United States Constitution, Article I, Section 8, Clause 11.
14. John Adams to United States Congress, 16 May 1797, *Founders Online*; John Adams to United States Congress, 3 July 1797, *Founders Online*; Fehlings, "America's First Limited War," 110.
15. James Madison to Thomas Jefferson, 2 April 1798, *Founders Online*.
16. Thomas Jefferson, "Notes on a Cabinet Meeting, 15 May 1801," *Founders Online*.
17. Secretary of the Navy, "Instructions to Commodore R Dale," 20 May 1801, *Naval Documents*, 1:463–69.
18. Alexander Hamilton (as Lucius Crassus), "The Examination, Number 1," *New York Evening Post*, 2.
19. Alexander Hamilton to James McHenry, 17 May 1798, *Founders Online* (emphasis in original).
20. Inquisitor, "Facts Against Facts" *Aurora General Advertiser*, 7 September 1801, 2. The article in the *Aurora* defends the Jefferson administration against claims quoted as published in the *Baltimore Federal Gazette* on 3 September 1801, which included that of unconstitutional authorization of force.
21. Truxton had been in command of the ship *London Packet* when it had been rumored to have been captured by Algerian corsairs with Benjamin Franklin onboard in 1793, and several falsified letters purportedly from Truxton had been printed in the newspapers describing their capture and captivity before it was clarified that this story was "widely discredited."
22. Captain Thomas Truxton to Secretary of the Navy, 13 April 1801, *Naval Documents*, 1:432; Samuel Smith to Thomas Truxton, 19 April 1801, *Naval Documents*, 1:428–29.
23. Captain Thomas Truxton to Captain Richard Dale, 22 May 1801, *Naval Documents*, 1:473–74.
24. *National Intelligencer and Washington Advertiser*, 8 June 1801, 2.
25. Secretary of the Navy, "Instructions to Commodore R Dale," 20 May 1801, *Naval Documents*, 1:463–69.

26. John Quincy Adams to James Madison, 25 June 1801, *Founders Online;* James Cathcart to Secretary of State, 4 January 1801, *Naval Documents,* 1:405–9; James Cathcart to William Eaton, 29 June 1801, *Naval Documents,* 1:493–95; Charles Iggestrom to Captain Richard Dale, 29 August 1801, *Naval Documents,* 1:563.
27. James L. Cathcart to Captain Richard Dale, 17 September 1801, *Naval Documents,* 1:576.
28. N. Frumerie to William Eaton, 14 October 1801, *Naval Documents,* 1:599.
29. Commodore Dale to various captains, 25 October–14 November 1801, *Naval Documents,* 1:603–20.
30. Richard Dale to David Humphreys, 28 October 1801, *Naval Documents,* 1:610–11.
31. Extracts from the journal of the USS *Essex,* 27 and 30 November 1801, *Naval Documents,* 1:626, 627.
32. Captain Richard Dale to Secretary of the Navy, 10 January 1802, *Naval Documents,* 2:16–17; Captain Richard Dale to Captain Daniel MacNeill, 18 January 1802, *Naval Documents,* 2:25–26; Captain Richard Dale to Thomas Appleton, 25 January 1802, *Naval Documents,* 2:28; Daniel McNeill to William Eaton, 28 January 1802, *Naval Documents,* 2:41
33. Richard Dale to Admiral Cederström, 2 February 1802, *MS 45 Letterbook of Commodore Richard Dale,* NAV.
34. Captain Richard Dale to Rufus King, 7 February 1802, *Naval Documents,* 2:52–53.
35. Charles Wadsworth to William Eaton, 17 May 1802, *Naval Documents,* 2:154; Extracts of the journal of U.S. Frigate *Constellation,* 22 July 1802, *Naval Documents,* 2:209.
36. Richard Dale to Robert Livingston, 7 February 1802, *Naval Documents,* 2:52–53; "II. First Annual Message to Congress, 8 December 1801," *Founders Online.*
37. "Circular to Naval Commanders, 18 February 1802," *Founders Online.*
38. Cantor, "A Connecticut Yankee in a Barbary Court," 102–3.
39. Swedish Consul Nordlingen to Swedish Consul at Genoa, 14 June 1802, *Naval Documents,* 2:174.
40. Captain Alexander Murray to Secretary of the Navy, 5 July 1802, *Naval Documents,* 2:192–93; Extract from the Captain's log, USS *Constellation,* 21 July, *Naval Documents,* 2:192–93; "Extract of a letter from a gentleman in Leghorn to his correspondent in this town, dated July 8th 1802," *Evening Post,* 2 October 1802, 3; Andrew Morris to James Cathcart, 22 July 1802, *Naval Documents,* 2:176–78.
41. Secretary of the Navy to Captain Richard Morris, 27 or 28 August 1802, *Naval Documents,* 2:277–78.
42. Captain Alexander Murray to Secretary of the Navy, 18 September 1802, *Naval Documents,* 2:278–79.
43. William Eaton to James Madison, 22 October 1802, *Founders Online* (emphasis in the original).
44. Joseph Barnes to Thomas Jefferson, 20 December 1802, *Founders Online.*
45. Rufus King to James Madison, 25 March 1803, *Founders Online.*
46. Mullen, *To Fix a National Character,* 64.
47. Joel Barlow, "Memoir on Maritime Law, written for the French Government," 5 December 1799, as printed in *National Intelligencer and Washington Advertiser,* 16 March 1801, 1.

48. Circular letter from Swedish Ambassador to France, Baron d'Ehrenswärd, 15 January 1802, as printed in *Aurora General Advertiser*, 20 March 1802, 2.
49. William Eaton to Secretary of State, 4 May 1802, *Naval Documents*, 2:142.
50. William Eaton to Captain Richard Morris, 26 January 1803, *Naval Documents*, 2:344-46; Journal of James Leander Cathcart, 29 January-14 March 1803, *Naval Documents*, 2:350-55.
51. Extract from Journal of Midshipman Henry Wadsorth, 1 and 5-6 March 1803, *Naval Documents*, 2:367-68.
52. Hammuda Bey of Tunis to Tobias Lear, 14 August 1805, *Naval Documents*, 6:226; Thomas Jefferson, "Message of President to Senate concerning differences with Tunis," 18 April 1806, *Naval Documents*, 6:418; Captain John Rodgers to Doctor James Dodge, 17 August 1805, *Naval Documents*, 2:234. The other consul switch in the regencies in this era was an exception to the naval officer pattern, partly because it was not sudden. Richard O'Brien had been requesting replacement for some time. After James Cathcart was rejected by Tunis, the Jefferson administration nominated him to the position in Algiers, but the dey of Algiers also rejected him. Finally, in 1803 the administration appointed Tobias Lear, former secretary to George Washington and consul to Saint-Domingue during the Quasi-War, to the position. He arrived in November 1803. O'Brien remained in the Mediterranean as his wife, Elizabeth, was pregnant and served as an adviser to Lear and to the navy throughout 1804. The O'Briens returned to the United States in early 1805.
53. Sidi Mohamet Ben Absalem Selawy to James Simpson and Peter Wyk, 10 May 1802, *Naval Documents*, 2:149.
54. James Simpson to James Madison, 5 June 1802, *Founders Online*.
55. James Simpson to James Madison, 26 June 1802, *Founders Online*; James Simpson to James Madison, 24 December 1802, *Founders Online*; James Simpson to James Madison, 17 June 1802, *Founders Online*; Captain Richard Morris to James Simpson, 19 June 1802, *Naval Documents*, 2:182-83.
56. James Simpson, "Circular letter to U.S. Consuls and Commercial Agents," 25 June 1802, *Naval Documents*, 2:183-84.
57. "Extract of a letter from an officer on board the United States schooner Enterprize, dated Malaga, 28th June, 1802," *Aurora General Advertiser*, 30 September 1802, 2; James Simpson to Captain Richard Morris, 16 August 1802, *Naval Documents*, 2:235-36.
58. Captain Richard Morris to Secretary of the Navy, 17 August 1802, *Naval Documents*, 2:236-37.
59. Morris, *A Defence of the Conduct of Commodore Morris*, 24-38.
60. Emperor Suleiman of Morocco, "Concerning the Tripolitan ship *Meshouda*," 17 September 1802, *Naval Documents*, 2:275.
61. James Simpson, "United States Passport issued to the Ship *Meshouda*," 27 September 1802, *Naval Documents*, 2:283.
62. James Simpson to James Madison, 24 December 1802, *Founders Online*.
63. Richard Morris to James Simpson, 19 May 1803, *Naval Documents*, 2:408-9.
64. James Simpson to Captain Richard Morris, 20 June 1803, *Naval Documents*, 2:456-57.

65. "Raiz Lubarez' Orders for Capture of American Vessels," 17 August 1803, *Naval Documents*, 2:507; William Bainbridge to James Simpson, 29 August 1803, *Naval Documents*, 2:518–19.
66. Emperor of Morocco to all Consuls resident at Tangiers, 11 September 1803, *Naval Documents*, 3:26–27 (as translated by James Simpson).
67. Captain Edward Preble to James Madison, 23 September 1803, *Founders Online*; James Simpson to Captain Edward Preble, 8 October 1803, *Naval Documents*, 3:115–17; Captain Edward Preble to James Simpson, 8 October 1803, *Naval Documents*, 3:119; James Simpson to William Jarvis; 12 October 1803, *Naval Documents*, 3:130; "An Act for the relief of the captors of the Moorish armed ships *Meshouda* and *Mirboha*," 19 March 1804, *Naval Documents*, 3:503; Captain William Bainbridge to Captain Edward Preble, 22 October 1803, *Naval Documents*, 3:159.
68. For more on British cooperation prior to this move, as well as some discussion of cooperation with the Sicilies, see Armstrong, "Against the Common Enemies." For naval cooperation and British basing in the United States during the Quasi-War, see Knox, *Naval Documents Related to the Quasi-War between the United States and France* (hereafter, *Quasi-War Documents*), specifically Secretary of State to Secretary of the Navy, 23 July 1798, *Quasi-War Documents*, 1:235; Captain Thomas Truxton to William Pennock, 27 December 1798, *Quasi-War Documents*, 2:127–28. Admiral Vandeput's name is also given in the records as Vandeport, Vandiput, and Vandevert. I have chosen the spelling given in the *Oxford Dictionary of National Biography*. For tensions in Malta and Gibraltar and the move to Syracuse, see "Extract from journal of Midshipman Henry Wadsworth, U.S. Navy on board U.S.S. *Chesapeake*," 14 February 1803, *Naval Documents*, 2:362; Captain Edward Preble to Royal Navy Captain George Hart, 22 October 1803, *Naval Documents*, 3:158; Captain Edward Preble to Secretary of the Navy, 23 October 1803, *Naval Documents*, 3:160–62; Midshipman Henry Wadsworth to whom not indicated, 10 November 1803, *Naval Documents*, 3:212–13; Captain Edward Preble to Secretary of the Navy, 10 December 1803, *Naval Documents*, 3:160–62.
69. Captain William Bainbridge to Secretary of the Navy, 1 November 1803, *Naval Documents*, 3:171.
70. Captain William Bainbridge to Secretary of the Navy, 1 November 1803, *Naval Documents*, 3:171.
71. Ray, *The Horrors of Slavery*, 11, 167.
72. James Cathcart to Secretary of State, 15 December 1803, *Naval Documents*, 3:272; Robert Livingston to Charles Maurice de Talleyrand-Perigord, 2 January 1804, *Naval Documents*, 3:308–9; Alexander de Worotzoff to Levet Harris, 25 January 1804, *Naval Documents*, 3:358; Thomas Jefferson to James Madison, 15 April 1804, *Founders Online*.
73. Thomas Jefferson to Robert Smith, 27 April 1804, *Founders Online*.
74. French chargé d'affaires to Tripoli Beaussier to Captain Edward Preble, 28 March 1804, *Naval Documents*, 3:542–44; Alexander de Worotzoff to Levet Harris, n.d., but enclosed in a letter dated 28 March 1804, *Naval Documents*, 3:541; *Aurora General Advertiser*, 15 March 1804, 2.
75. Ray, *Horrors of Slavery*, 89; "Log book of the U.S. frigate *Constitution*," 23 December 1803; For the renaming of the *Philadelphia*, see Anthony Zuchet to the Netherlands

Ministry of Foreign Affairs, 20 January 1804, as quoted in Marzagalli et al., *Rough Waters,* 122. Various sources give the name as *Gift of God, Gift of Allah, Gift from Allah,* and *God's Present,* but these are all translations of the same Arabic name.

76. Captain Edward Preble to Tobias Lear, 31 January 1804, *Naval Documents,* 3:377–79.
77. Captain Edward Preble to John Gavino, 18 February 1804, *Naval Documents,* 3:422.
78. "Concerning the participation of the ketch *Mastico* (subsequently captured and renamed *Intrepid*) in the capture of the *Philadelphia*," 2 February 1804, *Naval Documents,* 3:180–81; Lt Stephen Decatur to Captain Edward Preble, 17 February 1804, *Naval Documents,* 3:414–15; Midshipman Ralph Izard, Jr to Mrs. Ralph Izard, Sr, 20 February 1804, *Naval Documents,* 3:416–17; Salvadore Catalano to Secretary of the Navy, 26 November 1805, *Naval Documents,* 6:311, "Certificate of Salvadore Catalano, Pilot," 19 December 1825, *Naval Documents,* 3:421. For a more detailed narrative of this operation, see Armstrong, "A Ketch Named Mastico."
79. Lt Stephen Decatur to Captain Edward Preble, 17 February 1804, *Naval Documents,* 3:414–15.
80. Secretary of the Navy to Hon. John C. Smith, 21 December 1805, *Naval Documents,* 5:386; and Salvadore Catalano to Secretary of the Navy, 26 November 1805, *Naval Documents,* 6:311; "Certificate of Salvadore Catalano, Pilot," 19 December 1825, *Naval Documents,* 3:421.
81. Captain Edward Preble to Secretary of the Navy, 16 July 1803, *Naval Documents,* 2:488.
82. Joseph Barnes to Thomas Jefferson, 20 December 1802, *Founders Online.*
83. Robert R. Livingston, U.S. Minister to France, to Thomas Appelton, U.S. Consul to Leghorn, 16 March 1804, *Naval Documents,* 3:488.
84. *The Times* (London), 6 June 1804, 3.
85. Sir John Acton, Kingdom of Sicily Prime Minister of State, to Captain Edward Preble, 13 May 1804, *Naval Documents,* 4:97.
86. Captain Edward Preble to James Cathcart, 28 May 1804, *Naval Documents,* 4:126; Captain Edward Preble to John Broadbent, 28 May 1804, *Naval Documents,* 4:126.
87. For a detailed account of these engagements see Preble's after-action report: Captain Edward Preble to Secretary of the Navy, 20 February 1805, *Naval Documents,* 4:293–310. For Preble's commendations and employment of Massi, see Edward Preble to Prime Minister John Acton, 6 September 1804, *Naval Documents,* 4:523–24; Edward Preble, "Certificate concerning Don Antonio Massi," 14 October 1804, *Naval Documents,* 5:84; Edward Preble to Don Antonio Massi, 17 October 1804, *Naval Documents,* 5:89; and General Forteguerra to Captain Edward Preble, 21 December 1804, *Naval Documents,* 5:205.
88. Captain Edward Preble to Secretary of the Navy, 20 February 1805, *Naval Documents,* 4:293–310; Captain Edward Preble to General Forteguerra, 16 December 1804, *Naval Documents,* 5:194.
89. Captain Edward Preble to Tobias Lear, 23 December 1804, *Naval Documents,* 5:207–9; Master Commandant John Shaw to Secretary of the Navy, 8 January 1805, *Naval Documents,* 5:265; Secretary of the Navy to Commanders of Gunboats, 9 April 1805, *Naval Documents,* 5:493; Lieutenant Samuel Elbert to Secretary of the Navy, 8 June 1805, *Naval Documents,* 6:101.
90. James Cathcart to William Eaton, 29 June 1801, *Naval Documents* 1:493–95.

91. William Eaton to James Madison, 13 December 1801, *Founders Online*. Though Hamet Karamanli's given name was Ahmed, he was generally known by the Turkish variant Hamet, and as that is how he appears in most documents and other works, I have decided to retain that spelling. Some sources refer to him as Mohamet or Mahomet, possibly in the impression that Hamet is short for this name.
92. On early efforts to recruit Hamet and criticism of Eaton's unsanctioned spending, see William Eaton to Commander of American Naval Squadron, 12 May 1802, *Naval Documents*, 2:152–53; William Eaton to James Madison, 4 April 1802, *Founders Online*; William Eaton to James Madison, 4 April 1802, *Founders Online*; William Eaton to James Madison, 8 June 1802, *Founders Online*; Captain Alexander Murray to Secretary of the Navy, 22 August 1802, *Naval Documents*, 2:246–47; James Madison to Richard Harrison, 11 February 1804, *Founders Online*. On the revisiting of the project, see William Eaton to Thomas Jefferson, 2 February 1804, *Founders Online*; "Notes on a Cabinet Meeting, 26 May 1804," *Founders Online*; Franklin and Lowrie, *American State Papers*, 2:702.
93. Tobias Lear to Secretary of State, 3 November 1804, *Naval Documents*, 5:114–16; Captain William Bainbridge to Tobias Lear, 11 November 1804, *Naval Documents*, 5:135–37; Captain Samuel Barron to Master Commandant Isaac Hull, 10 November 1804, *Naval Documents*, 5:134. For further discussion of appropriate masculinity in the early American republic, see Foster, *New Men*. For similar discussion specific to Americans in North Africa, see Goodin, *From Captives to Consuls*, 34–52.
94. Captain Samuel Barron to Tobias Lear, 13 November 1804, *Naval Documents*, 5:139–40.
95. William Eaton to Captain Samuel Barron, 17 November 1804, *Naval Documents*, 5:146–47.
96. Sir Alexander John Ball to William Eaton, 16 November 1804, *Naval Documents* 5:144; William Eaton to Secretary of the Navy, 6 September 1804, *Naval Documents*, 4:525–26; William Eaton to Secretary of the Navy, 13 December 1804, *Naval Documents*, 5:186–89; William Eaton to Sir Alexander John Ball, 13 December 1804, *Naval Documents*, 5:190–92.
97. Samuel Briggs to Master Commandant Isaac Hull, 26 November 1804, *Naval Documents*, 5:161; William Eaton to Secretary of the Navy, 13 December 1804, *Naval Documents*, 5:186–89; William Eaton to Sir Alexander John Ball, 13 December 1804, *Naval Documents*, 5:190–92.
98. William Eaton to Secretary of the Navy, 13 December 1804, *Naval Documents*, 5:186–89.
99. Khurshid Ahmed Pasha to Hamet Caramanli, 9 February 1805, *Naval Documents*, 5:186–89. "Extract from the journal of William Eaton," 8 March 1805, *Naval Documents*, 5:398–99; William Eaton to Secretary of the Navy, 13 February 1805, *Naval Documents*, 5:350–51. The first of these documents is listed in *Naval Documents* as being from the "Vice Roy of Cairo," but its signature clarifies that it is from Governor of Egypt Khurshid Ahmed Pasha. It is also dated "about 8 February 1805," but the Hijri date of 9 Dhuʻ al-Qiʻdah corresponds to 9 February in that year.
100. Prentiss, *Life of Eaton*, 297–300.
101. Master Commandant Isaac Hull to Captain Samuel Barron, *Naval Documents*, 5:547–48; Nicholas Nissen to Captain Samuel Barron, 18 March 1805, *Naval Documents*, 5:421.

102. William Eaton to Captain Samuel Barron, 29 April 1805, *Naval Documents*, 5:550–53.
103. Captain Samuel Barron to Tobias Lear, 18 May 1805, *Naval Documents*, 6:22–23; Ray, *The Horrors of Slavery*, 152–58.
104. "Treaty of Peace and Amity between the United States and Tripoli," 4 June 1805, *Naval Documents*, 6:81–82; Tobias Lear to John Ridgley, 6 June 1805, *Naval Documents*, 6:93–94.
105. "The Moroccan-American Treaty of Peace and Friendship, 28 June 1786," *Founders Online*.
106. *Evening Post*, 2 September 1805, 2; *Evening Post*, 10 September 1805, 2.
107. *Evening Post*, 20 September 1805, 1; Captain William Bainbridge and twenty-two officers to Nicholas Nissen, 3 June 1805, *Naval Documents*, 6:79; Captain William Bainbridge to John Gavino, 27 July 1805, *Naval Documents*, 6:79; Nicholas Nissen to William Bainbridge 13 January 1807, *Naval Documents*, 6:500. "Resolution respecting N.C. Nissen, Danish Consul at Tripoli," 10 April 1806, *Naval Documents*, 6:415.
108. Thomas Jefferson to John Taylor, 29 March 1805, *Founders Online*.
109. Columbianus, "The New World: An Enquiry into the National Character of the People of the United States of America. No. X," *National Intelligencer and Washington Advertiser*, 30 October 1809, 1; Columbianus, "The New World," 25 October 1809, 1. For Coxe as the author of the above-mentioned essays, see Nash, "Race and Citizenship in the Early Republic," 95.
110. Tobias Lear to James Madison, 31 August 1812, *Founders Online*.

5. Changing Tides

1. The *Meshouda* in this account is not the same vessel blockaded in Gibraltar during the Tripolitan War. Meshouda was a common girl's name in North Africa, and thus also a common ship name, much as this study has featured multiple American ships named *Betsey*. Some sources give the *Meshouda* as the former Portuguese frigate captured by Algiers in 1805, though Decatur reported that both it and the brig in the second engagement were built in Algiers by a Spanish contractor. The brig is referenced as the *Estedio* in some secondary accounts, but I can find no primary source for that. The account above is based primarily on Decatur's reports to Secretary of the Navy Crowninshield, reprinted in Franklin and Lowrie, *American State Papers* (hereafter *ASP*), volume entitled *Naval Affairs*, 396; with input from Devoulx, *Le Rais Hamidou*, 113–25; "Decatur's Squadron," *Lancaster Intelligencer*, 1 September 1815, 3; and Panzac, *Barbary Corsairs*, 270–71.
2. For an example of the American version of the "end of the Barbary System" narrative, see Leiner, *The End of Barbary Terror*; for that crediting the Exmouth expedition, see, e.g., Symonds, "'A Squadron of Observation,'" 109.
3. George Davis to Secretary of State, 15 November 1806, in Knox, *Naval Documents Related to the United States Wars with the Barbary Powers*, 6:487 (hereafter *Naval Documents*); Charles Coxe to Secretary of State, 8 December 1806, *Naval Documents*, 6:491–92; Charles Coxe to Secretary of State, 26 December 1806, *Naval Documents*, 6:495; Charles Coxe to John Ridgley, 20 February 1807, *Naval Documents*, 6:507; Charles Coxe

to Secretary of State, 8 December 1806, *Naval Documents*, 6:491–92; Charles Coxe to James Madison, 20 October 1820, *Founders Online;* Captain Hugh Campbell to Secretary of the Navy, 26 January 1807, *Naval Documents*, 6:501.
4. Secretary of the Navy to Captain James Barron, 15 May 1807, *Naval Documents*, 6:523–44.
5. Captain James Barron to Secretary of the Navy, 29 June 1807, *Naval Documents*, 6:539–40; Secretary of the Navy to Captain Hugh Campbell, 14 July 1807, *Naval Documents*, 6:546–47; Captain Hugh Campbell to Secretary of the Navy, 3 September 1807, *Naval Documents*, 6:556–57; Extract from the Brig USS *Hornet*, Master Commandant John Dent commanding, 18 October 1807, *Naval Documents*, 6:572.
6. Tobias Lear to U.S. Consuls in the Mediterranean, 16 December 1807, *Naval Documents*, 6:583; *The Times* (London), 14 May 1808, 3.
7. *Gazette of the United States*, 30 June 1808, 1.
8. *Aurora General Advertiser*, 11 July 1808, 2.
9. *Evening Post*, 25 January 1808, 3; *Gazette of the United States*, 14 July 1808, 2; "An Act to interdict the commercial intercourse between the United States and Great Britain and France, and their dependencies; and for other purposes," 1 March 1809, Section 22, in Peters, *Public Statutes at Large*, 2:531; *Gazette of the United States*, 8 June 1808, 4; *Aurora General Advertiser*, 9 January 1810, 3; *Gazette of the United States*, 11 January 1810, 2.
10. Charles Coxe to John Gavino, 25 August 1810, as printed in *Gazette of the United States*, 13 December 1810, 3; *Evening Post*, 7 March 1811, 3.
11. Tobias Lear to James Madison, 29 July 1812, as printed in *Aurora General Advertiser*, 7 December 1812, 2–3.
12. Tobias Lear's notes on Prince Regent George to Dey Ali, 4 January 1812, as printed in Shaler, *Sketches of Algiers*, 118–19.
13. *Evening Post*, 18 November 1812, 2.
14. "An Act Fixing the Compensation of Public Ministers, and of Consuls Residing on the Coast of Barbary, and for Other Purposes," 1 May 1810, Section 4, in Peters, *Public Statutes at Large*, 2:609.
15. Tobias Lear to James Madison, 29 July 1812, as printed in *Aurora General Advertiser*, 7 December 1812, 2–3.
16. *Evening Post*, 9 April 1813, 3.
17. *Virginia Argus*, 29 April 1813, 1.
18. *Aurora General Advertiser*, 10 October 1812, 2.
19. Tobias Lear to William Lambert, 14 November 1812, as extracted in *Evening Post*, 19 January 1813, 3; *Gazette of the United States*, 7 August 1813, 7; *Gazette of the United States*, 14 August 1813, 5; *Susquehanna Democrat*, 21 October 1814, 3; *Gazette of the United States*, 8 October 1814, 6; M. M. Noah to Stephen Decatur, 25 July 1815, *ASP: Naval Affairs*, 397; Richard Jones to Stephen Decatur, 6 August 1815, *ASP: Naval Affairs*, 398;
20. *Lancaster Intelligencer*, 26 June 1813, 3.
21. Blaufarb, "The Western Question," 744.
22. James Madison, "Presidential Proclamation, 27 October 1810," *Founders Online*.
23. James Madison to Joel Barlow, 17 November 1811, *Founders Online*.

24. George Washington to Richard R. Keene, 28 December 1798, *Founders Online*.
25. Aslakson, "Immigrant Lawyers and Slavery in Territorial New Orleans," 37, 46; Richard R. Keene, Plaintiff in Error v. the Heirs of Daniel Clark, No. 35 U.S. 291, 1836. SCT.0000015 (U.S. Supreme Court, 1 January 1836); James Madison to Joel Barlow, 17 November 1811, *Founders Online*; Joel Barlow to James Madison, 30 December 1811, *Founders Online*.
26. Noah, *Travels*, 68–76, 142–44.
27. Noah, *Travels*, 147–60, v–vi.
28. Noah, *Travels*, 412; James Monroe to James Madison, 22 April 1815, *Founders Online*.
29. James Madison to James Monroe, 24 April 1815, *Founders Online*.
30. "Mordecai Noah's Mission to Algiers: Spanish-American Relations and the Fate of a Jewish Consul in Madison's Administration, 20 February (Editorial Note)," *Founders Online*.
31. Noah, *Travels*, 379 (emphasis in original).
32. John Adams to Mordecai M. Noah, 15 March 1819, *Founders Online*.
33. Noah, *Travels*, 412–13.
34. Noah, *Travels*, 215, 236, 241.
35. Windler, "Performing Inequality in Mediterranean Diplomacy," 948.
36. Windler, "Performing Inequality in Mediterranean Diplomacy," 954.
37. Prentiss, *Life of Eaton*, 59.
38. Noah, *Travels*, 257.
39. Windler, "Performing Inequality in Mediterranean Diplomacy," 952.
40. Noah, *Travels*, 393, 429–30.
41. Noah, *Travels*, 319–20.
42. James Madison to United States Congress, 23 February 1815, *ASP: Foreign Relations III*, 748–49.
43. James Madison to Benjamin W. Crowninshield, 20 April 1815, *Founders Online*.
44. Benjamin W. Crowninshield to James Madison, 1 May 1815, *Founders Online*.
45. James Madison to James Monroe, 2 May 1815, *Founders Online*.
46. James Madison to James Monroe, 9 May 1815, *Founders Online*.
47. James Madison to Benjamin W. Crowninshield, 10 May 1815, *Founders Online*.
48. Benjamin W. Crowninshield to James Madison, 1 May 1815; James Madison from Alexander J. Dallas, 12 May 1815; Alexander J. Dallas to James Madison, 23 May 1815, all on *Founders Online*.
49. James Madison, "Presidential Proclamation," 18 February 1815, *Founders Online*.
50. Sadosky, *Revolutionary Negotiations*, 204.
51. "The Late Colonel Wilcocks," *Lancaster Intelligencer*, 3 December 1814, 1; *Pittsfield Sun*, 6 July 1815, 3; *Susquehanna Democrat*, 21 October 1814, 3; Brown, *An Authentic History of the Second War for Independence*.
52. *The Times* (London), 30 December 1814, 2.
53. Secretary of the Navy to the committee of Ways and Means of the House of Representatives, 23 February 1815, as printed in the *Evening Post*, 13 March 1815, 2.
54. James Madison to United States Congress, 23 February 1815, *ASP: Foreign Relations III*, 748–49.

55. "An Act for the protection of the commerce of the United States against the Algerine cruisers," 3 March 1815, in Peters, *Public Statutes at Large*, 3:230.
56. "Expedition to Algiers," *Gazette of the United States*, 19 April 1815, 3.
57. James Madison to James Monroe, 15 April 1815, *Founders Online*.
58. John Quincy Adams to Abigail Smith Adams, 17 July 1815, *Founders Online*.
59. Stephen Decatur to Benjamin Crowninshield, 5 July 1815, *ASP: Naval Affairs*, 396; Stephen Decatur and William Shaler to James Monroe, 5 July 1815, *ASP: Foreign Affairs IV*, 6; *The Times* (London), 30 May 1815, 3; "Pathetic," *Lancaster Intelligencer*, 17 July 1816, 3.
60. Stephen Decatur to Benjamin Crowninshield, 31 July 1815, *ASP: Naval Affairs*, 397.
61. Richard Jones to Stephen Decatur, 6 August 1815, *Letterbook of RB Jones*, MS 40, NAV; Stephen Decatur to Benjamin Crowninshield, 31 August 1815, *ASP: Naval Affairs*, 398.
62. John Quincy Adams to Abigail Smith Adams, 27 December 1815, *Founders Online*.
63. Shaler, *Sketches of Algiers*, Appendix H, "Protocol of the Congress of Aix-la-Chappelle." For more on Europe's efforts to curtail Barbary corsairing during the era of the Congress system through the 1830s, see Gale, "Beyond Corsairs" and "Barbary's Slow Death."
64. Head, "Slave Smuggling by Foreign Privateers."
65. James Madison to Benjamin W. Crowninshield, 18 September 1815, *Founders Online;* Benjamin W. Crowninshield to James Madison, 18 September 1815, *Founders Online*.
66. James Madison to James Monroe, 11 July 1816, *Founders Online*.
67. *Lancaster Intelligencer*, 14 February 1816, 2; *Lancaster Intelligencer*, 16 February 1816, 3; "From the American Squadron in the Mediterranean," *Gazette of the United States*, 15 June 1816, 7; *Evening Post*, 27 June 1816, 2; Dey Omar of Algiers to James Madison, 26 April 1816, *Founders Online;* James Monroe to James Madison, 27 June 1816, *Founders Online*.
68. James Madison to Omar Bashaw, 21 August 1816, *Founders Online*.
69. *The Times* (London), 26 April 1816, 4; *Raleigh Minerva*, 27 September 1816, 4; Lord Exmouth to William Shaler, 2 September 1816, and William Shaler to Lord Exmouth, 2 September 1816, printed in *Lancaster Intelligencer*, 25 November 1816, 3; *The Times* (London), 17 September 1816, 2; *Gazette of the United States*, 26 October 1816, 3.
70. Shaler, *Sketches of Algiers*, 279–81.
71. Devoulx, *Tachrifat*, 88; *The Times* (London), 26 April 1816, 4.
72. *The Times* (London), 1 January 1817, 2; *Lancaster Intelligencer*, 28 February 1817, 2; *Evening Post*, 7 March 1817, 2; *Gazette of the United States*, 12 March 1817, 4; *Evening Post*, 13 March 1817, 2.
73. *Gazette of the United States*, 17 June 1817, 3.
74. *Lancaster Intelligencer*, 16 July 1817, 2; *Lancaster Intelligencer*, 28 November 1817, 2.
75. Shaler, *Sketches of Algiers*, 76, 171.
76. Shaler, *Sketches of Algiers*, 33, 35, 160, 164–65.
77. Devoulx, *Register of Prizes*, 104–6, 108–10.
78. Devoulx, *Register of Prizes*, 111; *Morning Chronicle* (London), 3 July 1827, 2; *The Standard* (London), 21 January 1830, 2; *Derby Mercury*, 14 July 1830, 2; *The Times* (London), 20 February 1840, 4; *Charleston Mercury*, 25 June 1847, 2.
79. Windler, "Performing Inequality in Mediterranean Diplomacy," 956.

Conclusion

1. For examples relating the Barbary contestation to the War on Terror, see Kilmeade and Yaeger, *Thomas Jefferson and the Tripoli Pirate;* Leiner, *The End of Barbary Terror;* and Symonds, "A Squadron of Observation." For World War II, see Wright and MacLeod, *The First Americans in North Africa.* For Libyan civil war, see Ian J. Byrne, "Raiding Tripoli: Part 3," *Minnesota Daily,* 28 March 2011.
2. On the provocative nature of the deployment, see Grant, *Personal Memoirs of U. S. Grant,* 1:68.
3. "Might and Right," *Public Ledger,* 9 January 1846, 2.
4. "The Course of Washington," credited to the *Detroit Advertiser* and reprinted in *Sunbury Gazette,* 24 April 1847, 2. For examples of reprints of the "Course of Washington" story with slightly different prose, see *Indiana State Sentinel,* 20 March 1847, 2; and *Tri-Weekly Nashville Union,* 26 January 1847, 2.
5. *Detroit Free Press,* 24 January 1847, 2.
6. *New York Daily Herald,* 21 June 1847, 2.
7. Peterson, "Beatrice Vernon," 1; *Vermont Union Whig,* 7 January 1847, 4.
8. Benton, *A Search for Sovereignty,* 116–20.
9. For excellent examinations of this contestation from other perspectives: Lambert, *The Barbary Wars,* explores it as a struggle for free trade in an Atlantic world context; Allison, *The Crescent Obscured,* and Peskin, *Captives and Countrymen,* offer excellent examinations of the cultural construction of Barbary issues in the early republic's "home front"; and the military history of the conflicts is well covered in Toll, *Six Frigates.*
10. Gould, *Among the Powers of the Earth,* 12.
11. During the Civil War, the Confederacy issued letters of marque, but the Union did not and "announced it would respect the principles of the Declaration for the duration of the hostilities." International Committee of the Red Cross, *Treaties, States Parties and Commentaries,* "Declaration Respecting Maritime Law. Paris, 16 April 1856," https://ihl-databases.icrc.org/ihl/INTRO/105. For more on Confederate privateering and the Union response, see Symonds, *The Civil War at Sea,* 61–65.

Appendix 1

1. *Pennsylvania Packet,* 3 May 1785, 2–3.
2. Shepherd, "Forrest's Curious Old Play."
3. *Pennsylvania Packet,* 17 February 1786, 2.

Appendix 2

1. Miller, *Treaties and Other International Acts of the United States of America,* 2:365.
2. Miller, *Treaties,* 2:371.

3. Miller, *Treaties*, 2:360. My attempt at a translation from the Arabic. I am indebted to Mohamed Nouri from the United States Air Force Academy for helping me work out the difficult handwriting. All remaining errors are my own.
4. Miller, *Treaties*, 2:371–72.

BIBLIOGRAPHY

Archives and Libraries

ANRS   American Naval Records Society
APS   American Philosophical Society
HL   Huntington Library
HSP   Historical Society of Pennsylvania
LOC   Library of Congress
LVA   Library of Virginia
NAV   United States Naval Academy Nimitz Library Archives
USNA   United States National Archives, District of Columbia
YLS   Yale Law School

Manuscript and Record Collections

American State Papers, LOC
Avalon Project: Documents in Law, History and Diplomacy, YLS
Founders Online, USNA
Journal of the Continental Congress, LOC
Journal of the Executive Proceedings of the Senate, LOC
Letterbook of Commodore Richard Dale, NAV
Letterbook of R. B. Jones, U.S. Consul at Tripoli, NAV
Naval Documents related to the Quasi-War between the United States and France, ANRS
Naval Documents related to the United States Wars with the Barbary Powers, ANRS
Papers of William Eaton, HL
Papers of Benjamin Franklin, APS
Papers of Richard O'Brien, HSP
Record Group 45, USNA
Record Group 59, USNA

Record Group 360, USNA
Revolutionary Diplomatic Correspondence of the United States, LOC
Virginia Navy Board Record Group, LVA

Newspapers

Aurora General Advertiser (Philadelphia, PA)
Boston Independent Chronicle (Boston, MA)
Caledonian Mercury (Edinburgh, Scotland)
Carroll Free Press (Carrollton, Ohio)
Charleston Mercury (Charleston, SC)
Derby Mercury (Derby, England)
Detroit Free Press (Detroit, MI)
Evening Post (New York, NY)
Freeman's Journal, or The North-American Intelligencer (Philadelphia, PA)
Gazette of the United States (Philadelphia, PA)
Independent Gazetteer (Philadelphia, PA)
Indiana State Sentinel (Indianapolis, IN)
Lancaster Intelligencer (Lancaster, PA)
Maryland Gazette (Annapolis, Maryland)
Minnesota Daily (Minneapolis, MN)
Morning Chronicle (London, England)
National Intelligencer and Washington Advertiser (Washington, DC)
New York Daily Herald (New York, NY)
Niles' Weekly Register (Baltimore, MD)
Pennsylvania Gazette (Philadelphia, PA)
Pennsylvania Packet, and Daily Advertiser (Philadelphia, PA)
Philadelphia Inquirer (Philadelphia, PA)
Pittsfield Sun (Pittsfield, MA)
Public Ledger (Philadelphia, PA)
Raleigh Minerva (Raleigh, NC)
The Standard (London, England)
Sunbury Gazette (Sunbury, PA)
Susquehanna Democrat (Wilkes-Barre, PA)
The Times (London, England)
Vermont Gazette (Bennington, VT)
Vermont Union Whig (Rutland, VT)
Virginia Argus (Richmond, VA)

Published Primary Sources

Arnold, Samuel. *The Veteran Tar, a Comic Opera, In Two Acts, As Performed At the Theatre-Royal, Drury-Lane*. London: J. Barker, 1801.

Barlow, Joel. *The Political Writings of Joel Barlow*. New York: Mott and Lyon, 1796.
Brown, Samuel. *An Authentic History of the Second War for Independence*. Auburn, NY: JG Hathaway, 1815.
Cathcart, James L. *The Captives, Eleven Years a Prisoner in Algiers*. La Porte, IN, 1899.
———. "The Diplomatic Journal and Letter Book of James Leander Cathcart, 1788–1796." *American Antiquarian Society Proceedings* 64, no. 2 (1954): 303–435.
Cooper, Samuel. "A Sermon Preached before His Excellency John Hancock, [. . .] of the Commonwealth of Massachusetts, October 25, 1780. Being the Day of the Commencement of the Constitution, and Inauguration of the New Government." October 25, 1780. http://www.belcherfoundation.org/samuel%20cooper%20sermon%20on%20constitution.pdf.
Cowdery, Jonathan. *American Captives in Tripoli, or Dr. Cowdery's Journal in Miniature Kept During His Late Captivity in Tripoli*. 2nd ed. Boston: Belcher & Armstrong, 1806.
Devoulx, Albert. *Le registre des prises maritimes: Traduction d'un document authentique et inédit concernant le partage des captures amenées par le corsairs algériens*. Algiers: A. Jourdan, 1872.
———. *Tachrifat: Recueil de notes historiques sur l'administration de l'ancienne régence d'Alger*. Algiers: Imprimerie du Gouvernement, 1852.
Foss, John. *A Journal of the Captivity and Sufferings of John Foss, Several Years a Prisoner at Algiers*. 2nd ed. Newburyport, MA: Angier March, 1798.
Franklin, Walter, and Walter Lowrie, eds. *American State Papers: Documents, Legislative and Executive, of the Congress of the United States*. 38 vols. Washington, DC: Gales and Seaton, 1843.
Gibbs, George, ed. *Memoirs of the Administrations of Washington and John Adams, Edited from the Papers of Oliver Wollcot, Secretary of the Treasury*. Vol. 2. 2 vols. New York: William van Norden, 1846.
Grant, Ulysses. *Personal Memoirs of U. S. Grant*. 2 vols. New York: Charles L. Webster, 1885.
Grotius, Hugo. *The Law of War and Peace in Three Books (1625) Translated into English by Francis W. Kelsey*. Oxford and London, 1925.
Harris, Kenneth, and Stephen Tilley, eds. *Journals of the Continental Congress*. 34 vols. Washington, DC: National Archives and Records Service, 1976.
Irving, Washington. *Letters of Jonathan Oldstyle, Gent*. New York: William H. Chalyton, 1824.
Keene, Richard. *A Letter of Vindication to Colonel Munroe, President of the United States*. London: Ambrose Cuddon, 1824.
Knox, Dudley, ed. *Naval Documents Related to the Quasi-War Between the United States and France*. 7 vols. Washington DC: US Government Printing Office, 1938.
———. *Naval Documents Related to the United States Wars with the Barbary Powers*. 6 vols. Washington DC: US Government Printing Office, 1939.
Lowrie, Walter. *Journal of the Executive Proceedings of the Senate of the United States of America, 1789–1873*. Vol. 1. Washington, DC: Duff Green, 1828.
Markoe, Peter, and Timothy Marr. *The Algerine Spy in Pennsylvania, or, Letters Written by a Native of Algiers on the Affairs of the United States in America, from the Close of the Year 1783 to the Meeting of the Convention*. Yardley, PA: Westholme, 2008.
Miller, David Hunter. *Secret Statutes of the United States: A Memorandum*. Washington, DC: US Government Printing Office, 1918.

———. *Treaties and Other International Acts of the United States of America*. Vol. 2. Washington, DC: US Government Printing Office, 1931.

Molloy, Charles. *De Jure Maritimo Et Navali; Or, A Treatise of Affairs Maritime and of Commerce*. 3rd ed. London, 1682.

Morris, Richard. *A Defence of the Conduct of Commodore Morris During His Command in the Mediterranean*. New York: I. Riley, 1804.

Noah, Mordecai. *Travels in England, France, Spain, and the Barbary States in the Years 1813–14 and 15*. New York: Kirk and Mercein; London: John Miller, 1819.

Peters, Richard, ed. *The Public Statutes at Large of the UNITED STATES OF AMERICA, from the Organization of the Government in 1789, to March 3, 1845*. 18 vols. Boston: Charles C. Little and James Brown, 1845.

Peterson, C. J. "Beatrice Vernon." *Ladies' National Magazine*, November 1846.

Prentiss, Charles. *The Life of the Late General William Eaton*. Brookfield, MA, 1813.

Ray, William. *The Horrors of Slavery or, The American Tars in Tripoli*. Troy: Oliver Lyon, 1808.

Riley, James. *An Authentic Narrative of the Loss of the American Brig Commerce: Wrecked on the Western Cost of Africa, in the Month of August, 1815*. New York: T. & W. Mercein, 1817.

Roberts, Priscilla, and James Tull. "Moroccan Sultan Sidi Muhammad Ibn Abdallah's Diplomatic Initiatives toward the United States, 1777–1786." *Proceedings of the American Philosophical Society* 143, no. 2 (June 1999): 233–65.

Rowland, Dumbar, ed. *Official Letter Books of W. C. C. Claiborne, 1801–1816*. 5 vols. Jackson, MS, 1917.

Shaler, William. *Sketches of Algiers, Political, Historical, and Civil*. Boston: Cummings, Hillard, 1826.

Sheffield, John Holroyd, Earl of. *Observations on the Commerce of the American States*. 3rd ed. London: J. Debrett, 1784.

Vattel, Emer de. *The Law of Nations, Or, Principles of the Law of Nature, Applied to the Conduct and Affairs of Nations and Sovereigns*. Indianapolis: Liberty Fund, 2008.

Wharton, Francis, and John Moore. *The Revolutionary Diplomatic Correspondence of the United States*. 6 vols. Washington, DC: Government Printing Office, 1889.

Zahhar, Ahmad. *Mudhakkirāt Al-Ḥājj Aḥmad al-Sharīf al-Zahhār, Naqīb Ashrāf al-Jazā'ir, 1168–1246 H 1754–1830 M*. Algiers, 1980.

Secondary Sources

Allison, Robert J. *The Crescent Obscured: The United States and the Muslim World, 1776–1815*. Chicago: University of Chicago Press, 2000.

Anooshahr, Ali. *The Ghazi Sultans and the Frontiers of Islam: A Comparative Study of the Late Medieval and Early Modern Periods*. New York: Routledge, 2014.

Armstrong, Benjamin. "A Ketch Named Mastico: North Africa Maritime Security Operations." *Small Wars Journal*, April 2011. https://smallwarsjournal.com/blog/journal/docs-temp/740-armstrong.pdf.

———. "Against the Common Enemies: American Allies and Partners in the First Barbary War." *The Trafalgar Chronicle*, Journal of the 1805 Club, new series, no. 2 (December 2017): 48–60.

Aslakson, Kenneth. "Immigrant Lawyers and Slavery in Territorial New Orleans." *Tulane European and Civil Law Forum* 31, nos. 31–32 (2017): 33–77.
Baepler, Paul Michel, ed. *White Slaves, African Masters: An Anthology of American Barbary Captivity Narratives*. Chicago: University of Chicago Press, 1999.
Ben Ahmadi. "An-Nashat al-Bahria Aljiza'iria Fi al- 'ahd al-'athmania, Hurub Bahria Mashru'aa Am Qursana Wa-Lasusia?" *Algeria Gate*, November 2016. http://www.algeriagate.info/2016/11/algerian-naval-engagements-during.html.
Bender, Thomas. *A Nation Among Nations: America's Place in World History*. New York: Hill and Wang, 2006.
Benton, Lauren A. *A Search for Sovereignty: Law and Geography in European Empires, 1400–1900*. Cambridge: Cambridge University Press, 2010.
———. "Legal Spaces of Empire: Piracy and the Origins of Ocean Regionalism." *Comparative Studies in Society and History* 47, no. 2 (n.d.): 700–724.
Berlin, Ira. *Many Thousands Gone: The First Two Centuries of Slavery in North America*. Cambridge, MA.: Belknap Press of Harvard University Press, 1998.
Blaufarb, Rafe. "The Western Question: The Geopolitics of Latin American Independence." *American Historical Review* 112, no. 3 (June 2007): 742–63.
Braudel, Fernand. *The Mediterranean and the Mediterranean World in the Age of Philip II*. New York: Harper & Row, 1972.
Bushman, Richard L. *The Refinement of America: Persons, Houses, Cities*. New York: Knopf, 1992; distributed by Random House.
Cantor, Milton. "A Connecticut Yankee in a Barbary Court: Joel Barlow's Algerian Letters to His Wife." *William and Mary Quarterly* 19, no. 1 (1962): 86–109.
———. "Joel Barlow's Mission to Algiers." *The Historian* 25, no. 2 (1963): 172–94.
Colley, Linda. *Captives*. New York: Pantheon Books, 2002.
———. *The Ordeal of Elizabeth Marsh: A Woman in World History*. New York: Pantheon Books, 2007.
Cox, Caroline. *A Proper Sense of Honor: Service and Sacrifice in George Washington's Army*. Chapel Hill: University of North Carolina Press, 2004.
Crane, Jacob. "Barbary(an) Invasions: The North African Figure in Republican Print Culture." *Early American Literature* 50, no. 2 (2015): 331–58.
Cutter, Nat. "Peace with Pirates? Maghrebi Maritime Combat, Diplomacy, and Trade in English Periodical News, 1622–1714." *Humanities* 8, no. 4 (2019): 179.
Dávid, Géza, and Pál Fodor, eds. *Ransom Slavery Along the Ottoman Borders: Early Fifteenth–Early Eighteenth Centuries*. Ottoman Empire and Its Heritage, vol. 37. Leiden: Brill, 2007.
Davis, Robert C. *Christian Slaves, Muslim Masters: White Slavery in the Mediterranean, the Barbary Coast, and Italy, 1500—1800*. Early Modern History: Society and Culture. Basingstoke: Palgrave Macmillan, 2007.
DeConde, Alexander. *The Quasi-War: The Politics and Diplomacy of the Undeclared War with France, 1797–1801*. New York: Charles Scribner's Sons, 1966.
Devoulx, Albert. *Le Rais Hamidou: Notice biographique sur le plus célèbre corsaire algérien du XIIIe siècle de l'hégire*. Algiers: A. Jourdan, 1859.
Dzurec, David J. *Our Suffering Brethren: Foreign Captivity and Nationalism in the Early United States*. Amherst: University of Massachusetts Press, 2019.

Farber, Hannah. "Millions for Credit: Peace with Algiers and the Establishment of America's Commercial Reputation Overseas, 1795–96." *Journal of the Early Republic* 34, no. 2 (2014): 187–217.

Fehlings, Gregory. "America's First Limited War." *Naval War College Review* 53, no. 3 (Spring 2000): 101–43.

Firges, Pascal, Tobias P. Graf, Christian Roth, and Gülay Tulasoglu, eds. *Well-Connected Domains: Towards an Entangled Ottoman History*. The Ottoman Empire and Its Heritage: Politics, Society and Economy, vol. 57. Leiden: Brill, 2014.

Foster, Thomas A., ed. *New Men: Manliness in Early America*. New York: New York University Press, 2011.

Freeman, Joanne B. *Affairs of Honor: National Politics in the New Republic*. New Haven: Yale University Press, 2001.

Fusaro, Maria, Colin Heywood, and Mohamed Salah Omri, eds. *Trade and Cultural Exchange in the Early Modern Mediterranean: Braudel's Maritime Legacy*. International Library of Historical Studies 67. London: Tauris Academic Studies; Palgrave Macmillan, 2010.

Gale, Caitlin. "Barbary's Slow Death: European Attempts to Eradicate North African Piracy in the Early Nineteenth Century." *Journal for Maritime Research* 18, no. 2 (2016): 139–54.

———. "Beyond Corsairs: The British–Barbary Relationship during the French Revolutionary and Napoleonic Wars." PhD diss., Oxford, 2016.

Garrity, Patrick. "The United States and Barbary Piracy, 1783–1805." *Comparative Strategy* 26, no. 5 (2007): 395–438.

Gøbel, Erik. "The Danish 'Algerian Sea Passes,' 1747–1838: An Example of Extraterritorial Production of 'Human Security.'" *Historical Social Research* 35 (2010): 164–89.

Goodin, Brett. *From Captives to Consuls: Three Sailors in Barbary and Their Self-Making Across the Early American Republic, 1770–1840*. Baltimore: Johns Hopkins University Press, 2020.

Gould, Eliga H. *Among the Powers of the Earth: The American Revolution and the Making of a New World Empire*. Cambridge, MA: Harvard University Press, 2012.

Greene, Molly. "The Ottomans in the Mediterranean." In *The Early Modern Ottomans: Remapping the Empire*, edited by Virginia Aksan and Daniel Goffman. Cambridge: Cambridge University Press, 2007.

Head, David. "Slave Smuggling by Foreign Privateers: The Illegal Slave Trade and the Geopolitics of the Early Republic." *Journal of the Early Republic* 33, no. 3 (2013): 433–62.

Hershenzon, Daniel. *The Captive Sea: Slavery, Communication, and Commerce in Early Modern Spain and the Mediterranean*. Philadelphia: University of Pennsylvania Press, 2018.

Irvin, Benjamin H. *Clothed in Robes of Sovereignty: The Continental Congress and the People Out of Doors*. New York: Oxford University Press, 2011.

Irwin, Ray Watkins. *The Diplomatic Relations of the United States with the Barbary Powers 1776–1816*. Chapel Hill: University of North Carolina Press, 1931.

Jessup, Philip, and Francis Deak. "The Early Development of the Law of Neutral Rights." *Political Science Quarterly* 46, no. 4 (December 1931): 481–508.

Jones, T. Cole. "'The Dreadful Effects of British Cruelty': The Treatment of British Maritime Prisoners and the Radicalization of Revolutionary War at Sea." *Journal of the Early Republic* 36, no. 3 (Fall 2016): 435–65.

Kidd, Thomas S. *American Christians and Islam: Evangelical Culture and Muslims from the Colonial Period to the Age of Terrorism*. Princeton: Princeton University Press, 2009.

Kilmeade, Brian, and Don Yaeger. *Thomas Jefferson and the Tripoli Pirates: The Forgotten War That Changed American History*. New York: Sentinel, 2016.

Kitzen, Michael. "Money Bags or Cannon Balls: The Origins of the Tripolitan War, 1795–1801." *Journal of the Early Republic* 16, no. 4 (1996): 601.

Lambert, Frank. *The Barbary Wars: American Independence in the Atlantic World*. New York: Hill and Wang, 2005.

Laughton, J. K., and Nicholas Tracy. *Vandeput, George (d. 1800), Naval Officer*. Oxford University Press, 2010. https://doi.org/10.1093/ref:odnb/28066.

Leiner, Frederick C. *The End of Barbary Terror: America's 1815 War Against the Pirates of North Africa*. New York: Oxford University Press, 2007.

London, Joshua E. *Victory in Tripoli: How America's War with the Barbary Pirates Established the U.S. Navy and Built a Nation*. Hoboken, NJ: Wiley, 2005.

Marr, Timothy. *The Cultural Roots of American Islamicism*. Cambridge: Cambridge University Press, 2006.

Marzagalli, Silvia, James R. Sofka, and John J. McCusker, eds. *Rough Waters: American Involvement with the Mediterranean in the Eighteenth and Nineteenth Centuries*. Research in Maritime History, no. 44. St. John's, NL: International Maritime Economic History Association, 2010.

McGerr, Michael. "The Price of the 'New Transnational History.'" *American Historical Review* 96, no. 4 (October 1991): 1056–67.

Moalla, Asma. *The Regency of Tunis and the Ottoman Porte, 1777–1814: Army and Government of a North-African Ottoman Eyâlet at the End of the Eighteenth Century*. New York: Routledge, 2010.

Montmorency, J. E. G de. "The Barbary States in International Law." In *Transactions of the Grotius Society, Vol. 4: Problems of the War, Papers Read Before the Society in the Year 1918*, 87–94. Cambridge: Cambridge University Press, 1918.

Morgan, Philip D. *Slave Counterpoint: Black Culture in the Eighteenth-Century Chesapeake and Lowcountry*. Chapel Hill: Published for the Omohundro Institute of Early American History and Culture, Williamsburg, VA, by the University of North Carolina Press, 1998.

"Morocco: The Bilateral Relations between Morocco and the USA." *MENA Report*, November 20, 2013.

Mullen, Abigail. *To Fix a National Character: The United States in the First Barbary War, 1800–1805*. Baltimore: Johns Hopkins University Press, 2024.

Nash, Gary B. "Race and Citizenship in the Early Republic." In *Antislavery and Abolition in Philadelphia: Emancipation and the Long Struggle for Racial Justice in the City of Brotherly Love*, edited by Richard Newman and James Mueller, 90–117. Baton Rouge: Louisiana State University Press, 2011.

Nichols, Roy. "Diplomacy in Barbary." *Pennsylvania Magazine of History and Biography* 74, no. 1 (January 1950): 113–41.

Norton, Mary Beth. *Liberty's Daughters: The Revolutionary Experience of American Women, 1750–1800*. Ithaca: Cornell University Press, 1996.

Onuf, Peter S., and Nicholas Greenwood Onuf. *Federal Union, Modern World: The Law of Nations in an Age of Revolutions, 1776–1814*. Madison: Madison House, 1993.

Oren, Michael B. *Power, Faith, and Fantasy: America in the Middle East, 1776 to the Present*. New York: W. W. Norton, 2011.

Panzac, Daniel. *Barbary Corsairs: The End of a Legend, 1800–1820*. The Ottoman Empire and Its Heritage, vol. 29. Leiden: Brill, 2005.

Parker, Richard. *Uncle Sam in Barbary: A Diplomatic History*. Gainesville: University Press of Florida, 2004.

Perl-Rosenthal, Nathan. *Citizen Sailors: Becoming American in the Age of Revolution*. Cambridge, MA: Belknap Press of Harvard University Press, 2015.

Peskin, Lawrence A. "American Exception? William Eaton and Early National Antisemitism." *American Jewish History* 100, no. 3 (July 2016): 299–317.

———. *Captives and Countrymen: Barbary Slavery and the American Public, 1785–1816*. Baltimore: Johns Hopkins University Press, 2009.

———. "The Lessons of Independence: How the Algerian Crisis Shaped Early American Identity." *Diplomatic History* 28, no. 3 (June 2004): 297–319.

Petrie, Donald A. *The Prize Game: Lawful Looting on the High Seas in the Days of Fighting Sail*. New York: Berkley Books, 2001.

Porter, Susan. "English–American Interaction in American Musical Theater at the Turn of the Nineteenth Century." *American Music* 4, no. 1 (Spring 1986): 6–19.

Randall, Henry, *The Life of Thomas Jefferson*. New York: Derby and Jackson, 1858.

Roberts, Priscilla, and James Tull. "Moroccan Sultan Sidi Muhammad Ibn Abdallah's Diplomatic Initiatives toward the United States, 1777–1786." *Proceedings of the American Philosophical Society* 143, no. 2 (June 1999): 233–65.

Rojas, Martha Elena. "'Insults Unpunished': Barbary Captives, American Slaves, and the Negotiation of Liberty." *Early American Studies: An Interdisciplinary Journal* 1, no. 2 (2003): 159–86.

Rouleau, Brian. *With Sails Whitening Every Sea: Mariners and the Making of an American Maritime Empire*. United States in the World. Ithaca: Cornell University Press, 2014.

Rousseau, Alphonse. *Annales tunisiennes, Ou aperçu historique sur la régence de Tunis*. Algiers: Bastide, 1864.

Sadosky, Leonard J. *Revolutionary Negotiations: Indians, Empires, and Diplomats in the Founding of America*. Jeffersonian America. Charlottesville: University of Virginia Press, 2009.

Sears, Christine E. *American Slaves and African Masters: Algiers and the Western Sahara, 1776–1820*. Palgrave Macmillan, 2012.

Shepherd, Mary. "Forrest's Curious Old Play: Or, Hopkinson's Disappointment." *Papers of the Bibliographical Society of America* 88, no. 1 (March 1994): 37–52.

Smiley, Will. "The Burdon of Subjecthood: The Ottoman State, Russian Fugitives, and Interimperial Law, 1774–1869." *International Journal of Middle East Studies* 46 (2014): 73–93.

———. "Freeing 'the Enslaved People of Islam': The Changing Meaning of Ottoman Subjecthood for Captives in the Russian Empire." In *The Subjects of Ottoman International Law*, edited by Lâle Can, Michael C. Low, Kent F. Schull, and Robert Zens. Bloomington: Indiana University Press, 2020.

———. "Let *Whose* People Go? Subjecthood, Sovereignty, Liberation, and Legalism in Eighteenth-Century Russo-Ottoman Relations." *Turkish Historical Review* 3 (2012): 196–228.

Sultana, Donald. "Coleridge, Stephen Decatur, and the Mysterious Duellist in Malta." *Modern Language Review* 89, no. 2 (April 1994): 282–88.

Symonds, Craig L. *The Civil War at Sea*. New York: Oxford University Press, 2013.

———. "'A Squadron of Observation': Thomas Jefferson and America's First War Against Terrorism." In *White House Studies Compendium*, vol. 4, edited by Robert W. Watson, 99–110. New York: Nova, 2007.

Tabarrok, Alexander. "The Rise, Fall, and Rise Again of Privateers." *Independent Review* 11, no. 4 (Spring 2007): 565–77.

Talbot, Michael. "Ottoman Seas and British Privateers: Defining Maritime Territoriality in the Eighteenth-Century Levant." In *Well-Connected Domains: Towards an Entangled Ottoman History*, edited by Pascal Firges, Tobias P. Graf, and Gülay Tulasoglu. Leiden: Brill, 2014.

Todd, Charles. *Life and Letters of Joel Barlow, LL.D., Poet, Statesman, Philosopher*. New York: G. P. Putnam's Sons, 1886.

Toll, Ian W. *Six Frigates: The Epic History of the Founding of the U.S. Navy*. New York: W. W. Norton, 2006.

Tucker, Judith, ed. *The Making of the Modern Mediterranean: Views from the South*. Oakland: University of California Press, 2019.

Tyrrell, Ian. "American Exceptionalism in an Age of International History." *American Historical Review* 96, no. 4 (October 1991): 1031–55.

———. "Ian Tyrell Responds." *American Historical Review* 96, no. 4 (October 1991): 1068–72.

Vickers, Daniel, and Vince Walsh. *Young Men and the Sea: Yankee Seafarers in the Age of Sail*. New Haven: Yale University Press, 2005.

White, Joshua M. *Piracy and Law in the Ottoman Mediterranean*. Stanford: Stanford University Press, 2018.

Windler, Christian. "Diplomatic History as a Field for Cultural Analysis: Muslim-Christian Relations in Tunis, 1700–1840." *Historical Journal* 44, no. 1 (2001): 89–106.

———. "Gift and Tribute in Early Modern Diplomacy: A Comment." *Diplomatica* 2 (2020): 291–304.

———. "Performing Inequality in Mediterranean Diplomacy." *International History Review* 41, no. 5 (2019): 947–61.

Wright, Louis B., and Julia H. MacLeod. *The First Americans in North Africa; William Eaton's Struggle for a Vigorous Policy Against the Barbary Pirates, 1799–1805*. Princeton: Princeton University Press, 1945.

Zeledon, James. "'As Proud as Lucifer': A Tunisian Diplomat in Thomas Jefferson's America." *Diplomatic History* 41, no. 1 (January 2017): 155–82.

INDEX

Abellino (privateer), 163, 176
Adams, John, 1, 5, 6, 48, 168; as peace commissioner, 50, 53–54, 57–58, 60–62, 64–65; as president, 82, 84, 96, 97, 110–11, 114, 118, 121, 122, 123–24
Adams, John Quincy, 114, 127, 175, 176
admiralty law, 13, 22, 28, 32, 71, 93–94, 113–14, 142, 161, 179, 187, 193, 206n48
Ahmed "Hamet" Karamanli, 15, 35–36, 117, 120, 145–49, 224n91
Algiers, xv, 2, 14, 15, 20, 26, 31, 32, 34, 37, 41, 43, 44, 46, 47, 48, 49, 50, 51, 52, 56, 58–59, 62, 63–66, 67, 69–70, 72, 73–78, 80, 84–88, 89, 90, 92, 93, 95–100, 101, 102, 103, 107, 109–11, 112, 130, 131, 139, 158, 159, 165, 169, 171, 178, 179–82, 185, 188–89, 193–95, 196–98, 217n97, 221n52; American captives in, 1–2, 20, 21, 22, 25, 27, 43–44, 60–61, 63, 66, 68, 81–82, 139, 157, 166–68, 207n56; American ships captured by, 20, 33, 58, 159–60, 163, 208n26; peace indemnities and annuities to, 53, 79, 82, 87, 104, 106, 152, 156; war with, 16–17, 124–25, 152, 153–54, 155, 156–57, 161–64, 171–76, 190, 225n1
Ali, dey of Algiers. *See* Dey Baba Ali of Algiers

Al Koraschi Ebnallad, fictional dey of Algiers, 70–71, 193–95
American Revolution, 2, 8, 11, 19, 35, 48, 49, 50, 52, 57, 59, 64, 67, 83, 193, 209n42
Argus, USS, 146, 147
Articles of Confederation. *See* Confederation, Articles of and governance under

Bacri, House of, 87, 95, 103
Bainbridge, William, 128, 129, 150, 157; as captain of *George Washington*, 109–12, 217n97; as captain of *Philadelphia*, 137, 139; as captive in Tripoli, 141, 174; commodore of squadron during Algerine War, 174–75, 176, 178
Barbary Wars. *See* Algiers: war with; Tripolitan War (1801–1805)
Barclay, Thomas, 57–58, 75–76, 78, 85, 149, 206n44
Barlow, Joel, 79–80, 82, 85, 87–91, 93–94, 95, 97, 101, 106, 130, 133, 166, 196, 213n23
Barnes, Joseph, 131, 143
Barron, James, 159
Barron, Samuel, 128, 144, 146–47, 149
Betsey (ship captured by Morocco), 47, 55–56, 58, 62, 77

{241}

242 INDEX

Bey Ali Karamanli of Tripoli, 145
Bey Hammuda of Tunis, 36, 91, 132, 133–34, 158, 161
Bey Mahmoud of Tunis, 170
Bey Yusuf Karamanli of Tripoli, 36, 79, 80, 102, 106, 113, 121, 145, 146, 148–49, 196–97
Boston, USS, 116–17, 129
Bynkershoek, Cornelius van, 30

Caille, Etienne, 52, 54–55
captives, x, 158, 181; consular support of, 60, 108, 139; status of, 13, 24, 41–45, 181, 190. *See also* Algiers: American captives in; Bainbridge, William: as captive in Tripoli; Cathcart, James: as captive in Algiers; Coffin, Zacheus; Cowdery, Jonathan; Morocco; O'Brien, Richard: as captive in Algiers; Ray, William; Tripolitan War (1801–1805): American prisoners; Tunis: captivity in
captivity narratives, 37, 43, 45, 59, 209n42, 221n52
Carmichael, William, 56, 60, 61, 64
Catalano, Salvadore, 120, 142–43
Cathcart, James L., 19, 140, 145–46, 150, 203n1; as captive in Algiers, 20–21, 25, 42, 43–44, 45, 59, 82, 85, 86, 87; as consul to Madeira, 163; as consul to Tripoli, 98–100, 101–7, 113, 127, 132
Cederström, Rudolf, 116–17, 129, 131, 143, 218n1
Chesapeake-Leopard affair, 16, 139, 156, 159
Coffin, Zacheus, 60, 66
Confederation, Articles of and governance under, 6, 14, 50, 53, 54, 65, 66, 69, 71–72, 77, 80
Congress, United States, 1, 4, 48, 50, 52–53, 54, 55, 56, 61, 63, 64, 65–66, 69, 71, 73, 74, 80, 84–85, 88, 91–92, 101, 109, 113,
115, 118, 121, 123–24, 125, 130, 137, 150, 162, 171, 174, 186, 188, 195
Congress, USS, 142
Congress of Aix-la-Chappelle, 171, 177, 182, 184
Congress of Vienna, 175, 177
Consolato del Mare, 92–93, 94
Constantinople. *See* Istanbul
Constellation, USS, 129, 130, 139, 153
Constitution, United States, 14, 50, 66, 67, 72–73, 77, 80, 88, 112, 118, 122, 124, 150, 189
Constitution, USS, 141, 159, 174
corsairing, xv, 6, 61, 155, 160, 190; compared to privateering and piracy, 9, 16, 21, 23, 25, 184; as diplomatic leverage in Morocco, 36–37, 57, 119, 135–36; dwindling of, 17, 155–56, 158, 170, 178–83; as economic staple, 21, 24, 25, 26, 37–38, 43, 57, 205n18; status in law, 7, 12, 21, 23, 28–36, 80–81, 170, 206n42; theories of British "unleashing" corsairs, 20, 67, 156–57, 161–63
Cowdery, Jonathan, 140
Coxe, Charles, 158–59, 161
Coxe, Tench, 151
Crocco, Giacomo, 53–54
Crowninshield, Benjamin, 172, 174

Dale, Richard, 16, 39, 116, 119, 126–29, 138
Dauphin (ship captured by Algiers), 47, 58, 59, 60, 74
Davis, George, 134–35, 158
Decatur, Stephen; commodore in war with Algiers, 16, 153–54, 157, 159, 172, 174–77, 178, 179, 225n1; in Tripolitan War, 120, 128, 142
Democratic-Republicans, 85, 121, 123, 162
Denmark, 15, 32, 55, 81, 83, 109, 112–15, 117, 132, 150, 182, 189

INDEX 243

Derne, 15, 117, 120, 145, 146, 148–49
de Souza, Gerardo Joseph (José) Betancourt, 80, 88, 196–98
Dey Baba Ali of Algiers (Ali), 27, 161, 162
Dey Baba Mohammed of Algiers, 62, 74
Dey Hassan of Algiers, 74, 86, 87, 97, 196
Dey Hussein of Algiers, 182
Dey Mustafa Baba of Algiers, 27
Dey Omar of Algiers, 175, 179–80
Dodge, James, 135, 158
Donaldson, Joseph, 81, 82, 85–87, 90–91, 95, 97, 106
Dutch. *See* Netherlands, the

Eaton, William, 38, 83, 99–100, 131, 145, 149, 170, 214n44, 215n67, 216n83; army career, 97–98, 104; consul to Tunis, 83, 100, 102–6, 107–8, 110, 112–13, 131, 133–34; Derne expedition, 120, 146–49; service to and gift from Denmark, 83, 112–13, 150
Edwin (ship captured by Algiers), 163
Egypt, xv, 15, 111, 117, 120, 146–48, 149
Eliza (ship captured by Tunis), 91–92
Embargo Act (1807), 152, 160, 190
England. *See* Great Britain
Enterprize, USS, 128, 130, 131
Epervier, USS, 154, 176, 179
Essaouira, 51, 55, 57, 137, 186
Essex, USS, 128–29, 139
Exmouth, Lord (Admiral Sir Edward Pellew), 155, 157–58, 178, 179–80, 183, 190
Expilly, Count de, 61

Famin, Joseph, 88, 91
Federalists, 85, 121, 123, 125, 149, 160, 162
First Barbary War. *See* Tripolitan War (1801–1805)
Floridablanca, Count de, 56, 57, 61

Fortune (ship captured by Britain), 95, 97
France, 8, 14, 29, 30, 34, 91, 93, 116, 126, 131, 132, 164, 177, 182, 183, 184, 190; diplomatic engagement with, 17, 48–49, 50, 57, 58, 62, 77, 111, 124, 140, 166, 171, 188; privateering by, 93–94, 95, 109, 113–14, 123, 156, 160–61, 182; Quasi-War with, 12, 40, 83–84, 93, 98, 109, 111, 112, 113–14, 118, 125, 133, 138, 150, 189, 190; Treaty of Amity and Commerce with (1778), 6, 11, 49, 52; war with and subsequent colonization of Algiers, 156, 158, 182
Franklin, Benjamin, 48, 56, 207n59, 208n26, 219n21; engagement with Morrocco, 52–55, 57; as minister to France, 1, 48, 52; use of Barbary rhetoric to support abolition, 69
Franklin (ship captured by Tripoli), 131
French Revolution, 89
French Revolutionary and Napoleonic Wars, 79, 88, 144, 147, 152, 190; the One Hundred Days, 171, 177; War of the First Coalition, 87; War of the Second Coalition, 83, 111; War of the Third Coalition, 145

Gallatin, Albert, 124, 125
Genoa, 27, 31, 42, 95, 134
George Washington, USS, 109–11, 128, 139
Ghent, Treaty of, 16, 154, 155, 157, 171, 173–74
Great Britain, 2, 6, 8, 12, 14, 19, 20, 30, 32, 33, 34, 37, 48, 49, 50, 51, 60, 72, 77, 83, 87, 93, 95, 111, 132, 163, 173, 176, 177, 178, 179–80, 181, 182, 184; cooperation in Quasi-War, 138; cooperation in Tripolitan War, 15, 117, 119, 120, 138, 145, 147; embargo against, 152, 160, 190; impressment of American sailors, 94, 139;

Great Britain (*continued*)
  Jay Treaty with, 150; Royal Navy, 16, 87, 93, 107, 109, 138, 155, 156, 159, 162, 174, 179–80, 182; as supposed sponsor of Barbary corsairs, 20, 48, 67, 77, 156, 160, 183, 188. *See also* War of 1812
Grotius, Hugo, 5, 29–30
Guerriere, USS, 153, 174

Hamet Karamanli. *See* Ahmed "Hamet" Karamanli
Hamidou, *rais* and admiral of Algiers, 153
Hamilton, Alexander, 18, 125
Hammuda, bey of Tunis. *See* Bey Hammuda of Tunis
Hassan, dey of Algiers. *See* Dey Hassan of Algiers
honor culture, 69, 110, 120, 127, 131, 218n5
Hopkinson, Francis, 71, 193–95
Hornet, USS, 158, 159
Hull, Isaac, 174
Humphreys, David, 51, 76–77, 78, 82, 85, 86, 87, 110, 128
Hurgronje, C. Snouck, 196–97, 198
Hussein, dey of Algiers. *See* Dey Hussein of Algiers

Indians. *See* Native Americans
Intrepid, USS, 120, 141–42
Islamic law, 13, 22, 23, 28–29, 45
Istanbul, 12, 30, 34, 109–11, 139

Jay, John, 52, 65–66, 74, 122. *See also* Great Britain: Jay Treaty with
Jay-Gardoqui Treaty, 56, 150, 188
Jefferson (Virginia State Navy ship), 59
Jefferson, Thomas, 4, 6, 10, 54, 90, 93, 108, 114; as minister to France and peace commissioner to the Barbary powers, 17, 50, 53, 54, 56–58, 60–62, 64–66; as president, 4, 17, 110, 118, 121–22, 125, 130, 132, 140–41, 146, 151, 160, 187, 188; as secretary of state, 1–2, 10, 66, 73–76, 77, 84, 208n18
jihad, 7, 21, 25–27, 28, 204n14
John Adams, USS, 136
Jones, John Paul, 75–76, 77, 78

Karamanli, Ahmed "Hamet." *See* Ahmed "Hamet" Karamanli
Karamanli, Yusuf. *See* Bey Yusuf Karamanli of Tripoli
Keene, Richard R., 157, 165–68
Khurshid Ahmed Pasha, 147–48
Koran. *See* Quran

Lamb, John, 57, 58, 59, 60, 61, 62–63, 65, 75, 77, 81, 82, 86, 87, 209n42
law of nations, x, 6, 7, 8, 12, 15, 22, 29, 42, 93, 94, 96, 119, 133, 134, 135, 151, 185, 187
Lear, Tobias, 100, 152, 156, 159, 160, 161–62, 221n52
Leve, Eliaho, 53
Lingua Franca (trade language), 32, 142
Logie, Charles, 20, 60, 61, 63, 67
Louisiana Purchase, 150, 164, 165, 167

Madison, James, 123; as president, 2, 157, 162, 166, 167, 168, 171–72, 174–75, 178, 179–80; as secretary of state, 96, 110, 112–13, 122, 124, 127, 132, 140
Malta, 24, 30, 42, 73, 102, 120, 126, 138, 142, 146, 147, 156, 161, 177, 205n18
Maria (ship captured by Algiers), 47, 58, 74
Markoe, Peter, 72
Marsh, Elizabeth, 37
Marshall, John, 114
Mastico (ship). *See Intrepid*, USS
Mathurin Order, 2, 65
McHenry, James, 90, 98

INDEX 245

McNiell, Daniel, 116, 129
Mediterranean Pass. *See* passports
Meshouda (Algerian ship), 153, 225n1
Meshouda (Tripolitan/Moroccan ship), 136–37, 139
Mexican-American War, 182, 185–87
Miller, Hunter, 89, 196, 213n23
Mogadore. *See* Essaouira
Mohammed, dey of Algiers. *See* Dey Baba Mohammed of Algiers
Mohammed III, emperor of Morocco, 37, 47, 49, 51–57, 65, 76
Monroe, James, 90, 157, 166–69, 179
Montgomery, Robert, 52–53, 111–12
Morocco, xv, 1, 19–20, 22, 33, 38, 49, 62, 65, 76, 77, 85, 188; corsairing practices of, 2, 3, 13, 24, 34, 36–37, 46, 47, 206n44; negotiations and 1786 treaty with, 14, 47, 49, 51–58, 149, 176; Tripolitan War and, 119, 132, 135–37, 138, 139
Morris, Richard, 131, 134–36, 137
Murray, Alexander, 130, 131, 143
Mustafa Baba, dey of Algiers. *See* Dey Mustafa Baba of Algiers

Naples. *See* Two Sicilies, Kingdom of the
Napoleon Bonaparte, 111, 140, 160, 164, 171, 172, 177
Napoleonic Wars. *See* French Revolutionary and Napoleonic Wars
Native Americans, 4, 17, 69, 72, 97, 104, 126, 127, 151, 155; captivity practices, 11, 13, 45; diplomacy with, 4, 5, 10, 13, 54, 188; perceptions of British control over, 12, 67, 163, 173
Navy, United States, 16, 109, 112, 134, 152, 156, 158–59, 162, 176, 178, 183, 186, 189, 190; in Algerine War, 157, 171–72, 174–75, 176; creation of, 10, 14, 65, 66, 73–74, 84–85, 109, 115, 121–22; in Tripolitan War, xii, 9, 113, 114, 116–21, 122, 125–26, 130–31, 137–40, 142–44, 148, 151, 187; in War of 1812, 155, 173–74, 175, 183. *See also individual member and ship names*
Netherlands, the, 17, 26, 30, 32, 34, 92, 107, 155, 160, 172, 179, 180, 190
Nissen, Nicholas, 113, 131, 139–40, 141, 149, 150, 158
Noah, Mordecai, 157, 165, 166–71, 181, 184
Norderling, John, 156, 162, 163, 166, 175

O'Brien (Robeson), Elizabeth, 99–100, 221n52
O'Brien, Richard, 21, 26, 60, 88, 89, 94, 97, 196, 201n1; as captive in Algiers, 45, 59, 60, 61, 63, 66, 67, 68, 74, 75, 76, 78, 79–80, 82, 85, 87, 209n42, 215n67; as consul general to Algiers, 82, 97, 98–100, 101–4, 106, 109–10, 111, 221n52; Revolutionary War service, 59
Omar, dey of Algiers. *See* Dey Omar of Algiers
orientalism, x, 69–70, 72, 170–71, 181
Osborne's Landing, Battle of, 59
Ottoman Empire, xv, 2, 15, 22–23, 24, 25, 28–30, 33–36, 42, 65, 73, 110–12, 117, 120, 140, 145, 147–48, 156, 158, 182, 184, 204n11, 206n42

passports, 11, 20, 31–32, 40, 48, 51, 55, 76, 79, 86, 100, 101–2, 135–36, 215n59
Philadelphia, 47, 55, 56, 60, 69–71, 87, 97, 98, 99, 101, 104, 151
Philadelphia, USS, 120, 128, 137, 138, 143, 150, 154, 161, 186, 193–95, 208n26, 210n46; burning, 141–43, 174; capture and crew imprisonment, 139–41, 146, 174
Pickering, Timothy, 83, 92, 97–98, 110, 114, 123
Pinkney, Charles, 71–72

piracy, 3, 21, 71, 96, 122, 131, 175, 186, 193; as distinct from licensed corsairing/privateering, ix, 2, 9, 11, 12–13, 23, 25–26, 33, 35, 45, 141, 155, 184, 187; as practiced by some claiming legal license, 19–20, 23, 187
plague, 20, 66
Pollard, James, 163
Porcile, Maria Anna, 83, 108, 216n83
Portugal, 14, 19, 39, 55, 58, 59, 64, 76, 156, 161, 163, 178, 182; truce with Algiers, 74, 76–77
Preble, Edward, 120, 137–38, 139, 141–44
President, USS, 126
privateering, ix, 2, 7, 9, 11, 12, 14, 16, 19, 20, 23, 26, 31, 33, 34, 39, 40, 45–46, 59, 81, 90, 92, 93–94, 95, 96, 103, 109, 123, 155–56, 158, 160–61, 163, 170, 176, 177–78, 182, 184, 187, 190–91

Quasi-War (1798–1800), 12, 40, 83, 93, 98, 109, 111, 113–14, 118, 121, 122, 123, 125, 133, 138, 150, 174, 189, 190
Quran, 28, 108, 205n24

Ray, William, 140
Register of Prizes (Algerian document), 33, 38, 41, 182
Rhode Island, 72–73
Ridgely, John, 150, 158
Riley, James, 57
Robeson, Elizabeth. *See* O'Brien (Robeson), Elizabeth
Royal Navy of Great Britain. *See under* Great Britain
Russia, 75, 140, 171, 177

Said, Edward, 170–71
Salé Rovers, 30
Second Barbary War. *See* Algiers: war with

Senate, United States, 74, 75, 90, 168
Shaler, William, 157, 175, 179, 180, 181–82
Sheffield, Lord John Holbrook, 9, 48
Sicily. *See* Two Sicilies, Kingdom of the
Sidi Mohammed. *See* Mohammed III, emperor of Morocco
Simpson, James, 135–37
Skjoldebrand, Matthias, 63, 81, 83, 85–86, 108
Skjoldebrand, Pierre Eric, 81, 83, 85–86, 108
Skjoldebrand (ship), 98
slavery, 4, 8, 11, 41, 47, 55, 57, 58, 62, 66, 68, 87, 109, 155, 158, 165, 167, 170, 175, 177–78, 180, 181, 190, 194, 195, 204n14, 206n44; ransom vs. chattel, 13, 20, 24–25, 41–45; use of Barbary example to critique American practices, 50, 67, 68–69, 140
Smith, George (American captain captured by Algiers in 1812), 163
Smith, George (American seaman captured by Algiers in 1785), 86, 108
Smith, Robert, 140, 141, 146, 159
Soderstrom, Rudolph. *See* Cederström, Rudolf
Sophia (ship), 79–80
Spain. 8, 10, 11, 14, 19, 20, 21, 26, 31, 33, 39, 42, 47, 49, 55–58, 59, 61, 62–63, 64, 65, 77, 87, 93, 97, 107–8, 116, 139, 153–54, 155, 157, 163, 164–65, 166, 168, 178, 179, 181, 182, 188, 214n44
St. Andre, Jeane Bon, 93–94, 95
Stephens, Isaac, 60
Sterret, Andrew, 128, 130
Suleiman, emperor of Morocco, 135–37

terrorism, analogies of corsairing to, 185
Thetis (Swedish frigate), 127, 128, 129, 218n1
Tripoli, xv, 2, 22, 27, 34, 35–36, 37, 40, 57, 65, 79–80, 82–93, 106–7, 111, 156, 158, 163,

176, 182; corsairing in, 38–39, 46, 79, 101–2, 180
Tripolitan War (1801–1805), xii, 3, 4, 10, 15–16, 17, 58, 113, 115, 116–52, 154, 183, 189; American prisoners, 68, 139–41, 149–50, 174; blockade of Tripoli harbor, 116, 129, 130–31, 135–36; constitutional issues, 118, 121–25, 174, 185–86; convoy operations, 125, 127, 128, 129, 130, 131, 135; Derne expedition, 120, 145–49; European countries and, 119–20, 131, 138–45; Morrocco and, 119, 135–38; Napoleonic Wars and, 144–45; Ottoman Empire and, 120, 147–48; peace negotiations, 148–49; Sweden, United States Navy cooperation with, 7, 116–17, 126–32; Tunis and, 119, 132–35, 158
Tripoli Treaty (1797), 82, 88–90, 168; Article 11 inconsistencies, 196–99
Tripoli Treaty (1805), 149–50
Truxton, Thomas, 110, 125–26, 138, 208n26, 210n64, 219n21
Tunis, xv, 1, 2, 30, 33, 57, 65, 79–80, 82, 83, 88, 90, 94, 97, 103, 105–6, 112–13, 132, 145, 156, 158–59, 160–61, 163, 170, 171, 176, 180, 182; captivity in, 41, 43, 91, 108; controversy over neutrality rules in Tripolitan War, 119, 132–35, 158; corsairing in, 27, 32, 37–39, 46, 91, 102, 131, 182; relationship with Ottoman Empire, 22, 25, 34–35, 36, 206n42

Two Sicilies, Kingdom of the, 15, 16, 117, 120, 131, 134, 138, 143–45, 149, 156, 176, 179, 181, 189, 218n3

Vattel, Emer de, 5–6, 7, 8, 22, 29–30, 33, 42, 119, 132–33, 150, 184, 188, 189, 191
Venice, 30, 34–35, 94
War of 1812, 12, 157, 165, 178, 179; Algerine War and, 16, 152, 156, 157, 161, 163–64, 172, 174, 183, 190; effect on American standing, 16, 17, 154–55, 172–74, 175, 177, 183; effect on Native Americans, 173

War of Independence. *See* American Revolution
Washington, George, 1–2, 74–75, 76, 85, 123, 165, 186–87
West Florida, 155, 164–65, 166
Westphalian system, 3, 4, 5–6, 10, 11, 155, 170, 173

XYZ Affair, 104, 124

Zahhar, Ahmad al, 27, 205n23

The Revolutionary Age

The Course of Human Events: The Declaration of Independence and the Historical Origins of the United States
STEVEN SARSON

Napoleon in America: Bonaparte and the Rhetoric of US Empire
MARK F. EHLERS

Before Manifest Destiny: The Contested Expansion of the Early United States
NICHOLAS G. DIPUCCHIO

Revolutionary Diplomacy: Spanish Statecraft and the Birth of the United States
THOMAS E. CHÁVEZ

Declarations of Independence: Indigenous Resilience, Colonial Rivalries, and the Cost of Revolution
CHRISTOPHER R. PEARL

Dishonored Americans: The Political Death of Loyalists in Revolutionary America
TIMOTHY COMPEAU

The American Liberty Pole: Popular Politics and the Struggle for Democracy in the Early Republic
SHIRA LURIE

European Friends of the American Revolution
ANDREW J. O'SHAUGHNESSY, JOHN A. RAGOSTA, AND MARIE-JEANNE ROSSIGNOL, EDITORS

The Tory's Wife: A Woman and Her Family in Revolutionary America
CYNTHIA A. KIERNER

Writing Early America: From Empire to Revolution
TREVOR BURNARD

Spain and the American Revolution: New Approaches and Perspectives
GABRIEL PAQUETTE AND GONZALO M. QUINTERO SARAVIA, EDITORS

The American Revolution and the Habsburg Monarchy
JONATHAN SINGERTON

Navigating Neutrality: Early American Governance in the Turbulent Atlantic
SANDRA MOATS

Ireland and America: Empire, Revolution, and Sovereignty
PATRICK GRIFFIN AND FRANCIS D. COGLIANO, EDITORS

www.ingramcontent.com/pod-product-compliance
Lightning Source LLC
Chambersburg PA
CBHW030616230426
43661CB00053B/2011